BRITAIN AND JAPAN IN THE TWENTIETH CENTURY

BRITAIN AND JAPAN IN THE TWENTIETH CENTURY

One Hundred Years of Trade and Prejudice

Edited by
Philip Towle and
Nobuko Margaret Kosuge

Published in 2007 by I.B.Tauris & Co Ltd
6 Salem Road, London W2 4BU
175 Fifth Avenue, New York NY 10010
www.ibtauris.com

In the United States of America and Canada distributed by Palgrave Macmillan
a division of St Martin's Press 175 Fifth Avenue, New York NY 10010

Library of International Relations 33

ISBN: 978 1 84511 415 2

A full CIP record for this book is available from the British Library
A full CIP record is available from the Library of Congress

Library of Congress Catalog Card Number: available

Printed and bound in India by Replika Press Pvt Ltd
From camera-ready copy edited and typeset by Oxford Publishing Services

CONTENTS

ACRONYMS AND ABBREVIATIONS

AJBVA	All Japan Burma Veterans Association
ANZUS	security treaty between Australia, New Zealand and the United States
ARF	ASEAN Regional Forum
ASEAN	Association of South East Asian Nations
ASEM	Asia–Europe Meeting
BTI	British Trade International
ASW	anti-submarine warfare
CEA	Council of Economic Advisers
CFSP	Common Foreign and Security Policy
CPA	Coalition Provisional Authority
CRP 2	Community Reintegration Programme: Phase 2
DFID	Department for International Development
EC	European Community
ESS	Economic and Scientific Section (of SCAP)
EU	European Union
EURATOM	European Atomic Energy Community
FCO	Foreign and Commonwealth Office
FDI	foreign direct investment
FEC	Far Eastern Commission
FEPOWs	Far East prisoners of war
FO	Foreign Office
FT	*Financial Times*
G8	Group of Eight (industrialized countries)
GARIOA	Government Appropriations for Relief in Occupied Areas

GATT	General Agreement on Tariffs and Trade
GDP	gross domestic product
GEM	Global Entrepreneurship Monitor
GSDF	ground self-defence forces
HMG	His/Her Majesty's Government
HMT	Her Majesty's Treasury
HSBC	Hongkong and Shanghai Banking Corporation
IFF	International Finance Facility
IMCO	Intergovernmental Maritime Consultative Organization
IMD	Institute for Management Development
IMF	International Monetary Fund
IPU	Inter-Parliamentary Union
ISAF	International Security Assistance Force
JETRO	Japan External Trade Organization
KEDO	Korean Peninsula Energy Development Organization
LSE	London School of Economics and Political Science
MFN	most favoured nation
MITI	Ministry of International Trade and Industry
MNF–I	Multinational Force–Iraq
MOFA	Ministry of Foreign Affairs
MOU	memorandum of understanding
MSDF	Maritime Self-Defence Forces
MT	Ministry of Transport
NGO	non-governmental organization
NYK	Nippon Yusen Kaisha
ODA	Overseas Development Administration
OECD	Organization for Economic Cooperation and Development
ONS	Office for National Statistics
ORHA	Office of Reconstruction and Humanitarian Assistance
OSCE	Organization for Security and Cooperation in Europe
OSK	Osaka Shosen Kaisha
PKO	peace-keeping operation
POW	prisoner of war
PSI	Proliferation Security Initiative
PSO	Peace Support Operations

R&D	research and development
RIMPAC	Rim of the Pacific Exercise
SCAP	Supreme Commander of Allied Powers
SDF	self-defence forces
STICERD	Suntory and Toyota International Centres for Economics and Related Disciplines
TFP	total factor productivity
UKLM	United Kingdom Liaison Mission
UNCTAD	United Nations Conference on Trade and Development
UNDP	United Nations Development Programme
USSBS	United States Strategic Bombing Survey
VE	victory in Europe
VER	voluntary export restraint
VJ	victory in Japan
WTO	World Trade Organization

ACKNOWLEDGEMENTS

The editors would like to thank the Japan Society for the Promotion of Sciences, the Daiwa Anglo-Japanese Foundation and the staff of the Japanese Embassy in London for their help and support for the Cambridge conference, which eventually led to the publication of this book. They were particularly delighted to be able to play a part in the Japan 2001 celebrations in Britain to which Sir John Boyd made such a major contribution. They would also like to thank Oxford Publishing Services for their editorial assistance and the Great Britain Sasakawa Foundation for their support for the preparation of the text.

PREFACE
Sir John Boyd

The Japan 2001 Festival, in its Cambridge dimension, was by universal consent a great success. Part of the secret was spirit, the other part cultural range. 'Culture' on this occasion was widely defined, and the Cambridge audience had an opportunity to witness or take part in events from botany and cell biology to drama, Meiji photography and Japanese theatre - economic history, too. The involvement of young people was particularly important.

Churchill College had the opportunity to host a number of events, not least the excellent conference on which this book is based. Organized by Philip Towle and his colleagues this was academically rigorous; but it also drew particular inspiration from Nobuko Margaret Kosuge and her colleagues and in the attendance of leading economic practitioners. It was a privilege to sit in on the discussions.

The central focus was economic relations between Britain and Japan over the past century - just about a hundred years since the Anglo-Japanese Alliance and Henry Norman's outstanding study of emerging Japan. The history of the subject, and its significance in a wider context, is well caught in the introduction, but there may be a few words to add.

I myself saw the bilateral economic relationship in a particularly positive phase during my time in Tokyo. Britain's exporters and bankers, not to mention Whitehall, had readily seized growing opportunities during the 1970s and 1980s in a series of positive campaigns. Japanese inward investment into the UK was flourishing - and bringing vital relief to key sectors of British industry. This was before the bubble burst but we should not despair about the fundamentals. A sound bilateral understanding on the economic questions remains of course fundamental to good relations between London and Tokyo. But I am struck by the way in which the bilateral agenda has broadened in recent years - with the growth of political contacts, technological, educational and youth exchanges, and ever deeper cultural cooperation; and a much sounder understanding than a few decades ago of ways in which Britain and Japan can and should support each other's strategies as we grapple globally with ever more daunting challenges.

Cambridge's own links with Japan may offer helpful clues. They rest on mutual respect and strong mutual advantage. They are strikingly varied and innovative. Academic exchanges as such flourish. So does sharing of ideas. Embedded laboratories make a signal contribution. Individual researchers flourish. The intellectually open and international character of our University is its own message. It strikes, I think, a reciprocal chord.

Our Meiji visitors spotted this already a century ago - look at Dairoku Kikuchi (1855–1917) in Cambridge and other important figures on other UK campuses. We take pride in intellectual rigour, placing great demands on ourselves and our students: but this is offset by the collegiate (and collegial) style. University life - and, yes, conferences - can be fun.

Britain and Japan share key ideas. That is as it should be. I was struck during my time in Tokyo by the growing appeal there of a 'British menu' of open markets, active trading abroad and structural reform at home. Japan's record in the organization of manufacturing, and her splendid contribution to inward investment in the UK, have left a permanent mark on UK thinking. Colleagues in the sciences at British universities, as well as electronics and engineering, have the utmost respect for Japan's own strengths in these fields. In other words, a healthy economic relationship, in modern terms described in broad terms, is both part of and a conditioning framework for other joint endeavours.

I often think that our shared 'enemy' is lack of confidence. Clearly Japan needs the political self-confidence to continue with her programme of economic and financial reform. The mid-nineteenth century record reminds us of her ability to grasp challenges to her national and cultural survival. But on a wider front too she could use voices of support from the UK, encouraging her to believe more strongly in her organizational and industrial strengths together with the virtues of her own outstanding culture - as displayed, precisely, in Japan 2001.

INTRODUCTION

Philip Towle and Nabuko Kosuge

In 1904, the Japanese politician and economist, Korekiyo Takahashi tried to raise loans in New York and London for Japan's war against Russia. At first, as Richard Smethurst points out, he found a general reluctance to assist his country, not least because there was a widespread expectation that Russia would be victorious. There was also a tendency to compare Japan with China and to ignore the rapid development that Japan was undergoing. From Takahashi's point of view these were ignorant prejudices; Japan had defeated China almost a decade before and forced the Chinese to pay for that war and for the rebuilding of Japan's armed forces. His country was the rising power in East Asia as the British government had recognized by signing the Anglo-Japanese Alliance in 1902.

In the end, Takahashi was able to raise the loans not just because of Japan's military successes but also because of the Russian government's anti-Semitism. Jacob Schiff, the US banker, was determined to do everything he could to damage the Tsar's government because of the horrific pogroms it allowed against the Russian Jews. Schiff was able to work behind the scenes in London to find the money for Takahashi and his government. There were prejudices all round, but the anti-Semitic prejudices of the Russians trumped the miscalculations of the British and American bankers about Japan's prospects.

It was a fitting beginning to the first 40 years of the twentieth century, which were to see Anglo-Japanese relations deeply affected by political, economic and national prejudices. Only too often one side blamed the other for its own problems or completely misjudged the motives for the other's actions. Even if statesmen accurately distinguished between the attitudes of politicians, business leaders, financiers, journalists, military officers and popular opinion on the other side, they only too frequently misunderstood the balance of influence between the various actors. Misunderstandings exacerbated tensions leading to political decisions that only made the situation worse. It was not until Mrs Thatcher's government in the 1980s that the two governments found a way of making their economies symbiotic and, even then, popular memories of the Second World War and excitable journalists looking for a dramatic story occasionally disturbed the harmony of the relationship between the two countries.

Within two decades of the successful fund-raising in London by Takahashi and Schiff, the warmth of Anglo–Japanese relations had begun to abate. Japanese nationalists complained of Britain's abandonment of the Anglo–Japanese Alliance in 1922, the construction of the Singapore base and London's growing hostility towards their country's Asian policies. The British elite became concerned about Japanese control of Korea and its ambitions in China. Japan was also increasingly seen as an economic threat by the textile manufacturers of Lancashire and the shipbuilders of the Clyde and Tyne.

Many believed the Japanese had taken advantage of Britain's preoccupations during the First World War to seize the country's traditional markets in India and elsewhere. However, Janet Hunter shows that it was not inevitable that this process would continue. If much of British industry was doomed, it was not by Japanese competition but by its own inefficient practices, and optimistic commentators in the early 1920s, who were unaware how sapping such practices would be, expected that Japan's wartime economic gains would be reversed. Hunter concludes that the optimists still tended to look on Japan as a late-industrializing country with many structural weaknesses and failed to perceive it as a serious competitor. What was needed was a balanced appreciation of the seriousness of the competition combined with a determination to change conservative British industrial practices.

If the conservatism of British industrialists was damaging to their industrial prospects in the 1920s and 1930s, Fumitaka Kurosawa argues, Japan was pulled between a Wilsonian and a realistic view of international economic and political affairs in the 1920s. Kurosawa analyses Japan's ideas on international politics and the economic order in the interwar period; he contrasts the new spirit of diplomacy with imperialist views of international order, arguments for free trade with arguments favouring economic self-sufficiency.

In the relatively benevolent economic climate of the 1920s business leaders worked to integrate Japan into the world economy and to show colleagues from elsewhere the progress their country was making. Christopher Madeley demonstrates that the World Engineering Congress held in Tokyo in 1929 was typical in this regard. The Congress attracted 4495 members from 43 countries, and delegates and guests were impressed by the hospitality they received. However, deterioration in the world's economic and political climate during the 1930s meant the Congress's aims and ideals were not achieved. The Congress failed to boost trade between Japan and the West, and the desire for an international fraternity of engineers contributing to world peace was swept aside by the prejudices of the nationalists and militarists.

Unfortunately, these became predominant after the Great Depression, and Britain's introduction of tariffs favouring imperial trade, further entrenched their position. Ironically, as Naoto Kagotani shows, British imperial interests were divided between financiers and manufacturers in Britain, and between the British and Indian governments. Such divisions and Japan's importance as a market for Indian raw cotton allowed Japan to increase its trade with India despite imperial preference. The British maintained the stability of the Indian currency, but in other ways they had the worst of all worlds. They gave the impression that they were discriminating against Japanese goods and thereby, not surprisingly, reinforced the view that they were the main obstacle to the achievement of Japanese interests, yet, at the same time, they failed to help the Lancashire cotton industry because it was increasingly uncompetitive. On the other hand, until 1937, Japan could maintain a certain level of interdependence with British India, the Japanese yen was linked to sterling at a devalued rate, and Japanese goods paid duty to the colonial governments and were profitable for Asian and European importers. On their side, Amery, Beaverbrook and the other British imperialists saw imperial preference as a way of knitting the empire together. Instead, by provoking Japan, it helped to expedite the empire's downfall. Rarely has the 'law of unintended effects' been more in evidence.

The Great Depression had a serious impact on both countries. Japanese silk growers were reduced to starvation and millions in both countries were thrown out of work by the effects of the crisis which swept the developed world. Following mercantilist ideas the Japanese armed forces began their imperial expansion in Manchuria arguing that this was the solution to these economic problems. Yet such advances into Manchuria and later into the rest of China naturally failed to solve Japan's economic difficulties, not least because the destruction of Chinese towns and villages and the disruption to trade during the fighting added to the economic woes of the 1930s and embroiled Britain with Japan in the calamity of war in December 1941.

The prejudices of the leaders of the Imperial Japanese Army blinded them to the impossibility of defeating the United States, the world's greatest economic power, or of solving economic problems in a highly integrated world through military action. But those who led the Allied coalition had their own prejudices. As the Romanian–British financial journalist, Paul Einzig argued in 1943, they should have given greater consideration to the possibility of reversing Japanese expansion by concentrating on its vulnerable maritime communications rather than by massive conventional battles. Perhaps a naval blockade would not have forced a Japanese rethink without the horrors of air bombardment or invasion, but Western leaders greatly underestimated its efficacy.

After the experience of the war many British industrialists were even more prejudiced against their Japanese counterparts than they had been in the 1920s. They hoped that the United States would delay Japanese industrial recovery for as long as possible. Inherently defeatist, despite the Allied military victory, they blamed Japanese success on 'sweated labour' and saw trade as destructive of their interests, rather than mutually beneficial. However, as Peter Lowe demonstrates, it was to the advantage of the US occupiers that Japan should be restored to economic health as quickly as possible, and Japanese industry responded magnificently. According to Lowe, British policy towards the economic revival of Japan in the occupation era and after was predominantly negative because of memories of the intense Japanese competition in the 1930s. The Labour government in Britain was committed to ambitious domestic reforms with the maintenance of full employment; the perceived Japanese threats to textiles, shipbuilding and the Staffordshire potteries, were thus taken very seriously. However, political realities compelled Britain to accept the comparatively generous terms for Japan favoured by the United States in the San Francisco peace treaty in 1951.

World trade, as seen from Newcastle or the Clyde, was a zero sum game in which Britain was increasingly the loser. As John Weste argues, Anglo–Japanese competition in the shipbuilding and the shipping sectors over the 1950s was a reflection of relative British economic decline, and of the challenges posed by the re-emergence of Japan to the UK's efforts to maintain its position as a power of the first rank. Despite recent defeat and occupation, Japan therefore continued to have an important impact on British relations with the United States and with the British Empire and Commonwealth.

It was not, however, until the 1980s that Mrs Thatcher's government made a major effort to encourage Japan to invest in Britain. Nissan, Toyota, Honda and other companies took up this challenge to mutual benefit. Hideya Taida, who played a major part in this success story, shows how this process developed and how shocked individual Japanese were, at the start of the process, by the anti-Japanese prejudices still widespread in Britain. Taida details Japan–UK business developments from the beginning of direct investments in Britain in the 1970s through 2001 and characterizes Japan–UK economic relations during this period as an outstanding example of mutual cooperation, in contrast to Japanese relationships with other European countries or with the United States. During the Thatcher administration Japanese enterprises were encouraged to become established in various non-metropolitan regions of the UK and, as a result of the increase in Japanese direct investments following the Plaza Accords, altogether some 103 Japanese firms were established in the UK by the end of the 1980s.

This was the first period since the start of the twentieth century when British opinion began to see the two economies as symbiotic. Today, Britain has come to terms with the disappearance of most of its traditional industries - steel production, coal mining, ship-building and textiles. Thanks to Mrs Thatcher's initiatives the British economic climate has been relatively benign, at least by the standards of the twentieth century. Unfortunately, the Japanese situation was for a while rather different. The economic growth rate slowed in the 1990s; Japanese banks groaned under excessive debts and unemployment rose. The size of its economy fell by 2.6 per cent in 1998 alone. Even though Japan remained an economic and technological giant with a gross national product second only to the United States ($4.1 trillion in 2001 against $10.2 trillion), it suffered something of the loss of morale that afflicted the British from the 1920s to the 1960s. The hopes expressed by commentators in 1990 that its GDP would equal that of the United States within a decade, gradually faded away.

However, given the excellence of so many Japanese technologies, Simon Lee warns against the prejudice now common among international financial institutions that leads them to dismiss the Japanese economy as easily as some once feared it. By 2004 and 2005 Japanese growth had resumed and the banks' debts had been paid off. Lee focuses on the fundamental stability and strength of contemporary Anglo-Japanese economic relations, and the way in which it has been promoted through Japan–EU negotiations and flows of foreign direct investment, principally from Japan to the UK. This bilateral stability is contrasted with the macroeconomic instability of global economic performance during the past decade. Having explored the microeconomic challenges confronting both the Japanese and UK economies, and the difficulty of making the transition to a more innovation-based economy, he argues that the greatest challenge and principal threat to Anglo–Japanese economic relations derives from the destabilizing effect of the neo-liberal orthodoxy of the 'Washington Consensus'.

Hugo Dobson further shows how the bilateral Japan–UK relationship has been conducted in one of the chief mechanisms of global governance: the G8. Since its creation in 1975, the G8 has come to occupy centre-stage in the calendar of international politics and provides the only opportunity for the leaders of these leading countries to meet. Japan and the UK have been members of the G8 since its creation and display certain similarities in their perspectives and behaviour that has facilitated cooperation. However, at the same time, there are core differences that have led on occasions to conflict. Dobson provides an overview of their respective positions within the G8, highlights these areas of cooperation and conflict before looking ahead to the future of this process of annual summit meetings. The G8 is currently facing a number of challenges and will continue to do so in the future, but two are particularly salient: reform of the summit process and engagement with civil society. Both Japan and the UK already have experience of addressing these issues, although there are significant differences between the two governments and their people.

The British and Japanese economies have followed very different courses over the last century. Britain suffered from a slow but accelerating industrial decline for over a hundred years from the 1870s to the 1980s when it finally abandoned the attempt to preserve its traditional industries. That was exactly the same period, with the exception of the Second World War, when the Japanese economy was growing most rapidly; hence the natural, if misguided and destructive, British envy and resentment. In the early period, the two economies were most symbiotic when Takahashi and Schiff were cooperating and this was also the era when their political and military relations were closest. Political, economic and military factors all encouraged cooperation.

Today, as two middle-sized island powers buffeted by the rapid pace of economic and political change, Reinhard Drifte argues that their relations are once more congruent in the struggle to encourage stability and find ways of achieving steady economic growth. Britain can help Japan overcome some of the prejudices that have inhibited its involvement in peacekeeping over recent decades. Drifte argues that in the wake of the global changes after 11 September 2001 and a more active Japanese foreign and security policy, opportunities for cooperation between Japan and the UK over security have expanded and are increasingly being seized. The participation of Japanese and British forces in Iraq and in the Indian Ocean has provided the most important area of such cooperation. Both countries realize that against a background of mounting demands for action, bilateral cooperation can supplement scarce resources and strengthen multilateralism. However, both countries have to recognize the limitations of such cooperation, which lie with different regional and alliance structures, different approaches to security and different political styles and cultural approaches. Having reviewed the development of cooperation in Iraq and Afghanistan in particular, Drifte concludes that the future of bilateral security cooperation between the UK and Japan lies in the areas of the peace-keeping operations (PKO), naval cooperation and anti-terrorist operations that are all becoming increasingly interlinked.

Nevertheless, Nabuko Margaret Kosuge shows how this harmony can still occasionally be upset by the bitter memories rooted in the Second World War which still affect the image of Japan. The 'anti-Japanese demonstrations' in China in the spring of 2005, which began with appeals over the Internet to boycott Japanese goods because of opposition to the idea of Japan becoming a permanent member of the UN Security Council, and dissatisfaction over the history textbooks given official approval in Japan, were an opportunity to reconfirm the fact that the precondition for realizing active and stable business partnerships is to have flexible and stable political and diplomatic relationships. The incremental fall in the average value of Nikkei-listed stocks that came in the wake of these large-scale demonstrations was further exacerbated in Tokyo market prices by the Chinese government's refusal to apologize or provide compensation for the damage these disturbances caused to Japanese premises. After the beginning of the twenty-first century, Japan's exports to China have greatly expanded and today, when the degree of economic interdependence is growing in this way, one often finds the phrase '*seirei-keinetsu*' (politically cold but economically hot) being used to describe contemporary China–Japan relations. In other words, although political and diplomatic relations are not necessarily warm, economic and business aspects are said to be 'hot' and to be progressing in the direction of mutually complementary relationships. The implication is that political and economic or business issues are mutually distinct, but can political tensions between the two countries really not have an influence on economic relations? Kosuge shows that in the case of Japan–UK relations the memories of mistreatment of British military prisoners and civilian internees by Japanese army personnel during the Second World War have continued to project a shadow over Japan–UK relations, which may otherwise be described as excellent. She examines the ways in which both countries have tried to come to grips with the heavy pressures of this bitter past.

In the twentieth century, international crises were often the result of externalizing domestic economic and political problems. If the Tsar and his government had known that Schiff's activities had exacerbated their military setbacks, no doubt they would have blamed 'the Jews', but it was their own anti-Semitism that caused the problem. If Britain suffered from economic decline from 1851 onwards, this was because of the inability or unwillingness of British industrialists and workers to innovate and modernize their practices. The most extreme consequence of the tendency to blame others for domestic economic difficulties was the expansionism of the Imperial Japanese armed forces in the 1930s, which was, in part, a desperate and hopeless attempt to solve their country's demographic, economic and social difficulties. The developed countries seem to have learnt the lesson that in an ever more integrated world, military expansionism can never solve internal difficulties, and neither could the artificial constraints that British manufacturers, for example, hoped to see imposed on Japanese industry in 1945. Nevertheless, ingrained prejudices still often prevent us from understanding and empathizing with the fears that trouble other nations.

Chapter 1

KOREKIYO TAKAHASHI AND JAPAN'S VICTORY IN THE RUSSO-JAPANESE WAR, 1904–5

Richard J. Smethurst

Economic historians know Korekiyo Takahashi (1854–1936) best for his counter-cyclical monetary and fiscal policies during the world depression of the 1930s. Takahashi, who served as governor of the central bank, prime minister and seven times as finance minister between 1913 and his assassination in 1936, devalued the yen, lowered interest rates, and began substantial deficit financing in 1931–32, a quinquennium before John Maynard Keynes published his seminal *General Theory of Employment, Interest, and Money* in 1936. Takahashi's monetary and fiscal stimuli were so successful in engineering Japan's economic recovery that one of his biographers, Gotō Shin'ichi, has gone so far as to dub him 'Japan's Keynes'.[1]

At the age of ten Takahashi began to study English with American and British missionaries in Yokohama in 1865. Subsequently, he used his language skill as the foundation for playing a central role in Japan's economic and political history even before the 1930s. Born the illegitimate child of one of the shogun's court artists and a 15-year-old family maid, Takahashi was adopted as an infant into the lowest rank of the warrior class. Accordingly, Takahashi received very little formal education. There is no direct evidence that he even attended a *terakoya,* the kind of school in which ashigaru (hereditary foot soldiers) matriculated in the late feudal period. Nevertheless, he parlayed his ability to speak, read and write fluently an essential foreign language into a long career in Japan's government – he began his first job, as an English-language instructor at Daigaku Nankō, early Meiji Japan's most important school for the study of Western languages and science, in 1869, at the age of 14.

While still a teenager in the 1870s, Takahashi interpreted for David Murray, an important American educational adviser to the Meiji government, and helped translate Alfred Marshall's *The Pure Theory of Modern Trade*; in the 1880s, he wrote, and then after a year of research in the United States and Europe, rewrote Japan's first copyright and patent laws, served as the founding commissioner of his nation's patent office, and managed one of Japan's initial overseas industrial ventures, a silver mine in Peru; in the 1890s, he oversaw the construction of the Bank of Japan's new building, one of the premier examples of Meiji architecture, and helped in the process that took Japan onto the gold standard in 1898; during the war with Russia in 1904–5 he sold £82 million worth of Japanese war bonds, almost half the total cost of the war, in London and New York to British, American, and later French and German investors; from 1906 to 1915, successively as vice-governor of the Bank of Japan, president of the Yokohama Specie Bank, governor of the Bank of Japan, finance minister and party leader, he strove to limit government spending to avoid Japan's defaulting on its wartime bonds. These efforts included opposition to railroad nationalization in 1906, to the addition of two extra divisions to the army in 1912, and to Foreign Minister Takaaki (Kōmei) Katō's issuance of the 21 demands to China in 1915; after the war, as finance minister and premier, Takahashi attempted, largely unsuccessfully, to devolve much of the central authorities' power to local government, and played a key role in the rise of Japan's political parties; and throughout the second half of his career, Takahashi fought courageously for civilian control of the army and navy and against excessive military spending, a battle that led to his brutal murder at the hands of young army officers during the 26 February uprising of 1936.[2]

The subject of this study is one chapter in the story of Takahashi's fascinating life: his fundraising activities in the City of London and on Wall Street in 1904–5. Looking at a variety of sources: the English-language diary, address book and list of vocabulary Takahashi kept while abroad; the letters and cables he sent to his superiors in Tokyo, which are stored in the archive of the Institute for Monetary and Economic Studies of the Bank of Japan; two later accounts of his time in Europe and North America, one written in English and the other in Japanese; materials from the Ing Baring, NatWest and HSBC archives in London; letters and other materials related to Schiff, including the fascinating Jacob Schiff correspondence with Takahashi in the American

Jewish Archives in Cincinnati and in the documents in the constitutional government room (*kensei shiryōshitsu*) of the National Diet Library in Tokyo; and secondary works such as Naomi Cohen's recent biography of Schiff and path-breaking articles by Gary Dean Best and A. J. Sherman, I have been able to put together a day-by-day account of Takahashi's efforts to sell Japanese treasury bonds to defray the costs of the war against Russia.[3]

On 12 February 1904, Count Kaoru Inoue, one of Japan's elder statesmen, called Takahashi to see him and said, 'We want to send you to London to look into selling government bonds. Count Matsukata also thinks you are the best person for the job.' Takahashi was instructed that Japan would need to raise 100 million yen (ten million pounds) abroad to pay for driving Russia out of the Korean peninsula, and more if the war expanded beyond the Yalu River. Little did Tokyo imagine as the war began that it would have to raise abroad eight times that amount before the peace. On 24 February, Takahashi and his amanuensis Eigo Fukai departed for Honolulu and San Francisco, crossed the United States by train, and spent five fruitless days in New York meeting bankers. The New York bankers he met, Takahashi later reported, saw the Japanese as 'plucky children challenging a powerful giant. While they sympathized with us, they did not have capital to spare and had little experience at issuing foreign bonds.' Thus, in early March he sailed empty-handed for England.[4]

On the Atlantic voyage Takahashi met and conversed with the actress Lillie Langtry about the techniques Japanese actors use to die on stage.

> Although Miss Langtry and her maids kept to themselves, one day she spoke to me on deck: 'When Japanese actors die on stage', she stated, 'the colour of their faces change. Do you know how they do this? I would like to know if they use some kind of make-up to do this.' I replied, 'I don't really know, but now that you mention it, the Japanese actors' faces do change colour when they die. I don't think they use make-up, but do it by psychological control.' She seemed not to believe me, and answered, 'I think you are wrong. Maybe you know, but won't tell me.' We then talked of other things.

Takahashi dutifully recorded her name and address in the address book he used for the next two years in London; one assumes he did not mention 'the Jersey Lily' at his audience with Edward VII the next year.[5]

As one can imagine, Takahashi faced formidable odds in selling

Japanese war bonds in London in the spring of 1904. Were British financiers likely to be any more sanguine about Japan's prospects of victory over Russia, the behemoth to the east, than New York financiers were? Yūki Yamakawa, manager of the London branch of the Yokohama Specie Bank, a quasi-official arm of the Japanese government, had cabled Takahashi while he was still in New York: 'There is no prospect whatsoever of selling government bonds here now. The Specie Bank has not a penny's worth of credit.' He went on to advise Takahashi to raise the money in New York, because if he came to London he would find only 'shame'. By shame, Yamakawa probably meant the kinds of terms demanded by those London banking houses willing even to talk about a loan to Japan in March 1904, terms that no Japanese government would consider unless absolutely necessary. For example, Baring Brothers and the Hong Kong and Shanghai Bank (HSBC) had floated the possibility of a Japanese loan before Takahashi left Tokyo, but the terms were the same as those demanded on loans to the government of late imperial China: high interest rates, low paying price, customs duty revenues as security, and a 12-month monopoly on all Japanese government foreign loans. And Baring Brothers and HSBC soon balked even at this much. On 7 March, the London office of HSBC notified the Yokohama branch that the bank would not act on the loans now because of a 'continental feeling'. They also wanted American participation before going forward on the loans. And New York's joining in seemed unlikely at this time.

On 4 March, Hugo Baring wrote from New York to his elder brother Lord Revelstoke (John Baring) that James Stillman, chairman of the National City Bank, was pro-Russian and thought Japan could not possibly win the war. On 8 March, Revelstoke wrote back to Hugo that the bank would not take part in the Japanese loans at all at present. According to him, 'the highest people prefer neutrality just now.' On 14 March, in another letter to Hugo, Revelstoke wrote: 'Neither you nor I are enthusiastic about the (Japanese) loan.' The desire for an American presence in the loan syndicate seemed crucial, and the odds on it did not seem to improve with time. On 6 April, Hugo cabled that Stillman, a key player in New York, was 'positive in declining Japan during the war'. The London market in April 1904 reflected an Anglo-American investors' view of Japan's prospects for victory; Japan's prewar bonds fell in value by 25 per cent in the first two months of the war.[6]

Takahashi did have several allies, one known and the others as yet unknown to him. The known supporter was Alexander Allan Shand (1844–1930), a Scots banker 'the Japanese could trust'. Shand was born and had his earliest banking training in Aberdeen. In 1863 he joined the Chartered Mercantile Bank of India, London and China in Hong Kong, and in 1864, at the age of 20, he became the acting manager of the bank's branch in Yokohama. From 1872 until 1877 Shand, as an adviser to the Ministry of Finance, persuaded the Japanese to abandon the American national bank system for the British model, based on a central bank, as a method of controlling the issuance of paper money and inflation, a major problem for Japan in the 1870s. After Shand returned to Britain in the late 1870s, he joined the Alliance Bank, which merged in 1892 with Parr's Bank, and for the rest of his life served as an important ally in the City for Japanese financial officials. He helped the Yokohama Specie Bank open a private account at the Alliance Bank in 1881, which Parr's Bank took over after the merger. In April 1904 Shand served as manager of the Lombard Street branch of Parr's Bank and was the first non-Japanese Takahashi met after his arrival in London.[7]

A day-by-day perusal of Takahashi's diary reveals the difficulties he faced, the perseverance he showed, and his luck. On 7 April, five days after his arrival in London, Shand visited Takahashi for the first time. Within a week, Takahashi had been introduced to Shand's superiors at Parr's, and over the following week he met Koch of Panmure Gordon, Mitchell of Samuel Samuel & Company, Cameron of HSBC, and Lord Rothschild and his brother. But his other two allies were neither anywhere in sight nor, as it turned out, even in Britain.

By mid-April an arrangement to issue Japanese bonds had begun to take shape, but the terms suggested were even harsher than those floated by HSBC and Baring Brothers in February, and they met only a third of Japan's immediate financial needs: £3 million at 6 per cent interest, repayment in five years, selling price of £92 (that is, the Japanese government paid principal and interest as if they received £100, buyers paid £92, and the Japanese government received £89 or £90), customs duty revenues as security, which was most insulting to the proud Japanese, only then regaining from the Western powers the treaty right to set their own customs duties. They were asked to acquiesce in the appointment of a British tariff commissioner, like Sir Robert Hart in China, to oversee the Japanese government's collection of its own import duties.[8]

Given his government's pressing need to pay for imported weapons, the concomitant outflow of Japan's gold reserves, which fell under seven million pounds in May 1904, and the widespread view in London that Japan would have to leave the gold standard, Takahashi was not in a position to quibble over the terms, but he 'would not hear' of the appointment of a tariff commissioner. 'It is a mistake for you to compare

Japan with China. The Japanese government has never fallen even one cent behind in repaying interest or principal. This is true for domestic as well as foreign bonds. It upsets me that you equate Japan with China.' Takahashi wrote that 'the bankers agreed with me and backed down, saying the pledge of security is enough.'[9] He then cabled the terms to his government in Tokyo, which replied that it could not do with less than five million pounds, which was still only half of what it urgently needed, and that the principal should be repaid in seven, not five years, and at a price of £93, not £92. The London bankers agreed to these changes, and the loan negotiations moved forward. Still, as Takeo Imamura, one of Takahashi's early biographers, wrote, these were 'colonial' terms, that is, the kind imposed by Western powers on Asians; a typical loan by London bankers to North American and other European countries would bear only 4 or 5 per cent interest, with repayment in 25 years, and often with no security required at all.[10]

Over the next few weeks, Takahashi continued to carry out daily negotiations to iron out the details of the first of four sets of Russo–Japanese war loans. As one reads through his diary, one finds the names of many of the most prominent London financiers and two new, significant names appear: Sir Ernest Cassel and Jacob Schiff. On 22 April a London banker named H. R. Beeton visited Takahashi and suggested that he try to enlist the services of one of London's first-rate financiers as Japan's primary adviser during the war. Takahashi wrote in his diary: 'In his opinion Sir Earnest [sic] Cassel (old Broad Street) is the man he would recommend, though he is not sure whether he will take into his hand or not. He says the Jews are the first-rate financier, and Cassel is most influential in London. He can invite Rothschild as well as Morgan and so on. Bring out big loans so as to make Anglo–American concern.' Thus, the name of Ernest Cassel enters our story for the first time. His name appears in Takahashi's diary a number of times over the next eight months, but Takahashi does not make an entry to report meeting Cassel until eight months later, when on 16 December he wrote: 'Met Sir Earnest Castle at the dinner at Mrs Schiff.'[11] On 3 May Takahashi wrote: 'At dinner at Hill's, many distinguished guests, among whom Mr Shipley of New York, Green of Rothschild, Junior Levita and his father who is a director of the Chartered Bk., Curzon of Panmure Gordon and Company, Speyers, etc.' Shipley is crossed out and Schiff inked in below. At Arthur Hill's dinner party, Takahashi met Jacob Schiff, senior partner of Kuhn, Loeb of New York. Schiff not only turned out to be the key to Japan's fundraising success in 1904–6, but also became Takahashi's lifelong friend and mentor.[12]

Born into a middle-class Jewish family in Frankfurt in 1847, Schiff emigrated to New York as a teenager in 1865, and by 1904 had become one of the richest men in the world. Through hard work, marriage in 1875 to Therese Loeb, his employer's daughter, and a discerning eye for a good investment, by the turn of the century Schiff had made Kuhn, Loeb the primary rival to the House of Morgan as one of New York's two great investment banks. Like Morgan, Schiff and the investors he brought into his circle helped finance the building of the American railroad system, and reaped the benefits as America expanded westward. And like many other rich men at the turn of the century, Schiff became a generous philanthropist who invested millions in various causes. Although Schiff contributed extensively to Christian and secular charities, the primary focus of his largesse was Jewish organizations, especially those that helped the new Jewish immigrants driven to America from eastern Europe by its pogroms. Schiff was committed to the idea that Jews should assimilate into American society, but without giving up their own religious beliefs, and that he personally had a duty to help newer and poorer immigrants go through this process. He was also committed to using his financial leverage to reform or, if necessary, bring down the anti-Semitic Russian monarchy.[13]

References to Schiff continue. Takahashi writes, for example, on 4 May: 'American firm is Kwun-Rose [Kuhn, Loeb] and Company. 1st rate financier in America.' Then on 6 May: 'American business is almost settled. Agreement between the American House and the issuing Bk. here. Has been settled on at 5 P.M. Prospectus was approved by the Americans.' On 7 May: 'Cameron when he came said Sir Ernest Casttle [Cassel, Takahashi's second still unknown benefactor] said if only English he will not take a penny but as Americans came in he will take 50,000. Schiff (written in Japanese syllabary) after audience to the King yesterday going to spend Saturday at Casttle's with family.' Then, on 9 May he wrote:

> Mr Shand came with Mr Schiff. He was the person with whom I dined with Mr Hill's. He said last Monday was Bk holiday and not in the city. On Tuesday he met Lord Revelstoke and told him that he sent telegram to his American house that now is the time to open business with Japan. Customs security and 6 per cent treasury bond will go very well. What do you think. Revelstoke looking at him told him the loan on something same basis has just been concluded. Want you take half of 10,000,000. On Thursday everything was settled. When Schiff saw the King in Audience, he

> was told the King was satisfied to the American participation. That show Anglo–American combination in the Far East. The King was glad that his country alone was not to supply money to Japan. These were all confidential. Schiff asked me to call on him (in New York) on way to Japan.

And finally, on 10 May, Takahashi writes: 'Mr Schiff came with Mr Otto H. Kahn [Kuhn] and Shand. They brought telegram of full prospectus. Agreement was duly drawn and signed and exchanged at this date. Mr Kahn says the King was very much pleased to see the Americans coming in.'[14] Amazingly, within a week of meeting Takahashi at Arthur Hill's dinner party, Schiff had agreed to help the Japanese raise the needed ten million pounds by underwriting five million pounds of Japanese bonds, an amount equal to that of all three issuers in London, through Kuhn, Loeb in New York; he had arranged for a contract to be drawn up and signed and a prospectus to be written in New York and cabled to London. And Edward VII even gave his approval. How and why did this happen so quickly?

As mentioned above, Takahashi left us two other accounts of his meeting with Schiff, both more coherent in their exposition because they were written after the fact. One comes in Takahashi's memoirs, published in the mid-1930s serially in the major Tokyo daily newspaper, the *Tōkyō Asahi Shinbun*, and then reissued as a book in 1936 after his murder. The other, ghost-written for Takahashi by Eigo Fukai, and revised by Takahashi, appears in Volume 1 of the official biography of Schiff, drafted by his close associate Cyrus Adler and published in 1929. According to this account, when Takahashi attended a party at the Hill residence he happened to sit beside Schiff.

> Over dinner, he [Schiff] asked me [Takahashi] detailed questions about the Japanese economy, the conditions of our production, and the people's morale during the war. I answered as well as I could. Near the end, I told him about my satisfaction over the agreement with the London bankers to issue five million pounds of bonds, but that the Japanese government wanted to issue ten million. The London bankers at this time thought that more than five million was out of the question, and I had reluctantly agreed. We talked of other things and parted.[15]

The next day Shand came to see Takahashi and told him that 'Schiff of Kuhn, Loeb, which was the Parr's Bank agent in New York, wants to issue five million pounds of Japan's bonds in New York.' Takahashi was 'dumbfounded' because he had never heard of Schiff or Kuhn, Loeb before Hill's party. Takahashi had no idea to what he should attribute his fortuitous meeting; he concluded after his talk with Schiff at Hill's dinner that Japan's 'good fortune occurred because of an accidental meeting'.[16] But the meeting was far less accidental than Takahashi knew.

It is widely accepted that Schiff supported Japan in 1904–5 because of his hatred of the Romanov dynasty and its anti-Semitism.[17] The sceptical historian, who thinks people tend to act out of personal self-interest and not for idealistic reasons, may question such a 'truism', but hard as I have tried to test it, the evidence I have seen tends to support the view that Schiff lent money to the Japanese out of his desire to help his coreligionists in Russia. From the 1890s until the Russian Revolution in 1917, Schiff was a leader in the movement to end the persecution and suffering of Jews in the Russian empire. He compared the plight of Russian Jews with that of their ancestors in Egypt and, according to Naomi Cohen, his most recent biographer, 'doubtless saw himself as another Moses'. Cohen quotes Schiff as writing in 1907, 'I am so grateful to God that He so placed me to be able to be of some help to our coreligionists' in Russia. She then adds that his 'struggle for Jewish liberation in Russia took on the emotional overtones of a personal crusade, almost as if the czar were hounding him, Jacob Schiff'.[18] For more than twenty years, Schiff poured millions of his dollars and hours of his time into lobbying officials like Presidents Roosevelt and Taft and their successive secretaries of state, into battling the public views of successive pro-Romanov journalists and American ministers to St Petersburg, and into using his power in the world of money to prevent investment in Russia by New York and London banks and financiers.

In the first week of February 1904, just before embarking on one of his frequent trips to Europe, Schiff held a meeting at his home of important New York Jewish leaders. He told them: 'Within 72 hours war will break out between Japan and Russia. The question has been presented to me of undertaking a loan for Japan. I would like to get your views as to what effect my undertaking of this would have upon the Jewish people in Russia.'[19] In other words, a month before Takahashi arrived in Great Britain, and two months before Schiff and Takahashi met at Hill's, Schiff was already considering a loan to Japan, and considering it although almost every other financier in New York thought the inevitability of Japan's defeat made the risks of such a loan too great.

Waiting for Schiff in Europe was his close friend and frequent travelling companion, the third of Takahashi's angels, Ernest Cassel.

While Cassel did not actually underwrite Japanese war bonds – he was one of the largest purchasers, however – and although he never came out of the shadows into the forefront of our story (Cassel and Takahashi apparently did not even meet until ten months after the latter's arrival in London, and when they did, it was at Schiff's home in New York),[20] he appears to have played an important role in bringing the key players together to form a loan syndicate. Cassel like Schiff was born in Germany, in 1852 in Cologne, and also emigrated as a teenager, in his case to London. He met Schiff in 1879 because of their mutual interest in investing in North American railroads. Over the next 40 years the men made many investments together (including Pittsburgh's Westinghouse Electric Company), while Kuhn, Loeb handled Cassel's financial affairs in America. The two men exchanged over 1500 letters (in German) on finance, family and politics for more than forty years. Cassel especially endeared himself to Schiff by saving his daughter Frieda from a mountain-climbing accident in Switzerland in 1890. In addition to being one of the richest financiers in London and along with Lord Rothschild and Lord Revelstoke, one of three key advisers to the Treasury and the Bank of England, Cassel served as primary financial adviser to Queen Victoria's son, both when he was Prince of Wales and when he became Edward VII; thus his sobriquet, 'Windsor Cassel'.[21]

Schiff arrived in London in 1904, in the aftermath of the 1903 pogrom at Kishinev, outraged over both the complicity of the Russian government and its repeated denials that there had been any atrocities at all. He arrived, however, not directly from New York, but from Germany, where he had gone after the February meeting with Jewish leaders. On his way back to New York via London, he met his friend Cassel in Frankfurt. Although there is no evidence that the two spoke of loans to Japan at the time, given Schiff's prior interest in the possibility of a loan and Cassel's closeness to Schiff and his own anger over the Russian pogroms, it seems likely they did. Moreover, before meeting Schiff in Germany, Cassel had been in contact with an important mutual business associate, Lord Revelstoke. Revelstoke and Baring Brothers wanted to help the Japanese government; as we have seen, they had floated a loan proposal even before Takahashi left Tokyo, but had stepped back and refrained from active participation for two reasons: they had extensive investments in Russia that they did not want to endanger, and they and their government did not want Britain to side with Japan unless New York money came in. Given Stillman's and National City Bank's opposition to loans to Japan, and the silence of Morgan's and other Protestant New York financial houses, Schiff's interest seemed god-sent. Thus, Cassel and

Revelstoke became the go-betweens in bringing British and American capital together to support Japan.[22]

While this is shadowy, there are fascinating bits of evidence that seem to indicate that Schiff's meeting with Takahashi was not accidental but arranged, probably by Cassel and Revelstoke, and these conjunctions explain why the loan arrangements moved forward so quickly. The Baring journals are instructive here. They indicate that on Tuesday 3 May, the very date on which Schiff and Takahashi met at Hill's in the evening, Revelstoke wrote a letter to one of his associates in which he stated that a loan to Japan of ten million pounds had been arranged, half to be handled by Parr's Bank and the Hong Kong and Shanghai Bank in London, the other half through Kuhn, Loeb in New York. In other words, Schiff and the banks, through the intercession of Cassel and Revelstoke, had completed an agreement to issue the bonds before Schiff and Takahashi met that evening. The next day, 4 May, Schiff wrote from Claridge's Hotel to tell Revelstoke that 'things were falling into place in New York'. He also said that he had met Takahashi the night before at Hill's, and that Sir Ewen Cameron, manager of the London office of HSBC, was also there. There is a note to Revelstoke from the foreign secretary, Marquess Lansdowne on 4 May, to say that he had informed the prime minister of the 'admirable arrangements', and that the latter wanted Revelstoke to brief him. Then, on 5 May, a meeting took place between Cameron, Schiff and Revelstoke to work out the final terms of the loan. And finally, on 8 May, Whalley of Parr's Bank wrote that Schiff, Revelstoke, Cameron and 'the Japanese gentleman' were coming to see him.[23] This was Takahashi's first meeting with Schiff since the dinner party five days earlier. The details of the loan had been worked out without the two key players meeting again and with one entirely outside the loop.

My interpretation of this evidence is as follows: Schiff wanted to lend money to the Japanese because of his hatred of Russian anti-Semitism. Through Cassel and Revelstoke he learnt of the London plans to issue Japanese bonds, which did not provide the Japanese with all the funds they needed. Schiff agreed to provide the other half of the money, and did so even before he met Takahashi. Cassel and Revelstoke arranged for Schiff and Takahashi to meet at Hill's dinner party to bring the Japanese government into the picture. While Cassel's role is nebulous, the Japanese government recognized its importance. It presented decorations for services to Japan to Revelstoke, Schiff, Sir Thomas Jackson, chairman of HSBC, Cecil Parr of Parr's Bank, A. M. Townsend of HSBC, and Cassel.[24] Shand, who did all of the legwork in bringing everyone together, received nothing.

I should add that Revelstoke and Cassel had an additional motive for supporting Japan, the desire to bring about closer cooperation between London and New York financiers. Cassel, who as we have seen would not buy Japanese bonds in May 1904 unless the Americans came in, explained it as follows in a letter to Takahashi in the summer of 1905:

> I was not in London at the time of the first issuance of Japanese bonds. I telegraphed Baring Brothers and bought 50,000 pounds worth. There was a reason for this. I wanted to bring the British and American people closer together. I saw that the Americans (Schiff) burned with true sympathy for Japan early in the war. I helped bring about the issuance of Japanese bonds in the two countries to unify their sympathy for Japan and to create intimacy between the United States and Great Britain, which had been previously estranged.[25]

It was the efforts to achieve this goal that impelled both Edward VII, who after all was related to the Russian dynasty, and Lord Lansdowne to praise Cassel, Schiff and the others for their 'admirable arrangement'.

The first Russo–Japanese war loans were issued on 11 May 1904, one-half by Parr's Bank, HSBC, and the Yokohama Specie Bank in London, and the other half by Kuhn, Loeb in New York. The Japanese government, desperately in need of money to meet wartime expenses, agreed to terms it would not have accepted three months earlier. Because the lenders considered the loans to be risky, they issued ten million pounds of bonds at 6 per cent, a selling price of ninety-three and one-half pounds, issuing fees of three and one-half per cent, so that the Japanese government received nine million pounds but paid back ten, for seven years, with customs duty revenues as hypothecation. Schiff's investment turned out to be a sound one. Several days before the bonds went on the market, the Japanese won a resounding victory at the Battle of the Yalu River. When the bonds went on the market in London and New York on 11 May, investors stood in queues two or three blocks long to place their orders, and the issuing banks closed by mid-afternoon. Demand reached twenty-six times the supply of bonds in London, nine times in New York.[26] The chance to buy reasonably low-risk, 6 per cent bonds at ninety-three and one-half came to market rarely.

Almost immediately, the Japanese government began efforts to raise more money. While there is not space to trace the ensuing negotiations over the next 18 months, let me summarize. Japan made three more bond issuances before the war ended in August 1905. It received better and better terms so that the two 1905 issuances, for a total of £60 million, were made at 4.5 per cent interest and for 25 years. All together, the Japanese government borrowed £82 million in four trenches. Of this amount, Kuhn, Loeb underwrote £39,250,000, or just under 48 per cent. Ten million pounds' worth, one-third of the final issuance in July 1905, was issued in Germany, where Schiff's son-in-law's family, the Warburgs, served as primary underwriters. It is probably safe to say that Kuhn, Loeb and related investment houses underwrote half of Japan's foreign borrowing, and thus one-quarter of the total cost of its victory over Russia.

Schiff ended up having the best of both worlds. On the one hand, as he said to Takahashi, he bought the Japanese bonds for reasons other than making money:

> I am not buying Japanese war bonds simply for profit. I do so because Japan is at war with Russia. Thus, my loans are indispensable money (for Japan). We are Jews. We have many Jewish brethren in Russia. But the Russians torment our brethren. The Russian tsars have a history of persecuting Jews. Saying 'stop torturing Jews', we sometimes lend money to the Russians. But after they have taken our money, they start the persecution again. Jews are disgusted with the tsars. We pray for the fall of the Russian monarchy. Now Japan has gone to war with Russia. If Japan wins the war, a revolution will surely break out in Russia. Thus, the monarchy will be buried. Because I pray for this, I am lending money to Japan.[27]

And Schiff made money too.

Epilogue

The Japanese government invited Schiff to Japan in 1906, and his account of the journey makes it sound like a progression of royalty, which it was: financial royalty. Schiff travelled across America in a private train on a series of railroads he had helped finance; the president or vice-president of each one boarded the train as it entered his territory, exited as it left. He sailed sumptuously across the Pacific to Yokohama, stopping only in Hawaii to meet Liliuokalani, the deposed queen. In Tokyo, he met most of Japan's major leaders and many minor ones: the elder statesmen Itō (who came from Korea expressly to meet Schiff), Yamagata, Inoue and Matsukata; the wartime prime minister, General Katsura, and his successor, Prince Saionji; the wartime military leaders, General Ōyama, and Admiral Tōgō, but oddly, not General Nogi; important members of the financial world with names like Mitsui, Iwasaki, and Shibusawa; various government ministers, past and present, including Takaaki Katō, who had recently resigned as foreign minister as a protest against the railroad nationalization, and two successive finance ministers, Sone and Sakatani, for example; Yukio Ozaki, the mayor of Tokyo; and of course, his new friend, Takahashi, vice governor of the Bank of Japan. The Meiji Emperor entertained Schiff at a Western-style luncheon, and he became the first person ever to toast the emperor: like George Washington, 'First in war, first in peace, first in the hearts of his countrymen.' The emperor presented Schiff with the highest decoration any foreigner had received from him up until that time. Schiff and his entourage then travelled to Kyoto, in another private train, this one provided for them by the Japanese government, which had nationalized the railroads only weeks before Schiff's arrival.[28]

Takahashi's wartime experience and his budding friendship with Schiff – for example, Takahashi's adolescent daughter Wakiko returned to New York with the Schiffs and lived with them there for three years – influenced Takahashi in ways too numerous to present in this essay. But I want to mention one of these influences here. Takahashi was certainly a nationalist, and if one can identify an overriding purpose to his career it was to make Japan and the Japanese rich enough to stand up to the West. But he learnt between 1904 and 1906 in London and New York the importance of cooperation with the British and Americans. For the rest of his life, Takahashi preached that Japan's economic development and national defence depended on Anglo–American capital, markets, raw materials, technology and goodwill. Because of these views, young army officers brutally murdered him in 1936, and their superiors led Japan in a more autarkic and ultimately disastrous direction thereafter. Luckily, Schiff was not alive when Takahashi was assassinated; nor was Takahashi alive when Japan met crushing defeat by the countries he thought should be its allies.

Chapter 2

BRITAIN AND THE JAPANESE ECONOMY DURING THE FIRST WORLD WAR

Janet Hunter

The contribution of economic factors to the tensions that led to war between Japan, Britain and the United States in 1941 has been much debated, and it is clear that during the 1930s economic frictions between Britain and Japan were a recurrent feature.[1] Those frictions had their origin in earlier decades, in the shifting balance of the economic power of the two nations within the international economy. Economic historians widely accept that the First World War marked a watershed in the structure and operation of the international economy, affecting profoundly the fortunes of both Britain and Japan, and hence their mutual economic relationship. With the benefit of hindsight it has not been hard to catalogue the nature of this transition. Analysis of the functioning of the international economy, and of both the British and Japanese economies, has revealed many reasons why Britain was less and less able to retain her pre-1914 dominance, and why Japan was able to build on the wartime circumstances to push forward her overall industrialization process.[2] In this chapter I do not seek to reject these explanations. I do argue, however, that it was far from easy for contemporaries to predict the divergence that was to occur in the relative economic fortunes of the two nations.

While in a number of instances it was apparent even during the war that the Japanese economy had benefited at the expense of Britain, making inroads into foreign markets formerly dominated by British exports, as well as Britain's own domestic market, this was far from true across the board. Moreover, even during the war years, and in the year or two that followed, circumstances seemed to provide powerful evidence that many of Japan's wartime gains were likely to be of a temporary nature. Many obstacles existed to Japan's sustaining her remarkable progress of the war years, let alone using it as a platform for further development. Problems stemming from Japan's position as a late industrializing economy were widely recognized in both Britain and Japan. In this chapter, by locating wartime trends in the context of more fundamental structural problems in Japan's economy, politics and society, I argue that the relative divergence in the fortunes of the two economies that occurred from the late 1920s, and the economic frictions it brought with it, were far from being either predictable or preordained.[3]

The chapter will start with a brief overview of the effect of the First World War on the functioning of the international economy, and the positions of Britain and Japan within it. Particular attention will be paid to the impact of wartime conditions on the Japanese economy, and the way in which they acted as a stimulus to longer term growth. I will suggest that analysis of published statistical data on trade between Japan, Britain and the British Empire over the years from 1913 to 1921 indicates that in most respects the shape of commodity trade seemed to be reverting to its prewar pattern by 1921, once the wartime boom had collapsed. In the second section of the chapter I focus on how the expansion of Japan's economy was perceived in wartime Britain. Contemporary British publications are used to identify those aspects of Japanese trade and shipping expansion that were of most concern to Britain, and to show how far British commentators were concerned about the longer term implications of what was happening. The main publications used are *The Times*, the *Economist* and the *Board of Trade Journal*, all of which were widely read by businessmen as well as officials and other opinion makers. In the final part of the chapter I discuss the potential and actual problems facing the Japanese economy over the years 1914–20 which indicated to contemporaries that the country's economic base was essentially weak. It will be shown that the existence of these structural weaknesses was widely recognized in Britain.

Recent scholarship has indicated that well before 1914 weaknesses had begun to appear in Britain's industrial structure, and many have questioned the ability of British entrepreneurs to cope with the fundamental changes required to sustain British leadership in the context of new industries and growing competition from countries such as the United States and Germany. The possession of empire, the extent of

British capital exports and the pivotal role of London in international financial dealings placed Britain at the centre of the international economic system, but British industry often found it difficult to obtain capital. Income and wage differentials were considerable, and only the very last years before 1914 saw the British government starting to initiate more equitable tax and budgetary policies to improve the welfare of the less advantaged. The demands made by war on the British economy were enormous, and policymakers only gradually moved away from a reliance on the private sector towards a more coordinated system of government directed procurement, production, pricing and distribution. By the end of the war, the government had instituted near total control over large parts of industrial and agricultural activity. Notwithstanding the diversion of millions of workers for the conflict, and the switching of capacity to war-related production, the total output of British industry remained fairly stable. Capacity in industries such as shipbuilding and steel production increased substantially, while a number of new industries appeared to substitute for imports from Germany. Indeed, the effective removal of Germany as Britain's most powerful trading competitor was of crucial significance for the British economy, although Germany's demise was partly counterbalanced by the rise of the United States.[4]

In financial terms, the war years were characterized by an increase in the national debt, substantial growth in taxation and a measure of inflation. It is the impact of the war on Britain's international position, however, that is of most concern to us here. Diversion of resources to war production contributed to a decline in the export trade, while British sales of shipping capacity and other invisibles likewise declined. Britain borrowed extensively, but continued to lend, now in the changed context of the suspension of the international gold standard system, and an increasingly dominant role for the United States in the international payments system. In the immediate aftermath of the war, industrial unrest and wage claims mushroomed. Some contemporaries, stunned by the Bolshevik takeover in Russia and the unrest elsewhere in Europe, perceived the situation as potentially revolutionary. Expanded industries were compelled to compete for limited markets with their counterparts in other countries whose capacity had expanded even more. The prewar problems of a perceived lack of entrepreneurial initiative, distortion of financial incentives and failure to cope with more efficient competitors, combined with the changed structure of international payments, widespread recession and growing protectionism contributed further to Britain's relative decline. The volume of international trade decreased, and Britain's industries were increasingly uncompetitive within a shrinking market. It is apparent that the war had a distorting effect on the structure of the economy, temporarily strengthening and sustaining Britain's old staple industries. In the immediate aftermath of the conflict economic policy and social unrest appear to have exacerbated underlying structural problems and confirmed labour-market rigidities, all of which undermined Britain's competitiveness in a worsening international situation. There is considerable debate among economic historians over the impact of the First World War on the longer term development of the British economy, but whatever the case, there is no doubt that the war and immediate postwar years generated changes in Britain's domestic and international situation that made any return to the pre-1914 *status quo* impossible. In the Japanese case, the part played by the war is often depicted as rather more clear-cut.

As an ally of Britain, Japan was technically a belligerent, but her military involvement was very limited. This position, it is argued, left Japan free to make the most of the changed imperatives brought about in the international trading system by the war, while avoiding the costs and burdens borne by other belligerents, as well as limiting the associated distortions in the domestic economy. While the Japanese economy was initially thrown into disarray by the problems in the international payments system, the reduction of imports from the enemy economies of Germany and Austro-Hungary, and the diversion of shipping capacity to war purposes, it is apparent that over the longer term the Japanese economy benefited in several ways from the war, and that Japan was able to capitalize on these changes in the progress of interwar industrialization and trade.

The advantages identified as having accrued to Japan from the upheavals in Europe are several. First, Japan was favourably placed to meet allied demands for war *matériel*, notably guns, ammunition, uniforms and provisions. This stimulated the production of industries already well established. Second, the cutting off of supplies of a range of commodities both from the countries with which Japan was at war, particularly Germany, and from her allies, who could no longer satisfy Japanese demand, stimulated a substantial element of import substitution, in which Japan established new indigenous industries to supply her own needs. Third, the war in Europe made it impossible for countries such as Britain to continue to supply many former markets in China, India and other parts of Asia, Africa and Latin America, and thus Japan was able to step into this gap with her own exports. Fourth, the war exigencies created an expanded demand for shipbuilding and the carrying trade, and during the four years of conflict Japan became one of the world's major cargo carriers, dominating in particular trade in Asia. This combined stimulus brought about substantial increases in industrial production, led to the growth of both existing and new industries, and the founding of large numbers of enterprises. The balance of commodity trade turned sharply in Japan's favour, and the country experienced a brief period of export-led growth.

It is recognized that the transition was not problem free. Prices soared and speculation was rampant. The financial basis of many enterprises was weak and many collapsed after the war. Japan was no more immune to popular unrest and labour discontent than most countries of Europe. However, there is a degree of consensus that most of the gains that were made were never really lost. Notwithstanding the self-evident problems of the earlier postwar years, the war was essentially a catalyst for interwar industrial growth and an agent for Japan's becoming a core player in the international economy. Britain's relative decline seems clearly juxtaposed against Japan's relative rise. It is harder to prove, however, that there was any direct link between Japan's rise and Britain's 'decline', and this is apparent if we look briefly at the issue of commodity trade.

The dramatic expansion in the volume of Japanese trade during the war has been well documented. The yen value of Japanese exports increased more than 300 per cent between 1913 and 1919, and the value of imports by almost as much.[5] With the belligerents unable to make freight space available, an increasing proportion of this trade was carried in Japanese ships. The tonnage of Japanese shipping increased dramatically and shipping receipts even more. A structural shift in export composition also took place. While textiles remained the most important export, there was a relative increase in the importance of items such as chemicals, industrial machinery and transport equipment. The significance of Europe, including Britain, as a source of Japanese imports diminished, while the United States became more important. There was a geographical shift in Japanese trade towards East, Southeast and South Asia, which together accounted for 51 per cent of all Japan's exports in 1920.[6]

Trading relations between Britain and Japan during the war were not always harmonious. Japan's apparent reluctance to cease trading with the enemy caused concern,[7] while a British ban on imports of non-essential goods from Japan early in 1917 threatened some important areas of Japanese production. Japan's cotton hosiery producers, for example, who were estimated to send around 30 per cent of their total exports to Britain, were particularly exercised by the prohibition, although intergovernmental recognition of Britain's necessary war priorities helped to override the sectional interest.[8] Even at the time Japan's trading success aroused antagonism in Britain. The fact that between 1913 and 1923 exports of British cotton piece goods to India declined by 57 per cent seemed to offer cogent evidence that Japan was taking markets from Britain.[9] However, the official figures for commodity trade do not confirm that Japan was necessarily gaining at British expense. Indeed, they suggest for the most part a return to the *status quo ante* by the early 1920s.

Anglo-Japanese trade was much more important for Japan than for Britain and remained so into the early 1920s. Over these years Japan never accounted for more than 2.5 per cent of the total value of British exports and 1.5 per cent of the value of British imports. The British share of Japan's exports by value increased considerably during the war, from just over 5 per cent before 1914 to a peak of over 12 per cent in 1917, but by 1920 the figure had fallen back to 5 per cent. Britain's share of the commodities imported into Japan showed a sustained decline from nearly 19 per cent by value in 1912 to only 4 per cent in 1918, but by 1921 the figure had risen again, although it remained significantly below the prewar level.[10]

In the years immediately prior to the start of the war Britain enjoyed a substantial surplus in her trade with Japan. Between 1912 and 1914 the value of Britain's exports to Japan was worth three to four times the value of imports from Japan. During the war years the position was reversed, and in 1917 Japan exported to Britain over three times as much (in value) as was imported from Britain. By 1919, however, the balance had again reverted in Britain's favour. In 1921 the value of Britain's exports to Japan was nearly six times the value of British imports from Japan.[11] These aggregate figures therefore suggest that in terms of bilateral trade, at least, many of the gains made by Japan could be seen in the early 1920s as essentially temporary ones, largely reversed once the wartime boom collapsed. Such a conclusion is also confirmed if we consider the composition of bilateral commodity trade.[12]

While the volume of foodstuffs and raw materials imported from Japan into Britain increased dramatically during the war years, almost all of the expansion had been wiped out by 1921. A similar pattern can be identified in imports of manufactured goods from Japan. Imports of some commodities, such as cotton yarn and china, were still substantially above their 1913 import level in 1921, but it is hard to extract from the trends any evidence of the war's allowing Japan to make conclusive and permanent gains in the British market. Japan's export strength in relation to Britain remained in 'traditional' items such as silk and cotton textiles, china, straw plaiting, haberdashery, curios and house wares. Looking at such an import pattern, both British and Japanese observers might be justified in thinking that Japan was hardly on a new trajectory. Even where gains had been made, it was difficult to conceive of Japan's sustaining competitiveness in the postwar world of renewed productive activity in Europe, a surplus of shipping capacity and dramatic falls in freight costs.

Whereas Japanese exports to Britain rose and fell over the war years, British exports to Japan fell and then rose. Some traditionally important export items, such as clothing, scientific instruments and machinery, were being exported on a much larger scale to Japan in 1921 than they had been in 1913. The one major exception to this trend was shipbuilding. In 1913 British-built ships and boats accounted for around one-fifth of the total value of British exports to Japan. After 1920 this item virtually ceased to figure in the data.

While aggregate figures of this kind indicate that many of the gains made by Japan were soon reversed, they also provide some indications that the relative positions of the two economies had perhaps been changed for good by the war. High levels of British manufacturing exports to Japan during the immediate aftermath of the war were buoyed by a backlog in demand, the high level of prices in Japan and the increased purchasing power of many Japanese. They were in themselves indicative of advances made in Japan's own manufacturing sector. Expanding industries needed to buy in capital goods and technology where they as yet possessed insufficient capacity and know-how to produce for themselves. The demise of British ship exports was a reflection both of the expansion that had taken place in Japan's own construction capacity, and the world's excess capacity in this area.[13] However, the extent of the general shift appears limited. Britain remained a crucial supplier of manufactured goods to Japan.

Even if we look at Japanese trade with the British Empire, an increasingly controversial issue, the evidence of irreversible change seems far from conclusive. It is well documented that Japan's exports to third countries expanded during the war, particularly in Asia, but while the British might have been expected over the long term to concede some of their substantial share of the China market to Japan, the British share of markets in the colonies and dominions, particularly India, Southeast Asia, Australia and South Africa, seemed likely to prove more resilient. British Empire trade accounted for one-quarter to one-third of Japan's trade during the war and early postwar years. No obvious trend is apparent between 1912 and 1921, but, if anything, the importance of the Empire to Japan declined slightly. Commentators during the war found plenty of evidence that Japan was exporting on a substantial scale to

British colonies and dominions, and expected that trade to increase, but despite an increase in the volume of Japanese exports to the Empire, Japan enjoyed a surplus in her trade with the Empire only in 1917–18. After 1921 the trading deficit did not merely reappear, but widened further. So, Japan did increase her exports to the Empire, in some cases at the expense of British and German producers, but remained far more dependent on the Empire for her imports than for her exports. Throughout the early 1920s the Empire provided 30–40 per cent of Japan's imports by value, while it took only around 20 per cent of Japan's total exports.[14]

In the all-important trade with British India, Japan was consistently in deficit, and in as far as raw materials imports were likely to become of even greater importance as Japan's industrialization proceeded, this trend appeared likely to continue. It may be suggested, therefore, that the direction of both bilateral and Empire trade with Japan provided little basis in the early 1920s for any conclusive judgement on what the wartime period might mean for the future of the trading relationship. The broader understanding that prevailed in Britain concerning the structures, weaknesses and strengths of the Japanese economy, and of its international position, only served to increase doubts about the future of the Japanese economy. It is to this broader understanding that we shall now turn.

It is too easy to forget that at the onset of the First World War Japanese manufacturing capacity was still relatively small by international standards. Her share of world trade was minimal, at only 1.8 per cent in 1913, by comparison with Britain's 15.2 per cent.[15] Her mechanized manufacturing capacity was limited. Her ability to respond to the stimulus offered by the war was therefore constrained by the structural weaknesses experienced by other 'relatively backward', late industrializing economies. A further constraint was the pressure placed on Japan's economy and society by the war itself. That these problems were recognized at the time, both in Japan and in Britain, is in itself powerful evidence against the legitimacy of any claim that the war was bound to lead to long-term gains for Japan, and that contemporaries who thought otherwise were short-sighted in the extreme.

The structural problems appeared gradually. The initial impact of the conflict was to throw the Japanese economy into confusion. The country was highly vulnerable to the dislocation in international trading and exchange networks that ensued after the autumn of 1914. Restrictions on financial operations in London spelt disaster for Japan, which had tended to hold free money in London, and to borrow there. A high proportion of foreign bills was payable in London, and export bills were almost all sent to London for discounting. In August 1914 there were bills due for payment in London, Japan needed to make remittances to meet those payments, but there were no export bills there on which money could be raised. Bills had hitherto been sent to London via the Siberian railway, but suspension of this route meant that Japan was in danger of defaulting upon her interest payments, a situation threatening national bankruptcy.[16] Commercial transport links, particularly in ocean-going shipping, were truncated and distorted by the conflict, as the belligerents commandeered vessels for war purposes and essential supplies. With less than 50 per cent of cargo entering and leaving Japan's ports in 1913 carried by Japanese ships,[17] the situation would have provoked severe problems had it not been for the slump in trade that also resulted. As insurers refused to indemnify shipping companies for war losses, the Japanese government was compelled to step in to give compensating financial guarantees. Even Japan's main exports of silk and cotton yarn were badly hit, while supplies of some of Japan's essential imports, such as pig iron, metals and drugs, declined or virtually dried up. The prices of many others soared. The *Asahi Shinbun* reported in September 1914 that:

> All imported goods are increasing rapidly in price, while exported goods are rapidly declining. The decline in hemp and straw braids amounts to 40 per cent, while manufacturers and merchants are selling shell buttons at a drop of 20 to 30 per cent. The goods shipped to Europe after the middle of June are still on their way, and it is uncertain whether those shipped to Germany will reach the consignees or be accepted. If they are refused, the drafts will not be honoured in Germany, and the exporters will suffer another blow.[18]

While Japanese shippers had the potential of higher freight earnings, it looked unlikely that there would be sufficient trade or capacity to capitalize on them. Late in 1914 the Osaka Chamber of Commerce commented on the fact that the blow given by the war to commerce was aggravated by the nervousness of the banking system, and that the all important cotton industry was among those industries hit by the recession. Prospects for a rapid recovery were deemed to be poor.[19] All in all, the initial outlook seemed very grim, and it took several months for the situation to stabilize into one in which the prospects for Japan looked more positive. Even then, it took a while for traders to cast off the caution engendered by doubt about whether any favourable conditions were likely to last. It was at this point that the obstacles to longer term gains by Japan became apparent. These obstacles can be broadly divided into four main categories. Three of the categories were associated with the production process, and related to inputs, capacity and output. The fourth category consisted of problems of infrastructure and the economy more broadly.

The problems of inputs and capacity were closely related. In 1914 the capacity of Japanese manufacturing to produce on a large scale for export was relatively small. As demand patterns shifted, and demand for Japan's exports grew, Japanese manufacturers sought to increase their output to satisfy this demand. Such expansion, however, was dependent on imports, both of the inputs necessary to produce, and of the capital goods required to expand production capacity. While the inflow of some imported inputs could be sustained by paying more in the face of rising prices, the supply of others was sharply limited by export bans and prioritization of supplies to the belligerents themselves for war purposes. While Japan was able to increase domestic supplies of some minerals, those such as zinc, copper and coal, iron ore and pig iron supplies, much of which were imported, continued to be a problem. Shortfalls in dyestuffs from Germany, the world's major supplier, were a threat to the textile industry. Expansion of shipbuilding production was hindered by the lack of steel plate, as producers in countries such as Britain diverted supplies to their own needs. Demand for woollen cloth for use by the Russian army soared, but Japan found it difficult to import the raw wool from which the cloth could be made. Obtaining wool from Australia proved problematic, and Japan turned for some of her supply to South Africa, only to have some of that diverted to British and Empire needs.[20] Demand for paper increased, but the industry found it difficult to obtain the supply of wood required to respond.[21] Zinc was another potentially expanding industry that faced problems with imported raw material supplies. In the case of some of these infant industries, such as dyestuffs, the input problem could be addressed by import substitution, namely by Japan developing her own industries to produce these inputs. Alternatively, she could try and switch her main sources of supply. As Britain and other belligerents proved unable to supply Japan with pig iron, for example, Japan turned to other Asian countries, particularly India. The shortfall in supplies of iron plates and sheets for shipbuilding was eventually made up mostly from the United States, but the United States itself placed bans on the export of steel.[22] Where raw materials were concerned, such as iron ore, raw cotton or raw wool, the problem would prove more intractable.

Just as serious were the constraints the war situation imposed on a rapid expansion in productive capacity. Such expansion required technology transfer, usually taking the form of importing machinery. Even assuming that such supplies could be imported, installation and operation of the new capacity required an expanded, and often skilled, workforce, and a growing population of engineers and other technical staff. Such changes could not be achieved overnight. The cotton industry, one of Japan's staples, is a good example of this problem. Since its inception Japan's modern cotton spinning industry had relied on imported machinery, most of it from Platt Brothers and other firms in Lancashire. The outbreak of the war posed an immediate threat to such imports, which were essential if Japan were to make the most of Britain's own inability to supply markets in Asia. Japanese demand for spindles rocketed, but difficulties in importing machinery were noted as early as 1915, and there were repeated reports that most of Japan's orders could not be filled.[23] British exports were restricted as metal making and engineering skills were diverted to war purposes, and as shipping capacity, too, was commandeered for alternative uses. The Japanese weaving industry had evolved largely on the basis of indigenous technology, so was relatively unaffected by lack of machinery imports, but it was damaged by shortages of the thread upon which it depended. Turning to alternative sources of machinery was not easy. Developing an indigenous capital goods industry was a slow process, requiring scarce know-how and investment, although it was reported by the Board of Trade in the spring of 1917 that a company in Kobe had achieved good results in the manufacturing of frames and spindles, and that a practical trial had been successful.[24] The United States was a potential alternative source of imports, but Japan was largely locked into the standards and patterns imposed by British machines.

> Practically all the existing mills are fitted with British machinery, and the workers are now so thoroughly accustomed to its use that although there has been a good deal of talk about introducing American machinery, it is unlikely that such a drastic step will be taken – at least in the near future. Conditions in the Japanese mills are said to be quite unsuited to the adoption of American machinery, and it is most probable therefore that the United Kingdom will remain the chief source of supply, though it must not be forgotten that Japan herself is producing spinning appliances and machinery in increasingly large quantities.[25]

The war itself therefore posed limits to import-substitution industrialization. But even allowing for Japan's ability to supply, her manufacturers did not always provide exactly what the British or Empire purchaser wanted; in other words, the output failed to reach the required standards. Much of the attraction of Japanese goods lay in their relatively lower prices. In 1915, for example, toys from Japan replaced those formerly imported into Britain from Germany as 'cheaper' Christmas novelties.[26]

Low prices were also an attraction to low income consumers in developing countries. However, for many purchasers cheapness could not compensate for lack of quality. Complaints regarding the low quality of Japanese products are familiar from the interwar period, and from the early decades after 1945. It is apparent, however, that many of the commodities exported by Japan during the First World War also appeared distinctly shoddy to many customers. It was suggested in 1919 that the poor quality of output was a key factor in the collapse of some of the more speculative Japanese shipyards founded to capitalize on the war boom.[27] Not just in Britain itself, but in other key export markets such as India, Australia and South Africa as well, there was vocal criticism of poor quality Japanese goods and inappropriate practices by Japanese merchants. The *Economist* repeatedly reported on a range of complaints over the quality and supply of Japanese commodities.[28] *The Times* summed up the situation in the autumn of 1917: 'The authorities have come to the conclusion that if the great development achieved by Japan's foreign trade since the outbreak of the war is to be permanently preserved, it is of urgent necessity to prevent the production of inferior goods.'[29]

An official sent to Australia by the Japanese Ministry of Agriculture and Commerce to investigate the situation listed a range of complaints, including shipments not coming up to sample, imperfect packing and in general the supply of inferior goods. He also noted that Japanese merchants had been repeatedly accused of breach of contract, 'sharp practices' and duplicity with regard to appointed agents.[30] Complaints over fraudulent trade-marking were also in evidence, and concern expressed over the absence of any Anglo–Japanese convention on mutual protection of trademarks in China.[31] The commercial counsellor in Tokyo, E. F. Crowe, commented in 1920 that it had to be acknowledged that there was substantial piracy in relation to trademarks, much of it undertaken by Japanese firms imitating the marks of British firms that did not actually do business in Japan, and that had hence not thought to seek protection under Japanese law.[32] His view was that such sharp commercial practices contributed to an alarming hostility towards Japan that he found in many British businesses.[33]

Japan's reputation as a supplier was therefore often poor. Low quality, unreliability and misleading publicity characterized a search for short-run gains, and second-rate commodities and suppliers who could only compete on price and were likely to be ditched once better alternatives were available. Yosaburō Itō, who worked for Mitsui in London, suggests in his memoirs that this reputation was not undeserved:

> Although there have been various restrictions on our trade with Japan we could easily sell whatever products we imported from Japan. At the last stage of the war we even thought of selling tofu (soya cake) or kairo (portable body warmers) in Britain. As we had imported every possible product we could buy in Japan, we were at a loss, after the end of the war, how to dispose of the mountain of shoddy goods which we had failed to sell.[34]

How far such a situation characterized Japan in particular was much debated, but late-industrializing economies have invariably been pushed to compete at the lower end of the market, the point at which they can capitalize on their low wage labour, limited skill and demand for low quality goods.

Finally, the very prosperity generated in Japan by the war exposed strains and weaknesses in the Japanese economy. The suspension of the gold standard meant that Japan accumulated vast balances overseas, and compensating currency issues and bank lending at home exacerbated inflation. This was compounded by labour shortages in some areas, increased purchasing power among some residents but not others, and speculation. The rapid expansion of businesses in response to the growth in demand, in conjunction with the financial difficulties and weaknesses in the banking system, meant that while many made enormous profits, others were highly speculative and inadequately capitalized. Once the war boom collapsed after 1919 many of these new businesses sank without trace, or were absorbed by those better able to withstand the depression. Infrastructure in general was inadequate. Ports such as Kobe were compelled to try to expand capacity to cope with the increase in the volume of trade. Freight space for non-urgent goods was often difficult to come by.

Inflation contributed to the heavy toll taken by the war on many members of Japan's population. The culmination of discontent in the rice riots of August 1918, the most serious incident of popular unrest for decades, was for many an indication of a fundamental instability in Japan's society and economy. *The Times* reported regularly on the course of the riots, attributing the unrest not just to the high price of rice, but more to the 'knowledge of the public of the ill-gotten gains of certain statesmen and commercial magnates'. In essence, the 'propertied classes' must bear the responsibility for the unrest.[35] The worsening labour discontent of the later war years and afterwards also signalled to observers the existence of severe strains in the Japanese polity. The *Economist* wrote in 1919 of 'the growing tendency among Japanese workers to exert themselves in defence of their interests, which have hitherto been largely at the mercy of their employers'.[36] It described how the divergent war and postwar fortunes of Japanese enterprises, the appearance of profiteers on one hand and the unemployed on the other, and the consequent extremes of wealth and poverty, were generating a 'state of social unrest' that had driven the government to agree to the organization of labour unions and echoed unrest in Europe.[37] It expressed concern that the social disaffection was an encouragement to socialism and Bolshevism.[38]

Awareness of all these problems generated considerable doubt in both British and Japanese minds over the extent to which any wartime gains made by Japan could be sustained once the conflict was over. That many Japanese recognized these problems is suggested by the fact that policymakers and businessmen took positive steps to address some of these issues. The head of the Ito Chu trading company viewed the war as the key to Japan's ability to challenge Britain's 'unassailable' position in South China, but recognized that sustaining Japan's position after the war would not be easy.[39] Concrete attempts were made to try and standardize the quality of some export items, while key industries such as cotton and iron and steel considered how best to secure their longer term position through means such as amalgamations, protective legislation and subsidies. Government committees were established to explore the possibilities for new and existing industries to consolidate wartime gains for the long-term benefit of the nation. The former finance minister, Tokitoshi Taketomi, was reported as having urged the need for Japan to prepare to meet postwar competition.[40] As the war ended, Japan seemed to feel increasingly vulnerable. A detailed report by the Ministry of Finance in 1918 emphasized the country's ongoing dependence on imports from Britain and the Empire, especially of raw materials, and the potential impact of any system of imperial preference.[41] Imports from British India were of particular concern, and by early 1919 Japanese officials were already reporting on the trilateral Britain–Japan–India commercial tensions that were to become so acute in later years.[42]

Awareness of Japan's own concerns is likely to have confirmed a feeling in Britain that the Japanese economy was still relatively weak. Opinion in Britain was divided on how far Japan could sustain its wartime gains in the long run, and how far the 1914 situation of 'business as normal' could be resumed once hostilities had ceased, but there were many who took the more optimistic view that Britain would largely regain her lost markets and that the favourable balance of trade with Japan would be soon resumed. This view, if anything, seemed to strengthen as the war progressed. In the case of the South African trade, 'a representative of one of the largest importing firms in the country was inclined to believe that after the war the trade with the United Kingdom will be better than ever',[43] while it was suggested that the inferior quality of the Japanese hosiery, matches, cotton textiles and cement being exported to India in large quantities 'renders it unlikely that she will be able to hold the market after the war when British exporters renew activity'.[44]

Early in 1917 the *Economist* stated that although the belligerents would take some time to get their economies back on track, the war had provided countries such as Britain with a valuable lesson in how to achieve efficiency and volume of output, and this lesson would be a crucial factor in postwar European–Japanese competition.[45] The journal was also optimistic about Britain's ability to turn back many of Japan's wartime gains in the China market.[46] Declining trends in parts of Japan's trade in the first half of 1918 seemed to confirm feelings that Japan's expansion had peaked,[47] while events in the aftermath of the Armistice appeared to underline the point further. Writing in 1920, the commercial counsellor in Japan, Hugh Horne, spoke of a Japanese mood of 'deep depression and gloomy foreboding',[48] while around the same time his colleague, Crowe, stated more diplomatically, 'I feel convinced that the future is rosy, and a great many orders will once more be placed in the United Kingdom for those types of British goods which have deservedly earned so high a reputation in Japan in the past.'[49] In the light of the shifts in trade that took place in the few years after the war, and the difficulty that Japanese goods had in competing given the artificially high value of the yen, such optimism does not seem to have been unduly misplaced. The essential structural weakness of the Japanese economy suggested that Japan could not, except under the exceptional circumstances of the war, be a serious competitor to Britain in most commodities.

Even amid this awareness, there was recognition that Japan had strengthened its international position. By the end of 1915 the *Economist* was already advising the Lancashire cotton industry and the major engineering firms to watch out for Japanese competition.[50] The Board of

Trade agreed that Lancashire must be prepared to lose some of its trade,[51] while the consul at Shimonoseki stressed how important it was in the context of the removal of German competition for British businesses to put positive efforts into gaining a foothold in Japan.[52] Some commentators predicted that in South Africa, where Japan had replaced Germany in supplying the cheapest goods, Japan would remain a formidable competitor after the conflict.[53] Noting the expansion in the output and exports of Japan's clockmakers, bureaucrats stated that it was likely 'that some portion of this new trade will be retained after the war'.[54] The Japanese danger to British machinery exports was also recognized, but in machinery it was the American producers who were by far the biggest threat.[55] The British representative in London of Japan's leading shipping firm, NYK, believed that while it was impossible to predict the future of Japanese trade and shipping, both were likely to continue increasing after the war had ended, and the previous dominance of Britain and other countries could not last. 'Other Countries cannot expect to retain for ever the advantages they possess. There must gradually be a levelling of the old with the new.'[56]

There were in addition reasons very specific to Britain's trade with Japan that made it more difficult for Britain to recover its position quickly in the immediate aftermath of the war, allowing the Japanese further time to consolidate their gains.[57] The British inability to supply generated by the emphasis on war production was unavoidable, and was recognized even during the war as damaging. The vice-consul in Osaka reported that British business had been unable to capitalize on the available opportunities as they were unable to accept orders for delivery on definite dates: 'Had British firms been able to accept the opportunities that have been offered, a large amount of business could have been transacted. These opportunities, however, were in respect of iron, steel, machinery, and chemicals, the very articles of which supplies are limited, and Japanese manufacturers have benefited as a result of British firms being unable to supply.'[58]

This inability to sell a range of commodities, particularly spinning machinery, persisted through into 1920,[59] and was accentuated and prolonged by circumstances that meant that the orders that were accepted were seriously delayed. In his report of 1920, Crowe noted that Japanese spinners had been ordering large amounts of machinery not just to make good the war backlog, but to prepare for the abolition of 24-hour working later in the decade:

> Unfortunately, owing to the moulders' strike and the great

> reduction in hours of labour in this country, it has proved impossible to ship the machinery at the dates when delivery was expected. This has caused some small amount of feeling in Japan, as conditions were not fully understood there, and it was thought that there had been discrimination against Japan, and that other markets were receiving their machinery, while Japan was not getting her full quota.[60]

Horne, too, tried to get through the message that the export of British goods to Japan was handicapped by high prices and delayed deliveries, and that there was a growing danger of British-dominated fields passing into the hands of the United States:

> It is hardly credible that such a contingency can escape the attention of British manufacturers, but there is a general impression that full efforts are not being made to retain and maintain the prewar position. The British reputation for quality and square deals is as high as ever, but cost and delivery are naturally very strong factors of decision when important contracts have to be placed.[61]

Horne's comments also hinted at what was considered to be a further problem. British business was in general failing to make sufficient efforts to promote its exports to Japan and its colonies, whether through appointing the necessary agents with powers to offer trade discounts and other inducements or try to dispel the widespread ignorance about Japan, for example in relation to assumptions about wage levels and working conditions.[62] As early as the beginning of 1917 the acting Japanese consul-general in London told the Japan Society: 'I am afraid the English merchants and manufacturers have not studied industrial and commercial development in Japan so much as could be desired.'[63]

The prejudice and ignorance about the circumstances of Japanese manufacturing production was, of course, to become progressively more evident through the interwar years, but the failure of businesses to have experienced representatives in Japan and its empire certainly did not help. In Korea, for example, high prices and export restrictions of British goods during the war years meant that much of the textile trade was captured by the Japanese and that in metals and machinery by the United States. However, despite the potential significance of this trade, 'there are only three British firms in Corea [*sic*]; while in Seoul itself, a city of over 240,000 inhabitants and the seat of the government of a country with a population of 16,000,000, there is not a single representative of British commerce.'[64] The criticism of British 'inadequacy' had already appeared. It may be suggested, then, that a combination of high cost, supply problems, industrial action and misperceptions of the nature of Japanese competition were important factors in making it harder for Britain to recover from a situation that had unavoidably strengthened Japan's position in the short term.

Conclusion

Even allowing for problems on the British side, it is apparent that the war caused a range of problems for the Japanese economy, and exposed serious structural weaknesses that in many respects constrained the ability of Japan to respond to the stimulus offered by the hostilities. The threat Japan posed to British trading interests remained insignificant in comparison with that posed by the United States, arguably the main beneficiary of the war. While the pattern of trade between Britain and Japan showed some significant changes, and Japan made some important inroads into third country markets, in some cases at Britain's expense, structural weaknesses were a serious threat to Japan's maintaining her position once Britain and the other belligerents were again in a position to compete. The existence of these weaknesses was recognized in both Britain and Japan, resulting in mixed views among British businessmen and policymakers.

With hindsight, it is easy to see how the economic rivalries that were a part of the broader antagonisms between Britain and Japan of the late 1930s can be dated back at least to the years of the Great War. Economic strains were a recurrent feature the years of the Anglo-Japanese Alliance, and were highlighted by events during the 1914–18 conflict.[65] However, there was insufficient evidence at the end of the war to persuade many informed contemporary observers that Japan would be a major beneficiary of Britain's relative decline. Writing in 1934 for the Carnegie Institute, F. W. Hurst roundly criticized the 1925 Balfour Committee's Survey of Overseas Markets for underestimating the significance of Japanese competition, but acknowledged that the committee's conclusion that many of Japan's gains would be temporary was a logical one in the light of the import surplus, high prices and limited industrial efficiency of Japan in the early 1920s.[66] Culpable British business may have proved to be in terms of, for example, inadequate business practices, or a failure fully to understand the factors that led to Japan's increasing competitiveness, but up to the early 1920s the change in the relative fortunes of the two economies was far from being a foregone conclusion.

Chapter 3

GREAT BRITAIN AND JAPANESE VIEWS OF THE INTERNATIONAL ORDER IN THE INTERWAR PERIOD

Fumitaka Kurosawa

In December 1921 during the international conference held in Washington under US leadership, Japan, Great Britain, the United States and France signed a four-power treaty. Although this quadripartite pact legally supplanted the Anglo-Japanese Alliance of 1902, a sense of nostalgia towards the formal partnership that had delivered multiple benefits to both sides persisted long after. As historians have pointed out, this lingering mutual attachment prompted Japan and Great Britain to explore ways to work cooperatively at a number of junctures from the late 1920s through the 1930s.[1] Why, then, did such periodic attempts for conciliation and collaboration fail to maintain peace between Japan and Great Britain? What kind of political and economic issues were at stake for Japan and Britain that set the two nations on a path to ultimate collision? I do not presume to offer any definitive answers to these questions in this chapter. Rather, I seek to propose a new way to address them by examining key Japanese leaders' views of the international order during the interwar period.[2]

In the aftermath of the First World War, Japan found itself in a world structured by the peace settlement reached at the Paris Peace Conference and a set of international arrangements made at the Washington Conference (1921–22). This international order had several distinct characteristics. First, it reflected a shift in key powers' diplomatic attitudes and a change in the driving motivations of international relations in general. These changes have been widely described by commentators as a transition from the 'old diplomacy' to a 'new diplomacy'. In this, the basic fabric of interstate relationships changed from imperialistic and bilateral deal-making in the form of military alliances and political ententes to a multilateral cooperative framework that emphasized fairness, openness and humanitarian justice. These concepts and visions formed the underpinnings of the League of Nations. Together, they signified a yearning for an economic organization encompassing the whole world,[3] or a political vision for an interdependent international economic order.[4]

The emergent international order was also characterized by a search for ways to deter the use of force in world affairs. In specific terms, such efforts entailed the peaceful arbitration of international conflicts. This shift in orientation can be best summarized as the transition from imperialistic international relations to peaceful coexistence. Here, the world was expected to go beyond the type of balance of power sustained by arms build-ups to form an alternative interstate structure reinforced by general disarmament.[5]

Although Japan was elevated to the ranks of the five superpowers after the First World War, it confronted a drastically different world where the two pillars of its pre-First World War diplomacy (the Anglo–Japanese Alliance and the Japanese–Russian Entente) had ceased to exist. How did Japan's ruling elite seek to deal with this new international order? Two main currents of thought existed within the Japanese leadership regarding this question. The first was to embrace the emerging trend in international relations. Those who subscribed to this line of thinking included Nobuaki Makino, who had served as Japan's plenipotentiary to the Paris peace conference, Prime Minister Takashi (Kei) Hara, and Kijūrō Shidehara, Japan's plenipotentiary to the Washington Conference and later to be foreign minister in the 1920s and then prime minister just after the Second World War.

In December 1918, Makino stated before the government Foreign Policy Search Commission that the passing of the 'old diplomacy' was one positive outcome of the recent war in Europe. He further noted that the core principles of the 'new diplomacy' were fairness, openness, and respect for humanitarianism.[6] He criticized Japan's diplomacy up to that point as 'expansionist',[7] 'aggressive', and 'militaristic'.[8] Shidehara similarly observed that the age of diplomatic machinations and expansionist policy was over and that the diplomacy of the new era must seek justice and peace and uphold 'the principle of coexistence'[9] among nations. He also stressed the importance of economic transactions based on 'rational principles'.

The new interstate system that gained the acceptance of this group of the Japanese political elite may be called the Wilsonian world order. In East Asia, this global regime was embodied in what many historians call the Washington Treaty System, the mainstays of which were the nine power treaty on China, the naval disarmament treaty, and the four-power treaty governing the Pacific. More importantly, this regional order was supported by a 'new atmosphere' of friendship, cooperation and mutual trust expressed by three key powers, which were Japan, the United States and Great Britain.[10] One may call this shared outlook 'the Washington Conference Spirit' or 'the Cooperative Spirit of Washington'. According to Shidehara, 'Japan will uphold and foster the lofty spirit embodied both explicitly and implicitly by the Paris Peace Conference and the treaties and resolutions coming out of the Washington Conference.'[11] Statements like this indicated willingness to work towards a world order on the basis of universal values such as 'humanitarian justice' and 'peaceful coexistence'. Identification with such an international system constituted one strong undercurrent of Japanese thinking after the First World War.

On the other hand, there were those within Japan's leadership who minimized the importance of the new trend in international relations and expressed scepticism towards the Washington Treaty System. This group of the Japanese ruling elite viewed the international relations of the post-First World War era as essentially the continuation of an interstate system dictated by traditional imperialism, a world driven by the principles of 'the survival of the fittest' and 'winner takes all'. Their worldview was predicated on the notion that the nation-state will pursue its self-interests and therefore conflict among nations is a natural state of affairs. Army Minister Kazushige Ugaki epitomized this way of thinking.[12]

Ugaki essentially saw the post-First World War world as dictated by the British and Americans intent on hampering the growth and expansion of late-starting powers such as Japan. In the view of Ugaki and his ideological cohorts, even the League of Nations was an artifice for maintaining a *status quo* that only served the convenience of Great Britain and the United States. At the same time, however, Ugaki was keenly aware of Japan's inferior position and understood that it was impossible for the moment to take on frontally the powerful Anglo-American coalition. Therefore, Japan, as a matter of expedience, must avoid outright confrontation with these superior powers. Cooperation within the framework of the League of Nations was thus deemed a practical necessity. Precisely because this group of Japanese leaders perceived the world to be dictated by the realities of power, they recognized the mandate for cooperation. One may call this position 'imperialistic international cooperation'.

In this school of thinking, Great Britain was considered at once the foremost rival and a potential partner because of its geopolitical interests in China. The replacement of the Anglo-Japanese Alliance by the Washington Treaty System did not mean the end of 'the spirit of the Anglo-Japanese Alliance' because the latter presupposed bilateral cooperation justified in terms of imperialistic calculations. These two main strands of thought existed side by side in the worldviews of Japan's political and military leaders in the 1920s. This hybrid nature of Japanese foreign policy was evident from Tokyo's simultaneous pursuit of a conciliatory China policy formulated by Shidehara and the more aggressive policies advocated by Ugaki.

Two additional points merit mention. First, the notion that the post-First World War world was dictated by British and American interests was widely shared by Japan's ruling elite at the time, and it by no means represented an extremist position. For example, Prime Minister Hara observed in an article he wrote for *Gaikō Jihō* (September 1921) that Great Britain and the USA controlled the lion's share of the world's resources but Japan, by comparison, languished under the combined weight of its vast population and resource shortage. According to Hara, the top agenda of the Washington Conference must be to remedy this unequal distribution of the world's resources and remove 'artificial' barriers to world trade and discrimination against certain national groups. Even Hara, who fundamentally embraced the basic tenets of the new diplomacy, positioned Japan as one of the 'have-not' nations counterpoised against the Anglo-American bloc when he called for 'the opening of the world'.[13]

Perhaps one of the best-known examples of this Manichean formulation was the essay by the young Fumimaro Konoe that appeared in the December 1918 issue of the popular magazine *Nippon oyobi Nipponjin*. Entitled 'Protestation against Anglo-American-centered pacifism', the essay set up a dichotomy between 'nations desiring to keep the *status quo* (the haves of the world)' and 'nations seeking to destroy the *status quo* (the have-nots of the world)'[14] with the Anglo-Americans being the former. Since this essay takes issue with an unjust *status quo*, it is often cited as the germ of the radical thinking of the man who, later as prime minister, signed the Tripartite Alliance with Italy and Germany and declared Japan's intent to build the Greater East Asia Co-Prosperity Sphere.

It is my position, however, that such interpretations project too much of

Konoe's behaviour as prime minister into his earlier utterances. For one thing, even though Konoe criticized Great Britain and the United States in this essay, he in no way saw them as a monolith. He was in fact critical primarily of Great Britain, a country that to him incarnated imperialism and colonialism. Konoe, on the other hand, saw in America's 'idealism' a possible constraint on Britain's 'imperialism'. Second, Konoe's call for dismantling the *status quo* was not a call for war. His opposition was confined to 'economic imperialism', and the removal of this form of fundamental injustice was considered a first step towards honouring the right of every nation to equal access to the world's resources. Should that right be denied, Japan would be forced to seek the destruction of the *status quo* for survival. Third, Konoe agreed that Germany had been a disrupter of peace and the main cause of the First World War. Although he was sympathetic to Germany as a fellow member of the 'disadvantaged parties in the *status quo*', he believed that the world censure of Germany's destructive behaviour was warranted. Finally, Konoe believed that Japan should resist the temptation to pursue narrowly-defined national interests at the expense of others, because such a policy represented 'an atavistic way of thinking not befitting the new world order'. By taking this position, Konoe was in effect embracing the new trend in the world towards democracy and humanitarianism.[15]

It must be also emphasized in this context that Konoe fundamentally embraced the Wilsonian world order, or American 'idealism'. He called for the removal of 'economic imperialism' and criticized the 'imperial power', Great Britain. In this sense, Konoe's thinking paralleled that of Prime Minister Hara who called for the 'opening of the world' through free trade and commerce. They both believed that economics was the key to stable international relations and hoped that a new system based on international economic interdependence[16] would emerge once commercial barriers among nations were removed. How they evaluated the post-First World War global order thus depended on its ability to move towards an equitable economic system. It was natural, therefore, that many Japanese leaders became disenchanted with the 'rampant economic imperialism' of Great Britain when the latter opted for an autarkic bloc economy to cope with the devastating effects of the Great Depression. This sense of alienation weakened their allegiance to the cooperative spirit of the Washington Conference that was already marred by nationalist China's 'Northern Expedition' and then by the 'Manchurian Incident'.

The second point to note relates to Japan's special interests in Manchuria and Inner Mongolia. The Washington Treaty System not only called for China's territorial and administrative integrity, the open door, and a level playing field for all interested parties, but it also reaffirmed the integrity of vested interests and existing concessions held by key nations. The American plenipotentiary at the Washington Conference, Elihu Root, sponsored a resolution concerning China prior to the signing of the Nine Power Treaty. It contained a provision that all parties 'agree to refrain from taking actions detrimental to the security of friendly nations', an implied acknowledgement that Japan's national security and economic survival depended on its vested interests in Manchuria and Inner Mongolia.[17] Japan's interests in these areas, therefore, remained unaffected under the Washington Treaty System, and, from Japan's perspective, the Spirit of Washington was compatible with its vested interests in the continent. Even Foreign Minister Shidehara regarded the safeguarding of Japan's special interests in Manchuria and Inner Mongolia as legitimate. When these interests came under assault, Japan's faith in the Spirit of Washington was badly shaken. This is one reason why Giichi Tanaka, who served concurrently as prime minister and foreign minister, reinvoked the spirit of the Anglo–Japanese Alliance in April 1927 as the Northern Expedition progressed.

As pointed out, the worldview of Japan's ruling elite after the First World War formed a continuum between Wilsonianism and imperialism, or between the Spirit of the Washington Conference and the Spirit of the Anglo–Japanese Alliance. One should not overlook, however, another equally important dimension to Japanese foreign policy at this time. That is an economic element, as many in the Japanese government articulated a vision for an interdependent world economy and called for the removal of economic and commercial barriers. By adding this dimension, one can appreciate fully the entire complexity of Japan's diplomatic thinking after the First World War.

The economic dimension should be understood in conjunction with the fact that the First World War was the first total war in the annals of human warfare. This new concern forced policy makers to formulate positions on the matter of autarky versus free trade. The First World War convinced Japanese leaders in many circles that they must construct a nation capable of total mobilization. That goal was to be achieved by a twin policy of radical internal reform and reconfiguring the system of international relations. On the domestic front, it was considered necessary to build a national economy capable of mass production and mass consumption. On the international front, it was essential to secure scarce resources and establish an economic regime of autarky. In the words of one army general who was instrumental in the 1918 enactment of the Munitions Industry Mobilization Law, 'valiant generals and soldiers alone can not win ultimate victory if they are not backed by robust industrial production and plentiful resource supplies.' From the perspective of national defence, it was thus 'ideal to achieve self-sufficiency in all resources central to military and arms production'.[18]

The Japanese government began making systematic efforts toward total war programmes with the enactment in 1918 of the Munitions Industry Mobilization Law. Following this pioneering legislation, the Kokuseiin (1920) was established as a general mobilization agency directly supervised by the cabinet, to be replaced by the Resources Bureau (1927) during the tenure of the Cabinet of Giichi Tanaka. Through this period, the Japanese army was particularly responsive to fundamental shifts in modern warfare. In 1920, the army compiled a comprehensive total war statement titled 'An Opinion Regarding Total National Mobilization'. This document was later adopted as the army's master plan for building a total war system and gave impetus to the army's political ascendancy in the 1930s. Let us now examine the issues of free trade versus autarky as they were perceived by the Japanese army.[19]

If one is to understand the evolution of the world order in the interwar period as a movement along the free trade versus economic autarky continuum, the world shifted from an open international community predicated on free trade (the Washington Treaty System) to a system of autarkies. In other words, it was a shift from reliance on Great Britain and the United States to a self-contained economic system rooted in the Greater East Asia Co-Prosperity Sphere, 'a form of regionalism'. To shed light on this critical transition, I would like to take a moment now to examine the army's strategic and geographical thinking.

After the First World War, the army envisioned a very wide area encompassing Siberia, China (including 'Manchuria' and Inner Mongolia), India, various Pacific islands, and Australia, as sources of materials needed to support the Japanese economy. The war underlined China's particular importance, adding a new dimension besides traditional imperialism to the argument of those who advocated advances to the Chinese continent. Securing advanced positions on the continent now came to be understood also in terms of resource acquisition and establishing an economic autarky.

Even though Chinese resources were deemed essential, accessing them was not an easy proposition because of the Japanese economy's heavy dependence on Great Britain and the United States, and the fact that the interests of several different powers intersected in China. This reality made it necessary for Japan to strike a delicate balance between the policy of carving out an autarkic economic zone comprising Japan and China and the mandate to foster open trade with the Euro–American world. It is instructive that the aforementioned 'Opinion Regarding Total National Mobilization' stated that it was particularly important to balance an international division of labour amenable to increasing the wealth of the nation with a policy of establishing autarky to enhance national security.[20]

A search for a way to achieve this two-pronged agenda produced two main strategies. The first emphasized the need for carving out an autarkic zone. For example, one young officer serving on the Army Chief of Staff stated: 'Our Empire's population increases by 600 thousand per annum, and the absence of key resources in its soil has placed the daily life of our populace in a precarious position. ... Once a naval blockade is imposed in times of crisis, it will be impossible to sustain the empire because supply lines with the continent will be severed.' It was therefore imperative 'for our Empire to master the continent and directly procure needed resources from the standpoint of national autonomy'. The First World War demonstrated the risks involved in the international division of labour (free trade), so Japan should seek a coalition with China and 'plan for 100 years of mutually beneficial partnership among the yellow race and reject the blandishments of the white race'. It follows from this that the Japanese Empire, as 'the leader of the Far East', would inevitably come head to head with Great Britain and the United States. If 'the Empire can marshal enough power to drive them out of the Far East', it would be possible to 'secure peace in the Far East'.[21]

Given the actual dependency of the Japanese economy on the West, advocates of this assertive policy were not blind to the need for cooperating with the rival camp. This acknowledgement, although grudging, of the need for a *modus vivendi* stemmed from a sense of national weakness and a fear of international isolation. Even powerful nations, once internationally isolated, were doomed to defeat, as the case of Germany and Italy in the last war had demonstrated. This fear of isolation tended to moderate the Japanese drive for autarky.[22] By understanding this moderating impulse, we can fully appreciate the significance of an opinion rising in the 1930s that 'isolation is a means to acquiring freedom of action'.[23] Proponents of such a unilateralist diplomacy pushed for territorial expansion and the dissemination of Japanese culture in the world.

There were also those who sought to obtain both free trade and autarky. General Kuniaki Koiso (who replaced Hideki Tōjō as prime minister during the First World War) was this camp's principal spokesman. He called for an economic policy that could work both in war and peacetime. According to Koiso, 'it is clear that nations capable of successfully running an autarkic system can win a victory in a long war of attrition.' It was thus necessary to construct an 'autonomous economy' before a war actually began and prepare for a smooth transition from peacetime to wartime economic management. But autarky was inherently 'a wartime imperative' and not 'ideal for peacetime, because the needs of a peacetime economy can be best met through an international division of labour'. After all, 'it is impossible to artificially suppress commerce during peacetime'. If the Japanese Empire should try to defy this immutable law of nature, it would 'run the risk of losing its access to resources in China in peacetime and being cut off from what would become the economic lifeline in times of war'. It follows from this that 'the best way to secure needed resources is by importing and the best way to increase imports is by promoting exports on the basis of an international division of labour.' The wealth of the empire, accumulated in this way, 'will form the foundation for an autarkic system during wartime' while 'helping us to build a winner's position in the structure of an international division of labour'.

As this statement shows, Koiso's strategy made a distinction between peacetime transactions on the basis of commercial exchange and the wartime imperatives of securing autarky. He, too, viewed with suspicion unconditional advocacy of free trade devoid of due concern for the need for economic self-sufficiency. This dual concern led Koiso to conclude that Japan's policy after the First World War should 'strive for both the maintenance of autonomy, which can be translated into economic self-sufficiency in times of war, and the maximization of economic interests within the system of international division of labour'.[24]

Arguments such as this seemed to enjoy widespread support within the Japanese army in the aftermath of the First World War. For instance, the army's Emergency Military Affairs Research Commission, a group that studied the ramifications of the First World War between 1915 and 1921, expressed such a view. Analysts on the commission observed that the nation should not dismiss the system of international division of labour if it were to augment its wealth in peacetime. It should be the nation's central concern to strike a proper balance between these parallel imperatives.[25] This position was premised on four theories about the workings of the international economy besides the basic proposition that the market economy is 'natural' and that it was 'impossible to suppress it'. First, the First World War was caused in part by 'Germany's obsession about constructing an autarkic nation'. Second, it was the prevailing trend in international relations 'for key powers to rely on the system of an international division of labour'. Third, it was impossible to 'achieve total economic self-sufficiency'. Finally, the nation should not 'indulge in a bravado that can not be followed through'.[26]

Thus, two competing visions existed over the question of free trade versus autarky, with one placing more weight on the push for autarky and the other placing equal emphasis on the simultaneous quest for free trade and autarky. The attainability of these visions depended on the ways in which the international economic order, centred on the UK and USA, functioned and on the state of Sino–Japanese relations and Japan's position in Manchuria and Inner Mongolia.

On the basis of the preceding discussion, I propose to schematize Japanese foreign policy as shown in Figure 3.1. One axis corresponds to the continuum between the Wilsonian worldview (the Washington Treaty System) and the Imperialist worldview (the Spirit of the Anglo–Japanese Alliance). The other axis runs between the two extremes of free trade (universal international order) and autarky (exclusionary regionalism).

Figure 3.1 Schema of Japanese foreign policy

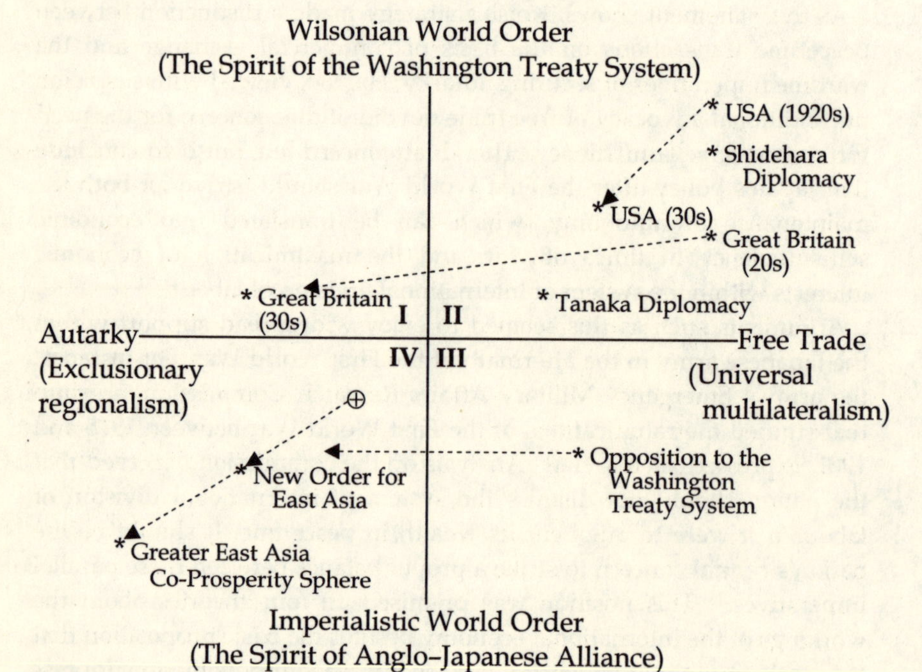

⊕ The Japanese Army (at the time of the Manchurian Incident)

Now, I would like to outline the orientations of Japanese foreign policy during the interwar period using this schema. I make a disclaimer here that the following observation by no means is intended as a microscopic analysis of the decision making process.

First, the international order of East Asia during the 1920s represented a state of détente based on a *modus vivendi* among Japan, Great Britain and the United States. Japanese foreign policy in this period could be placed in the Wilsonian free trade quadrant (Quadrant II). Typical of this category of policy was 'Shidehara diplomacy' and US foreign policy. To the extent that it embraced free trade, Great Britain was of the same mind as Shidehara and the USA. But in terms of commitment to the Wilsonian worldview, British foreign policy was oriented more towards an imperialistic worldview, as its lukewarm support of the Washington Treaty System indicated.[27] You will note that Shidehara's diplomacy, configured in this way, shared more in common with US foreign policy than did British policy.[28]

What, then, is significant about the diplomacy of Giichi Tanaka, who articulated another key element of Japanese foreign policy in the 1920s? It was fundamentally situated in Quadrant II as demonstrated by Japan's participation in the 1927 Geneva Naval Disarmament Conference and the signing of the Kellogg–Briand Treaty. It also possessed some attributes of 'the Spirit of the Anglo–Japanese Alliance', and in this sense it was closer to Britain, in contrast to the Shidehara diplomacy.[29] What is most revealing about Tanaka's vision comes from its position on the autarky-free trade continuum. It has seldom been pointed out, but I would like to remind you here that Tanaka's diplomacy was aimed at fostering cooperation between Japan, China and the Soviet Union in northern Manchuria and Siberia, while at the same time it sought to maintain a *modus vivendi* between Japan, Great Britain and to a lesser extent the USA.

Prime Minister Tanaka, who doubled as foreign minister, had been second in command on the Army Staff during the First World War and served as army minister in the Hara cabinet. He was a quintessential military man who tackled the question of how to prepare the nation for total war. Tanaka saw the universalistic cooperative framework with Great Britain and the United States as the overarching system, from which a regional subsystem based on partnership among Japan, China and the Soviet Union over northern Manchuria derived. It must be emphasized that Tanaka took care to pursue this closer relationship with China and the Soviet Union in ways that would not endanger Japan's relationship with Great Britain and the United States. For example, on 4 October 1927, Tanaka, in his capacity as foreign minister, asked British

Ambassador John Tilley to give his blessing to Japan's plan to negotiate with the Soviet Union.[30] The sentiment against the Washington Treaty System that became more potent in Japan as the 1920s progressed should be situated in Quadrant II (the imperialist worldview combined with sympathy for free trade).

The world in the 1920s was fundamentally in Quadrants II and III, while in the 1930s it was in Quadrants I and IV. The United States continued to subscribe to the vision of free trade (at least on the level of rhetoric). But Britain, to cope with the Great Depression, took itself off the gold standard and opted for the Ottawa Imperial Preference System and the sterling bloc economy (shifting towards Quadrant I). Meanwhile, Germany set out to divide up the world and impose a new world order on the basis of 'Lebensraum' (moving towards Quadrant IV). The world as a whole drifted towards autarky and exclusionary regionalism.

As for Japan, it moved towards the monopolistic acquisition of resources and the establishment of self-sufficient autarky when it instigated the Manchurian incident at the hands of middle-echelon army officers seeking to build a total war system (shifting towards Quadrant IV). After a succession of events, starting with the founding and recognition of 'Manchukuo' (1932), withdrawal from the League of Nations (1933), abandoning the naval disarmament treaty, and the acceleration of the infiltration of north China, a return to Quadrant II became extremely difficult. At the same time, it should be pointed out that Japanese foreign policy before the outbreak of the Sino-Japanese War was not singularly oriented towards an autarkic consolidation of the Japan–Manchuria–north China economic zone. Japan continued to seek avenues for cooperation with Britain and the United States, and upheld the basic principle of freedom of commerce in the light of its economic dependence on the Anglo-American world. It is doubtful, however, if imperialistic bilateralism along the line of Anglo-Japanese partnership was indeed a feasible policy option. Japan's autarkic designs on Manchuria and incursions into north China would have hampered any cooperative ventures. As the 'Amau Statement' of 1934 showed to all who cared to see, in the final analysis, Japan placed a premium on securing dominance in China.[31]

In addition, the existence of 'Manchukuo' and other factors made political cooperation with the British and Americans difficult, and cooperation with Britain could not help but be limited to practical economic matters. But even there, Japan came to see Britain with hostility because of the latter's perceived superior position in China. Once that happened, even a *modus vivendi* in the economic realm became all but impossible. Prior to a meeting between Finance Minister Eiichi Baba and British financial adviser Sir Frederick Leith-Ross in June 1936, a Japanese government position paper drawn up principally by the Foreign Ministry stated: 'Under the present circumstances, Great Britain possesses sizeable excess capacity for overseas investment compared to Japan. The country has a tendency to use Anglo–Japanese cooperation as a pretext to provide the Chinese with technical and financial assistance to recover its lost ground in the China market.'[32] In the final analysis, it was impossible for the Japanese leaders to tolerate a kind of economic partnership with Great Britain that might threaten Japan's dominance in China.

As I have shown, Japan's so-called 'international cooperation' with Britain and the USA could not go beyond bilateral economic deal-making, at least for the purposes of establishing autarky in Manchukuo and Japanese dominance in China. It did not seek conformity with the 1920s-type international economic order based on interdependence, or multilateral cooperation for that matter. As indicated by the Kōki Hirota cabinet's call for 'comprehensive national defence' and the notions of the 'national defence state' and the 'super defence state' it later enunciated, at the base of Japan's policy was always a determination to attain autarky so that a total war system might be successfully constructed. This fundamental orientation constrained and rigidified Japanese foreign policy.

We can see now that even in Quadrant IV Japan increased its orientation towards autarky and the imperialistic worldview as the 1930s progressed. This happened as Japan proceeded from the declaration of a 'New Order in East Asia' to the Greater East Asia Co-Prosperity Sphere, and from the Anti-Comintern Pact to the Japan–Germany–Italy Tripartite Alliance. Finally, as Great Britain entered the war in Europe in 1939, whatever remained of the basis for an Anglo–Japanese partnership ceased to exist. For a time in the 1930s, a possibility still existed for Anglo–Japanese cooperation on the basis of imperialistic bilateralism, but this too had disappeared by the decade's end. Now, before I close this chapter, I would like briefly to bring the United States back in. The United States occupied an important place in Britain's and Japan's respective policies towards each other. Once the distance between American and Japanese policies widened, it became progressively more difficult for Britain to accommodate Japan. Although the British and Japanese were closer together than Japan and the United States, they were just not close enough to make Anglo–Japanese cooperation a lasting reality.

Chapter 4

BRITAIN AND THE WORLD ENGINEERING CONGRESS: TOKYO 1929

Christopher Madeley

In this chapter I examine British preparations for, participation in and reactions to the World Engineering Congress in Tokyo in 1929, thereby demonstrating how industry reflected and supported the benevolent Wilsonian international scene that existed before the Great Depression. Though largely forgotten today and overshadowed by contemporaneous events – the opening day happened to coincide with the Wall Street crash – the congress was held on a grand scale, and it provided an opportunity for Japan to demonstrate to the world its progress in various engineering fields. Indeed, it was in a sense a coming-of-age for Japanese engineering, which had grown confident enough to show its achievements to both its former European mentors, notably Britain, France and Germany, and to developing countries in Asia, such as China, Burma and the Philippines. It was also an occasion for participating countries to demonstrate their engineering prowess not only to the host country Japan but also to each other. Some 43 countries participated in the Congress, with the largest overseas delegations coming from the United States, Britain, China, France, Germany, Italy, the Philippine islands and Sweden.

Japanese aims and preparations for the Congress

After the Meiji restoration of 1868, Japan was keen both to project a favourable image overseas and to learn from the outside world and frequently participated in international exhibitions from 1873 onwards.

Between 1873 and 1910 Japan contributed to an international exhibition almost every year, and in some years to more than one.[1] The convening of international events in Japan, such as the World Engineering Congress, was a further way in which Japan sought to achieve these aims. While an exhibition display overseas could reach a wide audience, there was no control over the nature of the audience. The contents of an exhibition display overseas could be carefully selected, but only a limited number of items could be displayed, and this might lead to accusations of image management. Japanese exhibits at international exhibitions might be unfavourably compared with or overshadowed by those of other participants. In addition, there might be a conflict between what Japan wanted to display and what would attract visitors. For example, while the British generally judged the Japan–British exhibition of 1910 to be a success, the Japanese were dissatisfied both with the image projected of Japan at that exhibition, due to the nature of certain exhibits deemed necessary to draw a crowd, and with aspects of the organization of the exhibition.[2]

An international event held in Japan, on the other hand, gave an element of control over the audience, particularly in the days before cheap mass transport. Selected visitors or participants could be invited to attend. A wider range of items could be displayed, and visitors or participants could also see Japanese attractions outside the event. Though there was a danger that they might see less desirable aspects of Japan, accusations of image management were less likely. The Japanese contribution was unlikely to be overshadowed by that of any other participant. The Japanese had the controlling hand in the contents and organization of the event. For these reasons international events held in Japan offered benefits in Japan's quests to project a favourable image overseas and to learn from others. The World Engineering Congress sought to achieve both these aims. While there were no physical objects on display, the presentations given by Japanese engineers revealed the progress Japan had made in this field. The Congress was accompanied by an extensive programme of excursions not only to tourist spots, but also to factories, civil engineering installations, research institutes and other places likely to be of interest to the overseas delegates, thus enabling them to see the fruits of Japan's progress in various fields of engineering at first hand. The Japanese could learn from the papers foreign engineers presented, and from comments or advice offered during the excursions. The World Engineering Congress was the first world congress devoted to the engineering profession, and it took place concurrently with the Tokyo sectional meeting of the World Power Conference. The meetings of the two events were held simultaneously in the prestigious location of the committee rooms of the Japanese Houses of Parliament. Participants were invited to submit papers and attend presentations at both events.

Details of Japanese preparations for the World Engineering Congress are set out in the first volume of its Proceedings.[3] While Japan had sent delegates to overseas engineering conferences in the past, and wanted to hold a similar conference in its own country, it was a suggestion from an American, Dr Elmer Sperry in 1925 that provided the impetus for the World Engineering Congress to be held. The Kogakkai, a federation of 12 engineering institutions in Japan, took on the role of organizing the congress. Government approval and financial support were secured. An organizing committee was appointed and, in August 1927, a preliminary announcement of the congress was made to all nations through the Japanese Foreign Office. His Imperial Highness Prince Yasuhito of Chichibu was invited and consented to accept the role of patron, and was installed in July 1928. A more detailed second announcement was sent out in August 1928. The Japanese were keen to secure British participation in the congress, and representatives of the British government, engineering institutions and industry were invited to a meeting at the Japanese embassy in London on 23 October 1928, where they were addressed by Dr Masao Kamo, professor of mechanical engineering at the Imperial University of Tokyo and chairman of the executive committee of the congress. Dr Kamo outlined the preparations that had already been made, the proposed programme for the congress, and stated 'The success of the Congress greatly depends on the cooperation of the several countries partaking in it, and to my mind the participation of Great Britain is the most important factor.'[4]

While this might be interpreted as flattery, Dr Kamo reminded his audience that Britain's Institution of Civil Engineers and Institution of Mechanical Engineers were the oldest such bodies in the world, thus their participation in the congress would be most welcome. On 3 July 1929 members of the diplomatic corps in Tokyo were invited to a dinner at the Industry Club of Japan, where their support for the congress was sought by Baron Koi Furuichi, president of the World Engineering Congress. Prince Chichibu delivered an address in English to the assembled guests, and Sir John Tilley, the British ambassador, responded on behalf of the guests.

Delegates were given free passes on the Japanese Government Railways, South Manchuria Railway, Chosen Railway and Taiwan Railway. Specially reduced fares with the Nippon Yusen Kaisha and Osaka Shosen Kaisha on journeys from and to Europe, Australia, Seattle, South America, China and India, as well as coastal journeys around

Japan were obtained. For Japanese travellers to the West during the mid- to late-nineteenth century, their first encounter with modern technology included the steamships and railways on which they travelled during their journey, and this created a deep impression on them.[5] The Japanese now wished to show the development of their own shipping and railway lines to the foreign delegates, though there is no record of whether any of the British delegates took up the offer of reduced fares on Japanese shipping and railway lines. Sir Alexander Gibb, one of the two British official delegates, probably did not. He visited Japan and the World Engineering Congress as part of a world tour that included Trinidad, Venezuela, Colombia, Cuba, Florida, Tokyo, Singapore, Rangoon, Calcutta, Baghdad, Jerusalem and Constantinople.[6] Richard W. Allen, a British delegate who played an energetic role in the congress, also visited Japan and the congress as part of a world tour, his fourth.[7]

The Japan Tourist Bureau handled hotel reservations. Several publications relating to the congress, to Japan and to its industries were distributed to the overseas delegates, in addition to the volumes of the proceedings that went on sale in 1931. Excursions were arranged both within and outside Japan, many of them to tourist spots such as Nikko, Hakone, Yokohama and Kamakura. Even these excursions were not without interest to the engineer. One excursion to Nikko combined a visit to the Toshogu Mausoleum with a visit to the Nikko Copper Refinery. Other excursions were of a more specialized nature, for example 14 inspection trips around Tokyo visited the Aeronautical Research Institute, Tokyo Imperial Industrial Laboratory, Tokyo Electric Company, Meiji Confectionery Company and the Imperial Fuel Research Institute among others. 'At every place visited, the party was welcomed and entertained, and technical explanations were given for the benefit of foreign delegates.'[8] The naval authorities welcomed the Yokosuka excursion, which inspected the Yokosuka Naval Works. The Chosen-Manchuria excursion visited Keijo where the governor-general of Chosen entertained the delegates. The group then proceeded to Manchuria where they visited the Fushun Colliery and the Anshan Iron Works. They were entertained by the South Manchuria Railway Company, the Engineering Society, and Ryojun Engineering College.[9] It is evident that the organizers of the World Engineering Congress went to great lengths and expense to create a favourable impression of Japan for their overseas guests. It is also evident that overseas delegates to the World Engineering Congress were given access to Japanese factories, research institutes, civil and military installations on a scale probably without precedent and one that was not to be repeated for many years, though not everything was open to view during the late 1920s, such as 'the great naval station of Sasebo (forbidden ground to the foreigner)'.[10] Nonetheless, delegates were, for example, able to visit the Yawata Government Steel Works. John F. Embree, writing of his later stay in Japan in 1935 and 1936, describes the city as 'Yahata, the great munitions centre, where no foreigner sets foot'.[11] Commenting on the village where he undertook his fieldwork, he states, 'Suye is far from any military zone, and thus our work did not come under any undue suspicion by the military. In any fieldwork by foreigners in Japan this is an important consideration.'[12] Clearly great changes had occurred between 1929 and 1935.

British aims and preparations for the Congress

The Department of Overseas Trade was at first lukewarm about British participation in the congress:

> The Institution of Mechanical Engineers have apparently appointed a Mr Allen to be their representative at the Congress and he says that there is an American Committee with Mr Hoover as chairman arranging for a strong American delegation. We do not know whether in fact there is a strong American delegation going, but I should not let that influence us very much. Americans notoriously like these congresses; Englishmen notoriously think they are a waste of time. I agree with the Englishmen. I would rather see our engineering people getting on with their job of getting trade to this country than attending congresses such as this which however much they appeal to the amateur do not teach the expert much.[13]

Other government departments were more concerned, however:

> The Japanese are not only going to do all they can to make this meeting a success, but that other countries are also seizing the opportunity to send powerful delegations, with the hope no doubt of business following. For instance, the United States have formed a committee under Mr Hoover and are arranging for 300 delegates to go from America. Germany will probably send a deputation of about 40. The Swedish Committee is going to get a special fund from the Swedish Government, etc. etc.[14])

An invitation to British institutions to participate in the World Engineering Congress appeared in the letters columns of *The Times*. The letter attributed Japan's rapid progress to 'The efficiency with which

Japanese engineers have applied modern engineering methods to problems relating to the utilization of their country's natural resources and the construction of railways, harbours, ships, and other engineering works'.[15] Britain's role in this was noted: 'The fact that a great many of the leading Japanese engineers received their early training in this country and that British engineers played no small part in the earlier developments in Japan will assure to all our engineers attending the Congress a very warm welcome.'[16] The letter was signed by Brodie H. Henderson, chairman of the British committee on the World Engineering Congress in Japan, and president of the Institution of Civil Engineers. By now the Department of Overseas Trade had modified its attitude and was supportive of British participation:

> The Congress, it appears, will be attended by large numbers of Americans, and it seems likely to carry still further the process of 'rapprochement' between American and Japanese industries. This tendency is on the whole inevitable, but it might be modified to some extent if a certain number of British engineers, as representatives of manufacturers as well as of institutions, could attend the Congress.[17]

Despite the fact that it was the United States of America that took the initiative in opening Japan to trade and contact with the outside world with Perry's expeditions of 1853 and 1854, Britain played an important role in Japan's modernization, industrialization and integration into world trade during the Meiji period (1868–1912). Britain, for example, provided 1034 foreign employees to the Meiji government, far exceeding the three other main providers, namely France (with 401), the United States (with 351) and Germany (with 279).[18] Up until 1890 British firms accounted for over 40 per cent of the total number of Western firms in Japan, and British residents for just under 50 per cent of the Western residents.[19] The Iwakura Mission, which left Japan in 1871, spent four months in Britain and devoted more pages to Britain it its official report than it did to any other country it visited.[20] Many Japanese students were sent to study in Britain – 31 per cent or 168 of the total 550 students sent abroad between 1868 and 1874. Thereafter, however, other countries, the United States and Germany, became favoured destinations for Japanese students.[21] The value of merchandise exported from Britain to Japan exceeded that of any other country during the Meiji period. In 1912, however, the United States overtook Britain as Japan's principal source of imports by value, and the value of United States exports to Japan generally exceeded that of

Britain thereafter.[22] American firms moved into Japan both as partners of Japanese firms and in their own right. Between 1899 and 1932 there were at least 13 cases of United States participation in Japanese manufacturing firms compared with six British ones, and between 1917 and 1929 at least six wholly United States-owned larger manufacturing firms were incorporated under Japanese law, but only one British firm.[23] The growth of American influence in Japan during this period was but one instance of a development occurring in many parts of the world:

> One of the most striking overall features to surface from my inquiry into American business abroad 1914–1970 has been the dramatic US corporate challenge to European enterprise worldwide. In 1914, only in nearby Mexico, Cuba, Panama, and perhaps parts of Central America did the amount of US business exceed the contributions of British investors. The decades after 1914 saw US capital triumph over European throughout the western hemisphere and as far away from home as Liberia and Saudi Arabia.[24]

Britain had good reason to be concerned about growing American influence in Japan, therefore, and this concern was voiced in connection with the Congress:

> In these days, when so much inaccurate information gains ready currency abroad and even in our own Press at home, that the day of Great Britain is over, it behoves us to take every reasonable opportunity of showing the world that we can still keep up our reputation of being in the van of progress. A number of cases have come to our notice, for instance, of opinions emanating from the United States, that British engineering was defunct, having been completely reversed when the holders of these views visited these shores and came into closer touch with us. It can only be, therefore, to our advantage to take an important share in the forthcoming Congress. It will be an opportunity of proving to others that we still share the ability to tackle problems of the first order, and it will thus undoubtedly redound to our professional and industrial credit if we are strongly represented.[25]

At first it seemed that Britain would have difficulty sending a sizeable delegation to the congress. 'The total British delegation is not likely to exceed twelve members.'[26] There was also the possibility that the British delegation would be subsumed under the American one:

> It has been our hope that a considerable number of European delegates would be able to join one of the American parties in New York and to travel with it at least as far as San Francisco. ... It is also the hope of both American committees that a considerable number of the European delegates will likewise accompany the American delegation from San Francisco to Tokio on the SS President Jackson.[27]

In June 1929, however, the executive committee was able to report positive developments. Some 75 papers had been received; about 35 delegates, members and guests were expected to attend the congress; accommodation had been reserved for the British party at the Imperial Hotel in Tokyo; Sir John Tilley had agreed to become honorary president of the British delegation; and Mr G. B. Sansom, commercial counsellor, and Mr R. Boulter, commercial secretary at the British embassy had agreed to become members of the delegation.[28] A list accompanying a letter dated 11 October 1929 from the World Power Congress to the Department of Overseas Trade contains 48 British and Empire delegates and members, and eight guests, of the World Engineering Congress and the concurrent Tokyo sectional meeting of the World Power Conference. The largest contingent of delegates was from the Institution of Civil Engineers (12), followed by the Institution of Mechanical Engineers (8), the Royal Aeronautical Society (3), the British embassy in Tokyo (3), the Iron and Steel Institute (2), the Institute of Electrical Engineers (2), and the North of England Institute of Mining and Mechanical Engineers (2). A number of other institutions, institutes and organizations sent one representative each, and there were six delegates with no given affiliation. Eight Japanese were listed among the 48 British and empire delegates; some were members of British institutes and institutions. The congress proceedings list 37 British delegates and members who attended sessions, 68 who presented papers but did not attend sessions, and 17 guests, a total of 122 and second only to the United States among the overseas delegations, which had a total of 374. There were 31 British participating organizations, again second only to the United States, which had 82.[29] In the space of a few months, therefore, Britain had been able to secure adequate representation at the congress, which, while less than the United States, was greater than any of the countries of continental Europe that participated.

Britain's contribution to the World Engineering Congress

Britain's contribution to the World Engineering Congress may be divided into professional, social and procedural. The bulk of the British contributions were in fuel and combustion engineering (8), mechanical engineering (8), power and electrical engineering (7), engineering science (6), aeronautical engineering (6), railway engineering (6), shipbuilding and marine engineering (6). A few papers praised British achievements, for example in town and regional planning. 'There are two examples of worldwide importance which indicate the way in which this industrial movement may be guided and planned successfully. Letchworth and Welwyn Garden Cities are the greatest measures of constructive reform which the age has witnessed.'[30] Others were critical of British practice. 'The "advanced" modern movement in architecture, as it is seen exemplified in many of the countries of central and northern Europe, can scarcely be said to exist in England.'[31] Some papers are historical records in their own right, for example the paper illustrated with photographs entitled 'An air route linking up the Occident and the Orient' contributed by G. E. Woods Humphery, general manager, Imperial Airways Limited. This paper describes the world's longest air route of 5000 miles, operated by Imperial Airways, linking England with India. The journey involved the use of aircraft, trains, and flying boats, departed from Croydon in London and was routed via Paris, Basle, Genoa, Rome, Naples, Corfu, Athens, Crete, Alexandria, Gaza, Baghdad, Basra, and Jask, finally reaching the destination Karachi after six and a half days that included six overnight stays. It was proposed to extend the service to Australia, which could be reached within 14 days in a similar manner.[32] The majority of the papers neither praised nor criticized, however, but tried to demonstrate to the Japanese and other delegates the variety and vitality of current British engineering theory and practice.

The congress was covered extensively in the *Japan Times and Mail*, which published 'Abstracts from Important Papers Read at the World Engineering Congress'. On 2 November three British papers were featured in this column, 'The Development of the Flying Boat in Great Britain' by W. O. Manning, 'The Design, Production and Use of Steel Aircraft' by H. H. Wylie and 'The Case for the Monoplane' by Henry Davies. On 5 November 'Commercial Aviation, and its Development toward a Self-Supporting Basis' by F. Handley Page, and G. E. Woods Humphery's paper described above were among the abstracts featured in the newspaper. It is evident that the press at least found most interest in Britain's contributions under the heading of aeronautical engineering.

The congress also had an active social programme. The proceedings state that there were 61 'Principal functions (Dinners, Luncheons, Soirees, Tea Parties, Garden Parties, Theatre Parties, etc.)' and that, between 25

October and 7 December 1929, 50 excursions were organized.[33] In his closing address R. L. Ranken, the delegate of the government of New South Wales pointed out: 'On the social side since October the 25th we and our wives have had arranged for us no less than 91 separate entertainments, each of which must have necessitated quite a lot of preliminary preparation.'[34] The *Japan Times and Mail* described some of these entertainments, including a welcome ball at the Imperial Hotel, a garden party at the Imperial Gardens in Shinjuku, and an imperial tea party at the Kasumigaseki Detached Palace.[35] The social programme ended with a farewell banquet at the Tokyo Kaikan, and a closing ceremony in the House of Representatives, at which speeches of thanks were given by representative delegates from Great Britain, the United States, Germany, Sweden, Russia, Belgium and Czechoslovakia.

This leads us to the third, procedural, aspect of the congress in the form of ceremonies and receptions, at which speech making was required. Mr E. F. C. Trench delivered a speech on behalf of the British and Empire delegates at the opening ceremony. Mr Richard W. Allen spoke at a reception, where he said:

> I am deeply impressed with the extraordinary eagerness and punctuality of Japanese engineers during the Congress. I marvelled at the manner they handled our English language to express with facility difficult technical subjects, and I was astonished at the wealth of their knowledge. There are over 800 papers presented in the Congress, and these will constitute another milestone in the record of progress.[36]

The closing of the World Engineering Congress was also reported in the British press: 'The visitors are returning well satisfied with the results of their voyage, delighted with their reception, and impressed by the vigour, enterprise, and engineering progress they have seen. The organization was efficient, the language difficulty was well handled, and the proceedings went smoothly and expeditiously.'[37]

Evaluation of the World Engineering Congress

The official Japanese evaluation of the congress was set out in the proceedings, which were published two years later, in 1931. The organizers recognized that, 'Strictly speaking, there may not be any direct result or effect of such a conference convened for so short a time, but the seed planted by the conference may grow and bear fruit.'[38] However, they hoped:

> The benefit Japan received as the convening country of the Congress was, of course, unlimited. Geographically situated so far from the centres of the world, Japan and her industry were formerly little known and often misunderstood. But during the Congress, the actual conditions of our industry were inspected by many of the Overseas Members who are specialists and leaders in their respective fields, and it is believed that the Congress was very effective in making our industry favourably known.[39]

The organizers expressed the hope that the congress would assist industrial progress and that friendships made at the congress would bring benefits in the future. Above all, however, was a desire to contribute to the establishment of world peace. 'Conflicts and rivalries among nations were often caused by economic competition in the past, and to promote the industrial peace of the world thus becomes a means of effecting permanent international peace.'[40] This sentiment was shared by British delegates such as Richard W. Allen, who wrote in his company's magazine upon his return to England, 'I cannot help feeling that it will have a beneficial effect on the peace of the world.'[41] The British embassy in Tokyo reported:

> As an exchange of technical information, the Congress was no better and no worse than such Congresses usually are. From the point of view of lavish entertainment and hospitality it was an eye-opener to even the most experienced of the delegates. From the point of view of making acquaintance with Japanese industrialists, etc. all the delegates found it useful, and most of them were astonished at the progress both theoretically and practically made by Japanese engineers. Some of the foreign community here complained to me that the whole show was advertisement of Japan, to which I retorted that I would rather see Japan overestimated by British manufacturers than under-estimated.[42]

The British ambassador reiterated the surprise of foreign delegates at the progress made by the Japanese.[43] On Anglo-American rivalry at the Congress he noted:

> The British Empire delegates and members, whom I entertained at a dinner and reception which Their Imperial Highnesses Prince and Princess Chichibu honoured with their presence, appear to have made upon their Japanese hosts a pleasing impression of

> dignity and modesty which contrasts favourably with the boastful manner of some of their American colleagues. The American engineers were inclined, as a whole, to use the congresses as a means of advertising commercial undertakings in which they were interested, and this was, I believe, resented by many of the Japanese professional men.[44]

Allen's lengthy account of the congress was published in the *Transactions of the Institute of Marine Engineers,* (now the Institute of Marine Engineering, Science and Technology).

He praised the Japanese for their skill and attention to detail in the organization of the congress. 'The World Engineering Congress was the first of its kind and considering the huge nature of the organization required, it was extremely successful from every point of view.'[45] Allen described the hospitality as 'overwhelming'. He felt that the greatest value of the congress was that 'it brought representatives of all nations together'. Of the Japanese hosts he had this to say. 'The Japanese pick up new ideas very quickly. If they can build a battleship, a 20,000 ton merchant ship, locomotives, aircraft, and huge hydro-electric power stations, they can do anything.'[46] Allen recognized that the learning process was not simply one way, however: 'The Japanese are a highly intellectual and noble people, and we have a lot to learn from them. It is a country I advise everyone to go to who can, as they will thoroughly enjoy the trip and will come home with a wealth of lasting information.'[47] For Allen, the only negative aspect of the World Engineering Congress was the lack of organization of the British delegation, particularly in contrast with the American delegation, whose 'organization was well thought out and complete in every detail'.[48] 'As regards the British Delegation while we were represented by men of outstanding ability, we had no organization, no plan of campaign, no office, no committee, no headquarters, consequently opinions were expressed, especially by those British delegates from Overseas Dominions of the want of coordination and organization.'[49] Allen expressed this view more forcefully elsewhere: 'I want to make it perfectly clear that I will never represent a British delegation again as long as I live. The present affair was organized in such a poor way as to be a positive disgrace to this country and to make one ashamed of his own connection with it.'[50]

It seems that Allen himself must, however, bear some responsibility. Sir Alexander Gibb, one of the official British delegates to the Congress, reported that R. W. Allen was jealous of Trench, president of the Institute of Civil Engineers, and leader of the party. On the one hand, Trench was not a good choice. 'Unfortunately, he was a man who had had very little experience of foreign countries, and no experience at all of big meetings of this sort. ... To that extent, therefore, Mr Allen's criticisms were right.'[51] R. W. Allen had usurped the leader's position, however:

> Mr Allen arrived in Japan some time ahead of the delegation, and had seized the opportunity to dictate to the Japanese what should be done. He arranged that if any speeches were to be made they should be made by Mr Allen, and both Sir Alexander Gibb and Sir Richard Threlfall, the official delegates were left out in the cold and never asked to speak.[52]

The World Engineering Congress was Allen's fourth visit to Japan and he had numerous contacts there in high positions: 'I was very glad to meet all my old friends again, especially Prince Tokugawa, Baron Hyashi [*sic*], Admiral Takarabe (Minister of Marine) and Lady Takarabe, Admiral Yamanashi (Vice-Minister), Captain Toyoda, Captain Ujiye, Commander Yanagihara, Baron Shiba, Dr Kamo, Baron Dan.[53]

Japan was an important market for W. H. Allen Sons & Company Limited's marine, pumping and power generation products, and before the First World War it had probably been the company's principal export market.[54] During the First World War a group of eight engineers from the Kawasaki Dockyard Company of Kobe had spent time at the company's works learning how to make auxiliary machinery for battleships.[55] Richard W. Allen had, therefore, more than a passing interest in Japan, its engineering products, and the successful conduct and outcome of the Congress as far as Britain was concerned. Nonetheless, the organization and success of the British delegation can hardly have been furthered by rivalry between its members.

While the Tokyo World Engineering Congress evidently made a deep and lasting impression on at least some of those who attended, to what extent was information about the congress and developments in Japan disseminated in Britain after the congress? In addition to the speeches and accounts mentioned above, the congress was the subject of a substantial report over several issues of the *Engineering* journal. The congress was said to have had several 'remarkable features', which were listed in order as 'hospitality', the desire of the Japanese to 'convince the world of their modernization' and 'the completeness of the preparations and organization of the Congress itself, including the very numerous social functions related thereto'.[56] A day-by-day account was given of the programme of the congress and the accompanying excursions. After describing the scale of the reconstruction works undertaken as a result of the 1923 earthquake, the writer stated, 'The Congress has probably made many realize as never before that the Japanese are a people with unparalleled determination, and of great force of character.'[57] The report then went on to describe in considerable detail some of the factories and installations visited on the excursions arranged once the congress had ended, and concluded 'Enough has probably been said to show that the country has now reached a high place in the engineering industry.'[58] Japan's progress in engineering was attributed to the need for import substitution during the First World War, when imports from Western nations almost ceased, attention devoted to research to develop and manufacture substitute products, and the widespread availability of cheap electricity generated by hydro-electric power stations. Despite progress made in engineering, Japan still faced balance of payment problems: 'The present excess of imports over exports is regarded with anxiety, and both financiers and industrialists are working hard to adjust the balance. The results of their endeavours will be watched with interest in this country.'[59]

Engineering also published summaries of selected papers presented at the congress[60] and announced the forthcoming publication of the proceedings of the congress. These were made available in both the standard edition comprising 20 volumes and sold by the set only, and the popular edition consisting of 39 paperback volumes that could be bought individually. The standard edition cost £25, or £20 if ordered in advance, and the volumes of the popular edition cost between eight and fourteen shillings each, with a two-shilling discount if ordered in advance. Thus the proceedings would not have been beyond the means of institutional or individual purchasers, who could buy the full set or just the particular volumes of interest to them.[61]

American Machinist published accounts of the congress and a series of articles describing factory and plant visits made by its editor Fred H. Colvin who attended the congress. These articles were extensively illustrated with photographs and showed the General Motors factory in Osaka, the Shibaura Electrical Engineering Works in Yokohama, the Kisha Seizo Kwaisha railway rolling stock factory in Osaka, the Omiya maintenance works of the Imperial Government Railways, the Shakako maintenance works of the South Manchuria Railway near Dairen and the Tokyo Gas and Electric Company's engineering factory at Omori amongst others.[62]

Other English-language publications accompanied the congress. One entitled *Industrial Japan* was a collection of papers by specialists on various branches of industry in Japan. The frontispiece stated 'this book is dedicated to the members from abroad of the World Engineering Congress Tokyo 1929.' Edited by the publications committee of the World Engineering Congress it seems this volume was distributed free to overseas delegates.[63] A book called *Industries of Japan* was issued in commemoration of the World Engineering Congress and, according to its introduction, was for distribution among delegates as well as consulates and chambers of commerce. This book took the form of a trade directory with company outlines and product descriptions submitted by enterprises in a wide range of fields. It also contained brief biographical details of the Japanese officers and councillors of the World Engineering Congress, showing their business interests and affiliations.[64] There was thus no shortage of published material for those who did not attend the congress but who wished to learn about Japan's current state of industrial development.

Conclusion

Both the organizers of and the participants in the World Engineering Congress entertained high hopes for its outcome. While the congress was an occasion for Japan to learn from others, it was also an occasion for Japanese industry to raise its profile and reputation overseas at a time when the country was suffering from an unfavourable balance of payments. Britain wished to enhance the reputation of British engineering in Japan, and regain some of the ground it had lost to the United States since the beginning of the Taisho period. Engineers believed that their profession could act as a positive force in the maintenance of world peace. These hopes were not, however, achieved. Though participating engineers might have learnt from their counterparts in the short term, in the long term opportunities to build on acquaintances and friendships made at the congress were limited. The Wall Street crash, which occurred on the same day as the congress opened, could hardly have gone unnoticed, particularly by the United States delegates, but its implications and repercussions were not immediately understood. During the ensuing worldwide economic depression the total value of Japan's exports declined between 1929 and 1932.[65] The value of exports from both the United States and Great Britain to Japan fell by half between 1929 and 1931, and though the value of United States exports to Japan had almost regained its 1929 level by 1933, that of Great Britain had not.[66] Economic depression fostered the growth of nationalism and militarism in many countries, and engineers found their skills were called upon for preparations for war. In retrospect, overseas delegates felt the blame did not lie with those who participated in the congress. With reference to the congress and other similar events, Sir John Tilley stated:

> When I think of all these gatherings which took place during my term of office, and of the really remarkable response which Britain and the British Empire made to every opportunity offered for showing friendliness and appreciation to Japan, I do feel that in this respect we left nothing undone which could have contributed to the maintenance of peace and amity. Unfortunately the Japanese with whom our visitors made friends were the cultivated class, men with wide views of human affairs, whose influence in their own country was diminishing in favour of the ultra-nationalists, who cared nothing for cooperation, intellectual or otherwise, with Europeans, unless it could contribute to the aggrandizement of Japan.[67]

Colvin is apologetic in bringing up the subject of the congress in his autobiography:

> A good number of my readers will be wondering why in the name of heaven the World Engineering Congress decided to hold its meeting in Tokyo when there were so many other places available. The veterans of the recent war, particularly those who fought through Okinawa, Iwo Jima, Buna, Hollandia, Aitape, Tarawa, Saipan - and those few who came back from Bataan and Corregidor, Wake Island, Guam, and a half-dozen other spots in the Pacific - will wonder why I should even devote part of a chapter to my visit to Japan.[68]

However, Colvin added, 'I don't think the average Japanese businessman wanted war.'[69] The spirit of openness and desire for cooperation and peace exemplified in the World Engineering Congress seem more typical of the 'Taisho Democracy', named after the Taisho period during which the idea of the congress was first proposed, than of the opening decades of the Shōwa period in which it actually took place. The World Engineering Congress was overtaken by world events in the economic and political spheres, and the opportunities it presented were lost to both the host country and the participating countries. The store of goodwill that existed in certain business circles in Britain towards Japan at the end of the 1920s was swept away by the events of the Second World War and took many years to recover.

Chapter 5

JAPAN'S COMMERCIAL PENETRATION INTO BRITISH INDIA AND THE COTTON TRADE NEGOTIATIONS IN THE 1930S

Naoto Kagotani

In this chapter I analyse Anglo-Japanese commercial relations during the 1930s, focusing on the problem of the international rivalry between the cotton industries of Britain and Japan in the British Indian market. The major trade friction between Britain and Japan was over cotton textile markets, as a result of the bitter commercial rivalry between the Lancashire and Osaka cotton industries. The nature of Anglo-Japanese relations in the 1930s is closely linked to the historical assessment of the course of Japanese expansion, both politically and economically.

In Japanese political historiography, many studies aim to show the continuity from the Manchurian incident of 1931 through the second Sino-Japanese War, which started in 1937, to Pearl Harbor in 1941. Historical studies on Japan's foreign policy have tried to trace these processes as the inevitable road to Anglo-Japanese confrontation. As an outline of Japanese imperialism, these explanations hold good. However, their emphasis on the continuity of Japanese imperialism during the 15 years from 1931 to 1945 encourages historians to ignore the economic aspects and the fact that there could have been alternative courses in the first half of the 1930s, thus reducing hostilities among some imperialist states, even though this possibility was slim.

Anglo-Japanese relations in the 1930s, especially the commercial aspects, give us a valuable opportunity to enquire into the possibilities of alternative courses. In the first half of the 1930s, Japan was able to take advantage of its proximity to the South and Southeast Asian markets, including the British and Dutch colonies, to compete successfully with European goods. The main factors behind the increase in exports of Japanese cotton textiles were their low prices, which had come about through the rationalization of the cotton industry from the mid-1920s and the drastic devaluation of the Japanese exchange rate in 1932.[1] As a result of the rationalization movement, which was stimulated by the Japanese government's policy of deflation to return to the gold standard in 1929, the process of concentration was intensified, especially in the spinning mills, and capital productivity increased. In the early 1930s, for example, ordinary rings were replaced almost entirely by more efficient high draft rings.

After abandoning the gold standard in December 1931 and devaluing the Japanese yen, Japan decided to link its currency, the yen, to sterling in 1932. Although it continued its efforts to expand the 'yen bloc' on the Chinese continent, the majority of Japanese trade in the first half of the 1930s was conducted with countries outside this yen bloc.[2] The fact that the yen was linked to sterling at a heavily devalued rate enabled Japan to shift its exports from East Asia to South and Southeast Asia. On the other hand, because the Indian rupee was linked to sterling at a high rate of 1s 6d from 1925 to 1947, this also helped increase exports of Japanese goods to these British colonies. The fact that the Japanese cotton mills, after the pound sterling's departure from gold and prior to the yen's devaluation, had bought up vast quantities of raw cotton at the old currency rate and these raw materials were utilized cheaply was to prove a major asset for promoting exports in the early 1930s.[3]

The increase in exports of Japanese textiles became central to the conflict in Anglo–Japanese commercial relations, and prompted Japan to hold trade negotiations with the government of India (which Britain controlled) in 1933.[4] In Japanese historiography, most scholars have seen these trade negotiations as part of the process of 'ironing out' the differences in industrial interests between the European and Japanese cotton industries.[5] Thus, they emphasize that each country's diplomatic policies toward the trade negotiations were formulated to serve the interests of its cotton textile industry, that is, to secure its markets abroad. Some have even suggested that the Asian-Pacific war was brought about partly by the tendency of the Japanese cotton industries to expand rapidly into Asian markets, most of which were under European control in the 1930s.[6] They claim that the increase in the exports of Japanese cotton textiles to the European colonies in Asia was a major factor in causing the European powers to intensify their protectionist policies, thus tending to isolate Japan from these colonial economies during the first half of the 1930s. The common understanding is that this isolation of Japan was intensified after the Indo–Japanese cotton trade negotiations of 1933. Japanese historiography has further supposed that the negotiations with the European colonial governments 'were broken off',[7] and that Japan abandoned its cooperation with industrial Europe. They conclude that Japan's diplomatic policy toward Europe in the 1930s was formulated to serve the interests of its industries, and was in the mid-1930s little interested in maintaining the *status quo*. Such a conclusion has encouraged Japanese historians to focus on Japan's offensive policy to secure raw materials and export markets in China after 1937. In other words, Japanese historians have thought that it was largely Japan's 'economic isolation from the world economy' in the first half of the 1930s that encouraged and aggravated her political and military aggression in China after 1937.

It is believed that the European countries blocked Japanese goods to protect their respective home textile industries. The argument is that they protected their industries by setting up 'tariff barriers' and 'quota systems' in those trade negotiations. The 'bloc' economies were created to preserve markets for the home textile industries by giving preference to goods produced within one or another 'empire'. However, as the figures from the *Cotton Statistics Yearbooks*, edited by the Japan Cotton Spinners' Association in Osaka, indicate, this argument does not hold. The value of exports of Japanese cotton textiles to British India was 85 million yen in 1935, compared with 61 million yen in 1930. The value of exports of British Indian raw cotton to Japan was 259 million yen in 1935, compared with only 147 million yen in 1930.[8] So the trade statistics do not correspond with the notion that Japan was forced into isolation from the world economy. In this short study, some factors that maintained the Japanese cotton trade at more or less an even level, even after Indo–Japanese trade negotiations, are discussed from the aspect of British financial interests.

The notion of 'gentlemanly capitalism' put forward by P. J. Cain and A. G. Hopkins offers an alternative interpretation for the motivations behind British policy in Asia.[9] Not only were the colonies expected to serve as markets for British goods, but they were also expected to pay interest on government loans, dividends on investments and many of the government-related costs associated with the 'home government'. The latter included the substantial 'Home Charges' in the case of British India. British India was not only the largest single market for British goods, but also a large debtor. The notion of 'gentlemanly capitalism' was based on the supposition that a main concern of British authorities after the First World War was to restore the flow of overseas investment and re-establish London's position as the world's leading financial services centre. If this were indeed the case, this perspective implies that the concerns of the City of London as the centre of finance were of pre-eminent significance to the prosperity of Britain, as opposed to those of Manchester, Birmingham or Glasgow, and that the City of London had an enormous influence on overseas and domestic policy. The economic relations between Britain and its empire were viewed from this financial perspective. Thus, the interests of the manufacturing sector were sometimes sacrificed for the sake of financial considerations.

Figure 5.1 (p. 75) shows that three kinds of economic policies were needed to enable the British colonies to pay such interest, dividends, and 'political costs' to the 'home country' on a regular basis. The first policy required that the colonial government should balance its own budget in order to assist the public credibility of sterling. In the case of British India, the government's revenues declined from Rs 1584 million in 1929–30 to Rs 1389 million in 1930–31; customs receipts dropped from Rs 513 million in 1929–30 to Rs 468 million in 1930–31. A substantial additional source of revenue was needed for the government if confidence in the rupee was not to slide. In order to balance the budget, the government of India tried to raise duties on cotton textiles in the early 1930s, for import duties on them were the largest source for the customs revenue. The amount of import duties on cotton textiles was Rs 42 million in 1935, which accounted for nearly 10 per cent of all the custom revenues, while the amount of duties on imports of sugar decreased from Rs 68 to Rs 20 million as the result of import substitution in the sugar industry.[10] The increase in import duties not only protected the Indian industries, but also kept up confidence in the rupee by balancing the budget. From the point of view of the government of India, Japanese goods were much more dutiable than Lancashire goods in the 1930s, since there was the gap of tariff rates between the preferential British and non-preferential tariffs. In 1932 the government of India increased the duty on 'foreign' cotton goods to 50 per cent, as compared with 25 per cent duty levied on imports from Britain.

The second economic policy was to maintain an export surplus in the balance of payments of the colonies, which was necessary for payment of their debts to Europe. British India's ability to service debts had been severely hit by the collapse of its export trade after the Great Depression. The colonies were encouraged to promote exports of primary products, such as raw cotton, to the industrial countries,[11] but these exports from the colonies met difficulties when the colonies were forced to maintain a relatively high exchange rate.[12] In British India, the level of the rupee was fixed at 1s 6d against sterling from 1925 onwards, despite efforts by Indian industrialists to decrease the level to 1s 4d to stimulate exports. Therefore, the home country had to encourage the colony's exports through certain political and artificial arrangements. This is why Britain was prepared to open its home market to the dominions and colonies through the Ottawa Agreement in the 1930s. In the Great Depression, those dominions and colonies suffered such a reduction in income from the export of primary goods that Britain had to expand their income by offering to buy more of their products for which it had a large demand, and in return it demanded tariff preference for its industrial goods. Actually, 'preferential arrangements' in the Ottawa Agreement led to a far more rapid rise in colonial imports into Britain than British exports to the colonies.[13] Without securing a significant slice of the British market, the dominions and colonies could not have paid their debts to Britain.

Goods for which Britain had relatively little demand required agreements with foreign markets, and this was encouraged by the diplomatic policies of the 1930s. In particular, the government of India expected to increase exports of raw cotton to Japan. Japan was a particularly attractive market both geographically and economically because its recovery from the Great Depression was quite rapid after the second half of 1932, due to the 'reflationary policy' of Finance Minister Korekiyo Takahashi.[14] The Indo–Japanese negotiations were completed in early January 1934. The agreement was on a barter basis. Japan was allowed to export 400 million yards of cotton textiles to India, provided that it imported 1.5 million bales of Indian cotton in return. This implied that the Japanese market was also necessary for British India in order to secure an export surplus to help maintain the stability of the rupee at 1s 6d and to maintain London's financial position.[15]

The third policy was, as mentioned above, to force the colonies in Asia to set their exchange rates relatively high, since exchange rate fluctuations were not desirable from the point of view of regular debt payments. The stability of the rupee at a highly appreciated level from 1925 was needed by British financial interests, even though the interests of British industrialists and exporters were also involved in the maintenance of India's exchange rate at 1s 6d. All experts in British India insisted that 'the budget be balanced, that the 1s 6d exchange rate be maintained and that there be no difficulties in transferring money to London'.[16]

In the interwar period, the British government continued to discourage

India's industrialization by keeping the value of the rupee consistently high. This high exchange rate thus aggravated deflation in the British colonies and stimulated Indian nationalism.[17] These deflationary tendencies induced in India very strong criticism of the currency policies the home country was imposing. It was necessary for the colonies to import cheap Japanese goods rather than home country goods because the purchasing power of consumers in the colonies had become so weakened in the 1930s.

Indian nationalism, which the deflationary policy stimulated, encouraged, from the 1920s, a political movement to raise the level of import taxes. In early 1930 the government of India announced its intention to raise tariffs on cotton goods. This was the first tariff to differentiate between British and non-British products. In April 1933, the government of India, through the British government, announced the abrogation of the Indo–Japanese Commercial Treaty of 1904, a change to come into effect in November 1933. This act coincided with the British decision to exclude West Africa from the Anglo–Japanese Commercial Treaty of 1911.

In June 1933, the government of India, with the consent of the British government, announced an increase in the duty on foreign cotton textiles from 50 per cent to 75 per cent, compared with 25 per cent on British cotton textiles. The Japanese industrialists in Osaka responded swiftly. The Japan Cotton Spinners' Association adopted a resolution of non-importation of Indian raw cotton. It anticipated that the boycott could hurt the majority of Indian cotton growers and India's trade balance with Japan, insofar as Japanese industrialists bought more cotton from India than Britain did. Some Japanese industrialists went so far as to suggest a boycott of all British Empire products, because they were convinced that Lancashire and the British government were behind the abrogation of the trade conventions.

But the government of India spontaneously planned and decided on the abrogation of the Indo–Japanese commercial treaty. After the government of India had adopted tariff preference on the import of cotton goods in early 1930, the gap between British and non-British goods widened with each tariff increase. By early 1933 the gap in the tariff rate between British and non-British goods exceeded the tariff preference in the provisions of the Ottawa agreement. Therefore, demands from Lancashire for increased preference could be met by counter-demands for its abolition from Indian nationalists.[18] Only the abrogation of the 1904 Indo–Japanese Commercial Treaty, which allowed the suspension of the 'most favoured nation clause', would allow for further discrimination solely against Japanese goods. The British government approved India's termination of the commercial treaty, and at the same time extended an invitation for new trade negotiations with the government of India. The latter expected to avoid both Indian and Lancashire resentment by consolidating the preferential gap between British and non-British goods through a new Indo–Japanese commercial treaty.

To iron out this serious situation, an international meeting to conclude a new Indo–Japanese Commercial Treaty was held before the Indo–Japanese commercial treaty of 1904 was abolished in November 1933. In view of the deteriorating relations between Britain and Japan, the Japanese government desired an appropriate settlement because it needed British recognition of the expansion of Japan's empire. Japan's withdrawal from the League of Nations in 1933 symbolized its opposition to the League of Nations' Lytton Commission report, which criticized Japan as an aggressor in China's three northeastern provinces, known to the rest of the world as 'Manchuria'. On the other hand, the government of India was eager to bring this meeting to a successful conclusion because it was being pressed to prevent a threatened Osaka-led boycott.

The conference opened in September 1933 and lasted until early 1934. At its outset, negotiations were conducted at both the industrial and governmental levels. Meetings were held separately between the Indian and Japanese industrial delegates and between the British and Japanese delegates. Negotiations in the Himalayan town of Simla between the Osaka and Bombay industrialists soon broke down, while negotiations between the Lancashire and Bombay industrialists, which had been in progress in Bombay, reached the 'Lees–Mody Pact' of October 1933. The 'pact' promised Indian support for tariff concessions on UK cotton goods and Lancashire's agreement to recommend effective action to increase imports of Indian raw cotton. The important task of negotiations fell to the governmental delegates of India and Japan.

Generally speaking, as Table 5.1 (p. 78) shows, four points were discussed in the Indo–Japanese governmental negotiations:

- the quantity of Japanese cotton textiles to be imported into British India per year;
- the quantity of Indian raw cotton to be exported to Japan per year, through a 'linking' of Japan's export of cotton goods to India with Japan's purchase of a fixed amount of Indian raw cotton per year;
- an allocation of Japanese textiles among the various categories, such as plain greys, bordered greys, bleached goods and coloured (printed, dyed and woven) goods; and

- the import tariff rate on non-British goods, in particular on Japanese goods, which was up to 75 per cent in June 1933.

Among these points, it is notable that the agreement reduced the level of duty to 50 per cent in the early stage of the negotiations, and that the Indian delegates granted Japan 'most favoured nation' treatment in exchange for Japan's recognition of voluntary control over her exports of cotton goods to British India at the same time. The Japanese delegates had as their chief negotiator Setsuzō Sawada (1884–1976), who was nominated as an ambassador plenipotentiary by the Ministry of Foreign Affairs due to his former appointment as secretary of the Japanese delegation to the League of Nations in 1931. Sawada did not indicate in the negotiations that there would be any retaliation against the Indians, despite the resentment among Japanese industrialists over tariff discrimination that had aroused boycotts against Indian raw cotton in June 1933.

It was fully recognized that high rates of customs duty had resulted in a serious loss of custom revenues from Japanese goods and that, if only the rates had not been prohibitive, Japan's share in Indian imports would not have declined. It was ultimately decided by each delegation that a 50 per cent tariff level was reasonable. Sir George Sansom, then commercial counsellor in Tokyo, was informed by Mr Saburō Kurusu, director of the Commercial Affairs Bureau of the Ministry of Foreign Affairs, that Kōki Hirota, the minister of foreign affairs (and a future prime minister), 'had hitherto hoped that some system of export control and quotas could solve the main difficulties caused by the competition of low-priced exports from Japan'. After acknowledging Japan's cooperative attitude, he went to British India to consult with the Indian delegates on Japan's diplomacy. Therefore, the problems of an import tariff barrier and Japan's self-restriction on her exports were not as serious an issue as might be assumed.

The crucial issue was whether or not Japan could import the quantity of Indian raw cotton that the Indian delegates proposed. Although the Japanese delegates basically agreed to the importation of raw cotton on a regular basis, the Japan Cotton Spinners' Association, which possessed 97 per cent of all the spindles and nearly half the mechanical looms at that time, adopted a resolution on non-importation of Indian raw cotton in June. The Japanese government had nothing to do with this boycott, but anticipated that, insofar as the Japanese market was larger for Indian raw cotton than the British, this measure, although drastic, would raise Japan's bargaining power *vis-à-vis* India. The Indian delegates were actually in a most unenviable position, since harvest time for raw cotton is usually in October. With the prospect of such continuing boycotts, the Indian delegates were inclined to agree to the Japanese demand in point three, namely that an allocation of nearly 20 per cent of all Japanese goods be bleached goods. It was the trade in bleached goods in which Lancashire took an interest where Japan was increasing exports, while the Indian cotton industry was not capable of competing well in this category.

When the Indian delegates made a series of concessions to the Japanese, the British government felt obliged to interfere in the negotiations in order to deprive the Japanese of their chief weapon, the boycott of Indian raw cotton.[19] The British government declared its readiness 'to replace Japan as the buyer of not more than 1.25 million bales by guaranteeing the Government of India against loss on purchases'.[20] The Treasury's guarantee enabled the Indian delegates to resist Japanese pressure. Sir Joseph Bhore, the chief Indian negotiator, told Sawada that the terms previously put forward by the Japanese were unacceptable. After some efforts by Japanese government officials to convince Osaka's industrialists to accept the final terms, the Japanese government issued a proclamation to accept India's terms.

The agreement, concluded at the beginning of 1934, limited Japan's exports to India to 400 million square yards, as against 552 million in 1932, and divided all Japanese cotton goods into four categories. And Japanese exports were made dependent on the purchase of Indian raw cotton. The Japanese could export the full quota of 400 million square yards only if they bought at least 1.5 million bales of cotton annually. Furthermore, the percentages for the four categories (plain greys, bordered greys, bleached goods and coloured goods) were 45, 13, 8 and 34 per cent, respectively. It meant that the Indian delegates, fortified by the definite financial guarantee from the British government, did not accept the terms previously put forward by the Japanese, which was a demand that 18–20 per cent of all Japanese goods be bleached goods. (See Table 5.1 for the Japanese proposals under point three made in November.) The Japanese government nevertheless persuaded the industrialists in Osaka to accept the final terms and to lift the boycott of Indian raw cotton. The boycott was lifted and a new trade agreement was formally agreed to in early January 1934. On 19 April, the new Indo-Japanese cotton trade agreement was initiated, which was effective until 31 March 1937.

Most studies view the Indo-Japanese trade negotiations as a process that revealed Lancashire's great influence over Indian commercial policy, since the government of India could insist on its proposed percentages for the four categories in which Lancashire took an interest, supported by the financial guarantee from the British government. However, it was also an important issue for the government of India to 'help in financing, including sterling financing, in order to protect the exchange position', after the United States' embargo of gold exports in April 1933.[21] As Figure 5.2 (p. 76) suggests, the depreciation of the American dollar from 1933 to 1934 had been a new and most important factor during the trade negotiations.

The British government was anxious lest Japanese industrialists 'were able, owing to the depreciation of the dollar, to find an alternative and cheaper source of supply in America', given the fact that the Japanese cotton mills could adapt easily to using American raw cotton rather than Indian cotton, as a result of rationalization carried out since the mid-1920s.[22] This change from Indian cotton to American was a serious problem for the government of India, causing a disturbance in the balance of payments with a consequent weakening of the exchange rate. If the devaluation of the dollar brought about serious losses in India's exports of raw cotton, the additional loss of the Japanese market, as a result of the breakdown of trade negotiations and the subsequent 'tariff war' with Japan, might well have created 'a disaster of the first magnitude in this country'.[23] Neville Chamberlain, the chancellor of the exchequer, said before the Committee on Indian Cotton (set up by the British cabinet and composed of five cabinet members): 'The Committee ought to envisage the worst eventuality. Japan might determine upon a permanent boycott of Indian cotton, might convert the machinery in her mills, and purchase all her supplies from the United States. We should then be faced with the permanent problem of disposing of the Indian cotton crop.'[24] This was the reason why the Treasury decided to give a guarantee to the India Office.

In the governmental negotiations, as mentioned above, the important points were the amount of primary products, such as raw cotton, Japan was willing to buy from British India annually, to enable the colonies to secure an export surplus, and the amount of cotton textile goods Japan would be regularly permitted to import into British India, which would be dutiable for the government of India. Thus the Japanese delegates accepted the Indian proposal, namely Japan's import of 3.75 bales of Indian raw cotton per one thousand yards of the Japanese cotton goods exported, as compared with 2.16 bales in the Japanese proposal of October 1933 (point 2/1 in Table 5.1). Thus, in order to protect the rupee, the government of India needed a new trade agreement that would enable Japan to purchase the Indian raw cotton regularly. Reflecting British financial interests, the government of India also tried to cooperate with third-country foreign markets, especially with Japan, in order to export food and raw materials and to secure smooth payments to the home country. Therefore, the decisive factor in the changing trend in the Indo-Japanese trade negotiations was not so much Lancashire's interests in securing the market as protecting the exchange position by maintaining Japan's regular purchase of Indian raw cotton.

The government of India argued that it was no longer its role to preserve Lancashire's interests. Instead, its aim was to take any action that would 'make this serious loss of trade by Lancashire as gradual a process as possible, to enable the necessary readjustment to be made'.[25] If there were very serious losses of custom revenues from Japanese piece goods due to the high rates of duty, 75 per cent during the negotiations, the government of India hoped to try 'to recoup its losses by imposing further duties on the products of Lancashire'.[26] Lancashire's influence on the Indian tariff policy was, however, limited.[27] In fact, Lancashire's interests were almost ignored by the government of India.

On the other hand, Osaka's influence on the Japanese delegates was also of a limited nature. The formal Japanese delegates in the Indo-Japanese trade negotiations did not include a representative of the cotton textile industry. The documents of the Japan Cotton Spinners' Association show that the representatives of this association voluntarily went to British India to report back to the association in Osaka.[28] This means that the interests of the private manufacturing sector, especially the Japanese cotton industry, were not directly reflected in these negotiations and that there was a discrepancy in the interests of the representatives of the Japanese government and the private sphere.

In the case of the Indo-Japanese trade negotiations, as mentioned above, the Japan Cotton Spinners' Association boycotted the import of Indian raw cotton from July to December 1933. However, the government had never participated in the decision to take this aggressive action by this private body. Instead, the representatives of the Japanese government were prepared to purchase raw cotton regularly without asking a private body, although the Japanese governmental delegates used the boycott movement as a lever to improve the conditions of the Indo-Japanese cotton treaty for Japan's benefit. Keizō Kurata, who was a leader of this boycott and an executive of Dai Nippon Bōseki Kabushiki Kaisha (Japan Cotton Spinning Company Ltd, one of the big five cotton spinning companies in the prewar period), pointed out that their boycott was not actually in effect in December 1933 because European and Indian merchants began to buy Indian raw cotton even while the Japanese trading companies maintained a policy of not purchasing raw cotton.[29] When the representatives of the Japanese government realized that the boycott, led by a private body, was no longer in effect, and that the British government had declared its readiness to replace Japan as the buyer of up to 1.25 million bales of Indian raw cotton, the Japanese delegation immediately concluded the trade agreement, conceding to the Indian delegates in December 1933 (see Table 5.3, p. 80).

It was important, however, that the real aim of the Japanese concession was to gain British recognition of Japan's political expansion in Asia in the 1930s, by showing Japan's cooperative attitude over the commercial issue. Kōki Hirota expected to make a link between Japanese trade cooperation and British concessions over China and the recognition of 'Manchukuo', the Japanese puppet regime in northeastern China. Clare Lees, a former president of the Manchester Chamber of Commerce, was inclined to give Japan a freer hand in China, so long as Japan restricted competition in the British Empire, since Lancashire's position would be helped by concessions to Japan in the China market and the recognition of Manchukuo. The British government, however, had never been prepared to accept Japan's foreign policy goals, though the arguments of the 'Treasury Group' had their own logic: gaining political concessions through economic understanding.[30]

The second Indo-Japanese cotton negotiations, which were held from late July 1936 to March 1937, before the first Indo-Japanese cotton trade conventions expired in March 1937, also show Japan's political aims. The second set of negotiations was expected to end easily with a minimum of revision, since both Japanese and Indian delegates tried to keep to the trade conventions, and the exchange rate of the dollar against the sterling was also stable (see Figure 5.2, p. 76). The Japanese delegation was small compared with the 40 or so who were in the first delegation. Kikuji Ishizawa, who was at the time Japan's consul general in Calcutta, was appointed to head the Japanese delegation. Ishizawa did not have the feeling that his mission was of first-class political importance as Sawada did in 1933. But the second set of negotiations were more prolonged than might have been expected, taking eight months, compared with four months in the first set of negotiations (see Table 5.1, p. 78). This was due mainly to changes in Japan's foreign policy and also to the fact that the Burma-Japanese cotton trade negotiations were being held at the same time because of Burma's separation from India in 1935.

This prolongation of the second set of negotiations was clearly related to Japan's foreign policy towards northern China, which had been formed in 1936. After the currency reform in China, led by Sir Frederick Leith-Ross's activities, which were successful in late 1935, the Japanese military wanted to destroy the new currency system in China. This threatened to bring about the economic unification of China, and the Japanese military set about creating an exclusive sphere of interest in northern China.

After the February 26 *coup d'état* attempt in 1936, Japan's foreign policy increasingly stressed that the creation of a Japanese sphere of influence in northern China should provide material resources to Japan, such as raw cotton, and Japan would not allow Britain to interfere in the expansion of Japanese influence in East Asia. It was important for the Japanese delegates in India that new Chinese raw cotton, cultivated in northern China, was substitutable for American raw cotton. The Japanese delegates pointed out that the Japanese cotton industry no longer needed Indian raw cotton, asking for concessions from the government of India.

But Japan's bullish attitude was drastically changed due to China's increasing tendency towards political unity after the Xi'an (Sian) incident of December 1936, in which political cooperation between nationalists and communists against Japanese aggression was agreed upon. In early 1937, the foreign, finance and war ministries demanded a joint economic development plan and political cooperation with Britain in northern China.

The ministries also strongly advised the Japanese delegates in India to make concessions in the Burma and Indo-Japanese negotiations. Table 5.1 (p. 78) indicates that the Japanese delegates made some dramatic concessions after February 1937, accepting an import tariff of 50 per cent and Japan's import of 4.19 bales of Indian raw cotton per 1000 yards of the Japanese cotton goods exported, compared with 3.75 bales in the first agreement. This was in compliance with the Japanese government's hopes for Anglo-Japanese cooperation after the Xi'an incident, which had further stimulated Chinese nationalism. It is important that Japan's diplomacy showed a cooperative attitude towards the British colonies at this time when the Japanese government did not have confidence that 'Japan alone should act as a stabilizing power in East Asia'.

Figure 5.1 The emerging 'Devaluation Sphere' in East Asia and the economic order of Asia in the 1930s

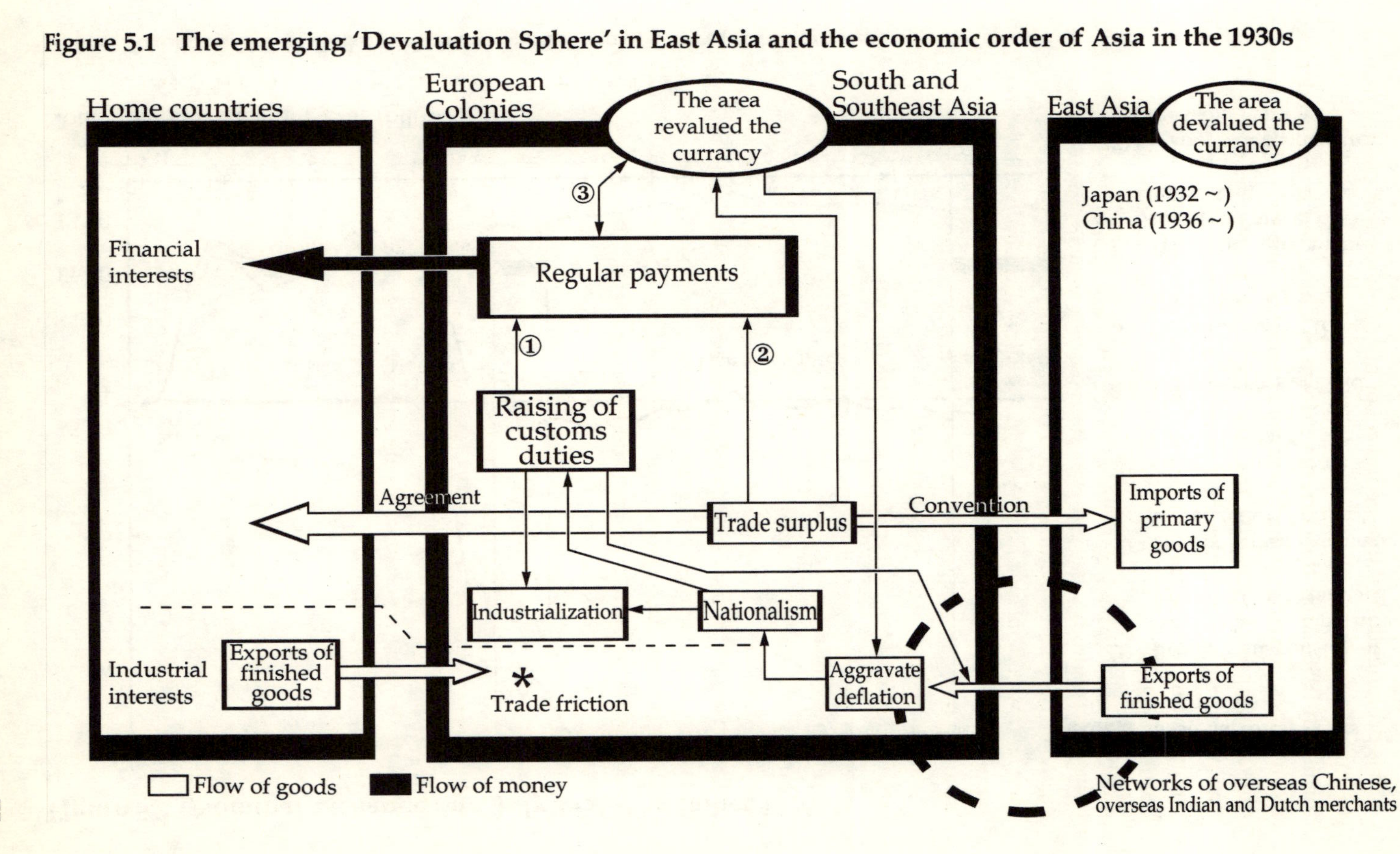

Figure 5.2 Nominal exchange rate, July 1931–December 1936

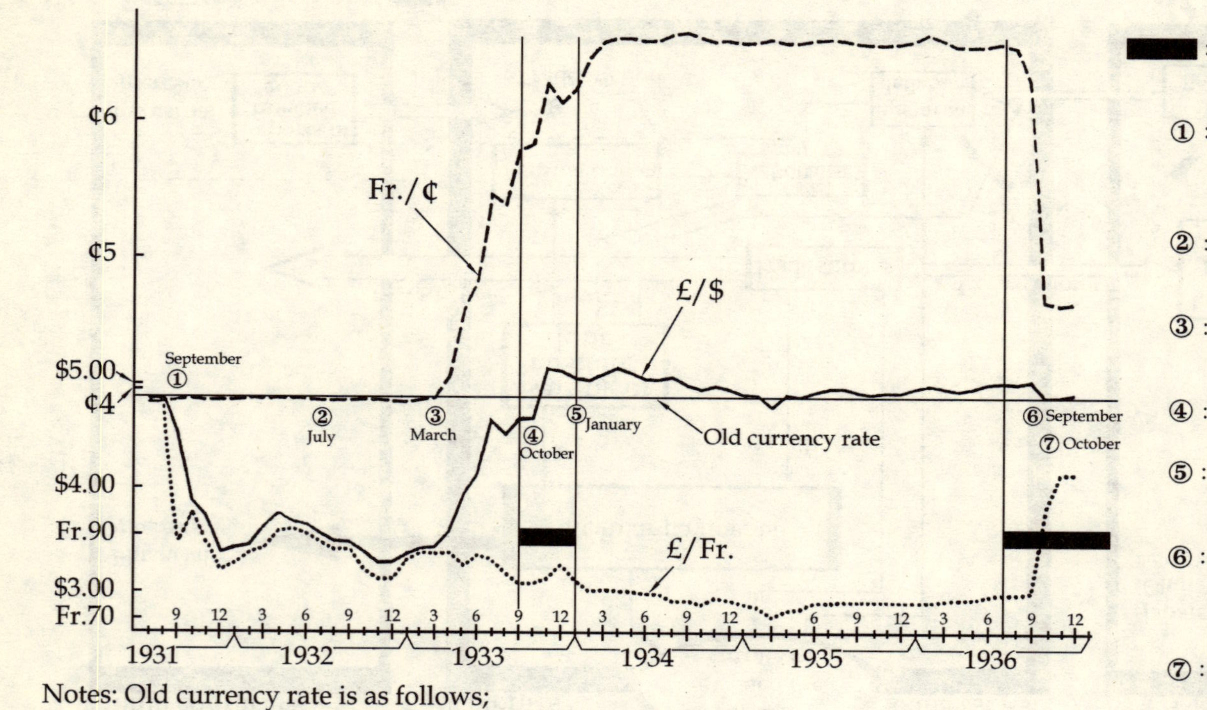

▬ : Indo–Japanese cotton negotiations.

① : Britain's suspension of convertibility, departure from the Gold Standard.

② : Start of British Exchange Equalization Account.

③ : US departure from the Gold Standard.

④ : US purchases of Gold.

⑤ : Devaluations of the US dollar.

⑥ : Tripartite Agreement between France, USA and UK.

⑦ : France's departure from the Gold Standard.

Notes: Old currency rate is as follows;

£1 = $4.866 £1 = Fr.124.21 Fr.1 = ¢3.9174

Source: Yokohama Shokin Ginko [Yokohama Species Bank], *Greppo* [A monthly report].

Figure 5.3 Price fluctuations, export and stock of Javanese sugar, 1929–1939

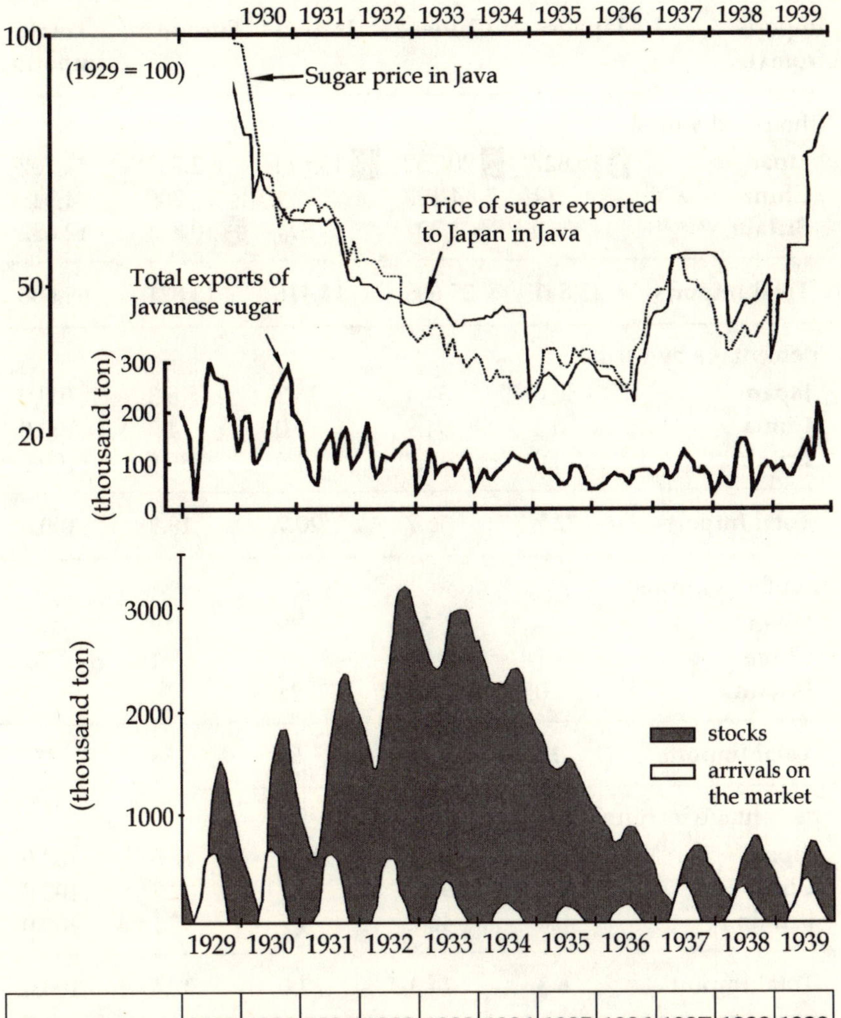

Exports to:	**1929**	**1930**	**1931**	**1932**	**1933**	**1934**	**1935**	**1936**	**1937**	**1938**	**1939**
West of Suez	12	0	9	24	15	12	1	14	41	53	37
British India	44	48	31	24	24	26	23	11	2	8	27
Japan	10	13	8	7	14	13	25	20	18	0	0
Hong Kong	11	18	23	14	16	17	15	20	9	11	8

Source: Nihon Sato Kyokai [Japan Sugar Association], *Sato Nenkan* [The Yearbook of Sugar] (Tokyo, 1929–1939).

Table 5.1 (a) Imports of cotton textiles into Singapore from main countries and by main merchants, June to December 1934

Imports from\by	**Japanese**	**Chinese**	**Indian**	**European**	**Total Imports**
(thousand yards)					
Japan	1 15,827	2 20,252	3 13,844	2,782	52,707
China	14	4,127	1	205	4,348
Britain	0	1,227	571	4 10,833	12,632
Total Imports	**15,841**	**25,608**	**14,416**	**13,821**	**69,688**
(percentage by yards)					
Japan	30.0	38.4	26.3	5.3	100.0
China	0.3	94.9	0.0	4.7	100.0
Britain	0.0	9.7	4.5	85.8	100.0
Total Imports	**22.7**	**36.7**	**20.7**	**19.8**	**100.0**
(number of firms)					
Japan	14	32	39	18	103
China	1	34	1	1	37
Britain	0	39	24	34	97
Total Imports	**15**	**105**	**64**	**53**	**237**
(percentage by number of firms)					
Japan	13.6	31.1	37.9	17.5	100.0
China	2.7	91.9	2.7	2.7	100.0
Britain	0.0	40.2	24.7	35.1	100.0
Total Imports	**6.3**	**44.3**	**27.0**	**22.4**	**100.0**

Notes: British merchants were not included under 'European' in 1938.
1–4 correspond with the equivalent in Table 5.2.

Source: Table 5.1(a) was based on Nanyo Kyokai [The Japanese South East Associations in Singapore], *Eiryo-Maraya ni okeru Menpu* [Cotton Textiles in British Malaya], November 1935.
Table 5.1 (b) (overpage) was based on Straits Settlements, *Annual Report on the Administration of the Quota System Regulating the Importation of Cotton and Artificial Silk during January to December 1938*, p4. CO852/224/3.

Table 5.1 (b) Imports of cotton textiles into Singapore from main countries and by main merchants, January to December 1937

		Japanese	Chinese	Indian	European	Total Imports
	(thousand yards)		(percentage by yards)			
Japan	34,208	28.9	27.4	38.9	4.8	100.0
China	10,287	0.0	99.1	0.3	0.6	100.0
Dutch East Indies	2,945	0.0	42.9	52.0	0.1	100.0
Netherlands	1,239	0.0	0.0	0.0	100.0	100.0
		(percentage by number of licences)				
Japan		11.9	24.8	48.6	14.7	100.0
China		0.0	78.8	18.2	3.0	100.0
Dutch East Indies		0.0	30.4	67.4	2.2	100.0
Netherlands		0.0	0.0	0.0	100.0	100.0

Table 5.2 The main description of textile goods by each importer in Singapore, June to December 1934

Number	Japanese 1			Chinese 2		
1	W.Shirtlings	2,824	I5	D.cotton	4,888	E2
2	Print.Poplin	1,649	I2	W.cotton	3,941	E1
3	G.T.cotton	1,199		Print.cotton	2,894	E3
4	D.Poplin	973		B.cotton.	1,720	E5
5	G.Shirtlings	954	I6	C.cotton	910	
6	B.Shirtlings	812		C.Poplin	846	I3
Totals		8,411			15,199	
Grand totals		**15,827**			**20,252**	

Number	Indian 3			European 4		
1	W.Rayon	2,337		W.cotton	3,446	C2
2	Print.Poplin	1,250	J2	D.cotton	1,886	C1
3	C.Poplin	1,045	C6	Print.cotton	1,415	C3
4	Print. Shirtlings	1,037		Gcotton	1,227	
5	W.Shirtlings	902	J1	B.cotton	594	C4
6	G.Shirtlings	691	J5	Str.Poplin	575	
Totals		7,262			9,143	
Grand totals		**13,844**			**10,833**	

Notes: E = Europe, C = Chinese, I = Indian, J = Japanese

Source: Same as Table 5.1.

Table 5.3 The main course of the first and second Indo–Japanese Cotton Trade Negotiations

Date		1 Import of Japanese cotton goods into India (mill. yds)	2 Export of Indian raw cotton to Japan (million bales)	2/1 x 1000 (bales/ thousand yards)	3 Allocation of 1 Japanese cotton goods imported into India (percentage)						4 Import tariff on non-British goods (percentage)	
					Plain greys	Bordered greys	Bleached	Coloured: Prints	Coloured: Dyed	Coloured: Woven	Greys	Others
17 October	1933	300–350	1.25–1.50	4.28	45	13	8	15	9	10	**50**	**50**
23 October		578	1.25	2.16							50	50
9 November		**325–400**	1.00–1.37	3.43	45–60		20–35		35–50		50	50
15 November		325–400	**1.00–1.50**	**3.75**	**45–50**	13–14	8		**34–37**		50	50
21 November		325–400	1.00–1.50	3.75	45–55	13–23	8–18		34–44		50	50
5 January	1934	325–400	1.00–1.50	3.75	45–50	13–16	8–10		34–37		50	50
30 July	1936	325–400	1.00–1.50	3.75	40–48		20–24		40–48		40	
20–27 August		275–350	1.00–1.50	4.29	40	13	10	20	17		50	50
15 September		325–425	1.00–1.50	3.53	45–54		15–18		40–48		45	
3 October		325–364	1.00–1.26	3.46	35–39	13–16	12–14		40–44		45	45
9 November		300–360	1.00–1.40	3.89	40	13	10		37		45	45
19 February	1937	283–358	0.93–1.43	3.99	**40–44**	**13–16**	**10–12**	28–37	9–11			
27 February		325–400	n.a.		40–44	13–14	10–11	20–21	17–18			
6 March		283–358	**1.00–1.50**	**4.19**	40–44	13–16	10–12	25–28	12–13			
20 March		283–358	1.00–1.50	4.19	40–44	13–16	10–12	**20–22**	17–19			
late March	1937	283–358	1.00–1.50	4.19	40–44	13–16	10–12	20–22	17–19		50	50

Notes: [shaded] is the Indian side's proposal. The upper section refers to the first negotiations, the lower to the second. The numbers in bold type refer to the first proposals to lead to an agreement in each negotiation.

Source: Naoto Kagotani, *Ajia Kokusai Tsudho Titsujyo to Kindai Nihon* [The International Trading Orders of Asia and Modern Japan 1880–1940] (Nagoya Daigaku Shuppan kai, 2000), Chapters 6 and 7.

Table 5.4 The exports of Japanese cotton goods to the Dutch East Indies by each merchant in Kobe and Osaka, 1932 to 1935

Nationalities	1932				1935				
	Greys	Bleached	Coloured	Totals 1	Greys	Bleached	Coloured	Totals 2	2-1
European	4,137	9,532	63,153	76,823	20,589	16,805	108,446	145,841	69,018
Japanese	57,272	49,045	180,138	286,456	57,674	35,939	171,069	264,684	∇ 21,772
Indian	301	1,376	14,388	16,066	167	1,367	23,014	24,549	8,482
Chinese	277	374	11,028	11,680	761	1,340	5,086	7,187	∇ 4,492
Totals	61,989	60,328	268,709	391,027	79,192	55,503	306,053	440,749	49,722
European	5	12	82	100	14	12	74	100	
Japanese	20	17	63	100	22	14	65	100	
Indian	2	9	90	100	1	6	94	100	
Chinese	2	3	94	100	11	19	71	100	
Totals	16	15	69	100	18	13	69	100	
European	7	16	24	20	26	30	35	33	
Japanese	92	81	67	73	73	65	56	60	
Indian	0	2	5	4	0	2	8	6	
Chinese	0	1	4	3	1	2	2	2	
Totals	100	100	100	100	100	100	100	100	

Notes: The figures in the top section are in thousands of yards. In the middle and bottom section the figures are percentages. ∇ indicates that there was a decrease in exports from 1932 to 1935.

Source: Naoto Kagotani, Ajia Kokusai Tsusho Titsujyo to Kindai Nihon [The International Trading Orders of Asia and Modern Japan 1880–1940] (Nagoya Daigaku Shuppan kai, 2000), Chapter 8.

Chapter 6

PAUL EINZIG AND THE JAPANESE EMPIRE IN 1943

Philip Towle

Japan's attempts to seize control of China and Southeast Asia in the 1930s and 1940s were justified by its spokesmen and military leaders as a necessary response to its lack of raw materials and markets, and to the growing protectionism of the Western powers. But when this expansion led to war with the United States and Britain in December 1941, it exposed the fragility of the new empire, which depended crucially on maritime trade and on the ability to move warships and troops from Japan to the conquered provinces. The Imperial Japanese Navy was, however, so obsessed with the surface battles that it was waging against US warships that it largely ignored the threat to its trade from submarines. Consequently, by the end of the war, its maritime links had been severed and much of Asia was reverting to a subsistence economy.

In this chapter I look at the work of the economist Paul Einzig who saw from the start where Japanese weakness would lie and tried to persuade the British and American governments to attack this 'centre of gravity'. It explains why his strategy was ignored and speculates on what might have happened had his 'economic' approach been adopted.

Einzig was a prolific financial journalist and writer of Romanian origin who worked in Britain from the 1920s to the 1960s. He wanted not just to report on events but to influence policy. As the reviewer of his autobiography commented in *The Times Literary Supplement* in 1960: 'To Mr Einzig journalism was not so much a profession as a crusade. He was always seeking not simply to record events, not even simply to comment on them, but to shape and influence them.'[1] He engaged in vitriolic controversies with many of the leading experts of his time, including J. M. Keynes, and he took on the British government in 1939 for giving Czech gold to the Germans and in 1944 for accepting the Bretton Woods agreement.[2] But he was not just a polemicist; his most enduring contributions to economic thought were on exchanges, gold movements and the Bank for International Settlements. The *American Economic Review* claimed in 1963 that his *Theory of Forward Exchanges* had been the standard work on the subject for 30 years. His books were reviewed in countries as far apart as India, Australia, Russia and Japan.[3] His writing in 1943 showed that he was also capable of very perceptive analyses of strategic issues.

It was in that year that Einzig published an assessment of the *Japanese New Order*, which illustrates very clearly some of the strengths of Japan's empire and its fundamental economic weakness, the fragility of its maritime communications.[4] He had both personal and political reasons for publishing this analysis. He had made his reputation in the 1930s as one of the chief writers on the London *Financial News* owned by Brendan Bracken. This was the main rival to the *Financial Times* and the two papers were to be amalgamated after the war. It was the *Financial News*, which was much livelier and more innovative than the older paper, that began the index of share prices, the first of its kind in the world, which is now known as the FT index.[5] But Einzig had only been naturalized in 1929 and, needing to display his loyalty to his adopted country and with his family still living in Romania, he became only too well aware in the 1930s of the Nazi threat to Eastern Europe. He fed anti-appeasement politicians, like Hugh Dalton, with information to help them fight government policy and, when the war began, he had good reason to see it as a crusade.[6]

In mid-1942 Einzig's old journalistic master, Bracken, became minister of information in the Churchill government. He was a tough, dominating minister who sacked many of the civil servants in his then unpopular department.[7] He had always been very close indeed to Churchill, helping him in his election campaigns, and there were erroneous rumours during the war years that he was the prime minister's illegitimate son.[8] Bracken encouraged his former subordinate to make a contribution to the war effort by writing books on the economics of the conflict. In January 1942, he wrote, 'it is about time we had another Einzig book.'[9] Einzig also had some cooperation at this stage from Keynes at the treasury who supplied him with statistics that he needed for his work.[10]

Einzig was worried about the survival of the Churchill government, following the loss of British possessions in Asia and continued reverses in the Middle East.[11] He boasted in his autobiography that his greatest political achievement was to persuade Neville Chamberlain's supporters in the Conservative Party to back Churchill after Chamberlain was forced to resign as prime minister in 1940.[12] Plainly, he was a passionate supporter of the prime minister and he was afraid that only the lack of an alternative kept Churchill in office in the worst period of the war. Indeed, he even worried that a combination of Conservative and Labour malcontents might rally round the austere left-wing figure of Stafford Cripps and there was a brief period in 1942 when Cripps rivalled Anthony Eden as the favoured candidate to succeed Churchill if he died. In fact Churchill himself was supported by over 80 per cent of the population for much of the war and a coup against him would have been deeply unpopular.[13] Nevertheless, *The Japanese New Order in Asia* was then Einzig's response to Bracken's encouragement and his contribution to the stability of the government and to the war effort in 1943. It was intended to demolish Japanese economic justifications for the conflict and to tell the public and the government where the weak points in Japan's empire were to be found. As he put it himself: 'It is of the utmost importance that the public of the United Nations should avoid developing an inferiority complex, and for this reason it is to be deplored that up to the time of writing the gigantic mistakes committed by Japan received no adequate publicity.'[14]

Einzig's book has to be placed in the context of the long-standing British debate on Japan. Much of the work published in Britain by military and economic experts in the 1920s and 1930s had been sympathetic to Tokyo's problems. Both the leading London institutes, the Royal Institute of International Affairs and the Royal United Services Institution, had given prominence to Japan's point of view. As A. V. Alexander, MP, told Chatham House after attending a conference of the Institute of Pacific Relations in 1936:

> I do not need now to explain the general case of the Japanese for expansion, since it is so well known. But it is perhaps just as well to mention the factors which do give them a strong case: a rapid industrial revolution; an increasing population, so rapidly increasing that they must find work for an additional two hundred to two hundred and fifty thousand people each year; a limited territory, and a limited portion of the limited territory available for really effective agricultural production.[15]

The very next month, the Japanese author and well-known intellectual, Yūsuke Tsurumi addressed Chatham House on Japan's internal situation and external policies. Tsurumi also stressed Japan's 'ever-growing population' and emphasized the general feeling among the Japanese that it was only their army that was supporting their legitimate interests in Manchuria.[16]

British military observers like Malcolm Kennedy and F. S. G. Piggott explained Japanese expansionism in the same way.[17] On the other hand, Einzig did not believe in leaning over backwards to see the other nation's point of view, an 'English' attitude he had denounced in a book published in 1942.[18] He pointed out that in peacetime Japan could import as many raw materials as it wished and that it could pay for these because 'the competitive capacity of Japanese exporters was proverbial'.[19] Einzig noted that Japanese manufacturers cut prices below what was necessary to capture markets, partly to overcome prejudices against Japanese goods and partly because of competition between the Japanese exporters themselves. Moreover, precisely because Japanese products were good value, they sold well in a period of economic depression.[20] He turned the Japanese armed forces' argument for expansion on its head with a typical Einzig touch: if Japan had a balance of payments problem between 1931 and 1941, it was largely because of its military preparations and actions overseas. As Japan was self-sufficient in food, despite its increasing population, it was in a far stronger position in that respect than Britain, Germany or Italy. Its lack of raw materials only became a problem when it so antagonized the United States and other Western states, after the intervention in Indochina, that they restricted exports. The remedies that the Japanese armed forces proffered were in fact the cause of the problem.[21]

Having demolished the economic arguments for Japanese expansion to his own satisfaction (although he was wrong about Japanese self-sufficiency in food), Einzig went on to argue that the Japanese had created an empire that could be largely autarkic as far as raw materials were concerned, provided they could be transported to Japan. But that would require peace, and peace was impossible because even if the West were defeated, Japan would, eventually, find itself involved in a war with Germany.[22] Japan's consumption of coal was about 70 million tons and home production 54 millions. The deficiency would have to be made good from Manchukuo, the rest of China and Indochina. Such resources were adequate but the extent to which they were available to Japan's war industries was debatable and entirely dependent on shipping.[23] Einzig estimated Japan's production of oil at a mere 400,000 metric tons, plus

250,000 tons from Sakhalin, to which he added under one million from the synthetic oil plants imported from Germany. Peacetime oil consumption was four million tons a year and, though civilian consumption would have been cut, this would have been more than offset by military demands. He estimated that Japan's deficit was thus some five million tons a year. Some of this could eventually be made good by production from the Dutch East Indies, Burma and Borneo, and in the meantime the Japanese would have to draw on reserves that the Western nations had foolishly allowed them to build up.[24]

Japan was also deficient in iron ore, Japan and Korea together producing some four million tons against estimated steel production of seven to eight millions. The deficit could be made good by imports from China, Manchukuo, Malaya and the Philippines.[25] Accordingly, Japan's prewar dependence on scrap imports from the United States could be more than offset by the expansion of its empire: 'The supply of iron ore for the Japanese steel industry is thus largely a problem of shipping space.' Previously, Japan had also imported manganese from British India but its conquests would more than make good the loss of this source. Copper could present a greater problem, but Einzig believed that Japan had built up reserves of 150,000 tons before the war and that these, together with limited imports from the colonies, would meet requirements for a number of years. Lead would have to be imported from Burma, Indochina and the Philippines, and zinc would have to come from Indochina, Burma and existing stocks.[26] Aluminium and tin would be plentiful in the Co-Prosperity Sphere, but nickel, cobalt, molybdenum and mercury would be in short supply.[27] The need for cotton might explain Japan's ambitions to expand towards India while 'the desire to secure wool supplies accounts partly for the keenness of Japan to conquer Australia and New Zealand', particularly as wool would be needed if Japan were to take on the Soviet Union.[28] In general, however, Japanese conquests meant that far more raw materials were available in Asia than could ever be absorbed by Japan. Rubber producing countries, such as Malaya, were being forced to switch to food production, while the Philippines had to replace sugar cane with cotton.[29] This was, however, unlikely to be effective because cotton requires a subtropical climate and because the cotton crop season would coincide with the monsoon.[30]

Agriculture would be hard hit by the New Order because Japan could only absorb a fraction of the foodstuffs that the new territories were capable of producing.[31] Moreover, Japan was unable to produce anything like enough tractors and other agricultural machinery for the rest of Asia. The consequence of this shortage, he quite correctly observed, was that 'the rubber and cane sugar plantations destroyed under the "scorched earth" policy or abandoned as a result of the invasion, were not restarted.'[32] Meanwhile, to use what cane sugar and rubber was being produced, the Japanese were experimenting with converting them into 'aviation spirit' and oil.[33]

Einzig explained the general Western underestimation of Japan's military potential before 1941 partly in economic terms.[34] Many Westerners had continued to think of Japan as a predominantly agricultural nation even when it was rivalling the USSR in the 1930s as the country industrializing most rapidly.[35] Wishful thinkers in the West had also convinced themselves that Japan had no machine tool industry and that the arms industry would break down as soon as the machine tools imported from the United States had worn out. But, as Einzig pointed out, the fact that the number of employees in the machinery and machine tool industries increased from 158,000 to 692,000 between 1931 and 1937 spoke for itself. The value of machine tool output represented 10 per cent of industrial output in 1932 and 20 per cent six years later.[36] Further expansion of all Japan's industries would be hampered not by shortages of machine tools but by a dearth of steel and shipping. Either the Japanese would have to invest effort in using low grade ores from the homeland or they would have to take up shipping capacity to import.

The overwhelming difficulty for Japan, which was the focus of Einzig's strategic analysis, was in fact lack of shipping and the circular nature of the problem:

> It is because of this difficulty that Japan is unable to expand her steel industry in accordance with requirements, and the lack of steel supplies provides in turn a handicap to the development of all other industries, not in the last place of shipbuilding. Lack of shipping space is also responsible for the necessity of producing in Japan foodstuffs and raw materials which could otherwise be imported from the conquered territories.[37]

According to Einzig's figures, in 1939 Japan had 5.6 million tons of merchant ships compared with over 20 million tons owned by Britain and 11.9 by the United States. Japan had lost some ships in the early stages of the war but had more than compensated by seizing 200,000 tons of allied shipping. These figures correspond with postwar estimates of 6.3 million tons available to Japan.[38] Nevertheless, the highly censored Japanese press had reported that 12 million tons of goods were held up for lack of shipping and that Burma had a rice surplus that could not be exported. According to the sources available to Einzig in 1942 and 1943, Japan was trying to build large numbers of small ships, particularly wooden ones and even sailboats, to meet its deficiencies. It could concentrate on merchant ship production, as Britain and the USA were doing, but only if it could bring enough coal and iron to Japan by sea, and if the armed forces were prepared to release steel for this purpose.[39]

What Einzig had produced was a typical intelligence assessment of Japan's economic and military potential. He was a voracious reader and it is possible that he was inspired by the earlier work of the strategic analyst, Hector Bywater. Although Bywater was a naval strategist rather than an economist, he was also a journalist and it is more than likely that the two had met in Fleet Street. All Bywater's books lavished praise on the Imperial Japanese Navy at the same time that they warned against the danger to all concerned of a war between the United States and Japan. They also noted Japan's dependence on imports of raw materials. Bywater's recent biographer has argued that his books were so prophetic that they gave the Japanese admirals the strategic ideas they followed during the war. Einzig agreed with Bywater's analysis of Japan's weaknesses, though Bywater's references to Japanese trade routes were peripheral, whereas Einzig made them the central issue.[40]

Whatever their source, Einzig's conclusions are clear: Tokyo had conquered an empire, which, according to the ideas of the geopoliticians, could be self-sufficient in most raw materials and have an abundance of food. But this could only be protected by fighting the USA and the colonial powers. Yet the seaborne empire that Japan had created was entirely dependent on shipping, which in turn was limited in quantity and was becoming vulnerable to allied action. Einzig predicted that the Japanese authorities would undoubtedly concentrate in that direction all the energies they could spare. It would be a mistake to underestimate the organizing capacity or the 'industrious character and selfless patriotism of the Japanese people who will undoubtedly exert themselves to the utmost to increase the output of steel and to expedite shipbuilding'.[41]

Of course, Einzig made miscalculations. He underestimated Japan's vulnerability to interdiction of oil, partly because he exaggerated its stocks and partly because he believed Japanese planning was far more efficient than was the case. He assumed that the Japanese would focus on overcoming their shipping problems and their shortages of raw materials.[42] But, from an economic point of view, he was clearly right about the economic centre of gravity in the Pacific war: 'What is essential', he wrote,

> is that the Allies should concentrate all the naval power and air power they can spare on a relentless warfare against Japanese shipping. It is much more urgent and important to sink a million tons of Japanese merchant ships than to reoccupy some of the lost territories. Inter-allied strategy in the Far East should be guided primarily by this consideration. Successful operations of ocean-going submarines and long distance bombers against Japanese shipping would cripple Japan's efforts to make good the deficiencies in her economic war potential. Time can be prevented from working in favour of Japan if the Allies could sink more ships than Japan is capable of building.[43]

Immediately after the Second World War President Truman sent the members of the US Strategic Bombing Survey to Germany and Japan to assess the effects of the allied air offensives. Volume VII of their report, written by Paul Nitze and his colleagues, concluded: 'Japan's merchant shipping fleet was not only a key link in the logistical support of her armed forces in the field, but also a vital link in her economic structure. It was the sole element of this basic structure which was vulnerable to direct attack throughout a major portion of the war.'[44] Volume IX of the report argued that 'the Japanese were peculiarly and astonishingly unprepared to convoy and protect their merchant marine against attacks whether by sea or air', given that Japan was more dependent on shipping than any other major country. Merchant ships were not armed, guns were not available to arm them and there was a great shortage of convoy escorts. The shortage of guns was all the odder because British publications, such as Brassey's, had stressed the importance of arming merchant ships if submarines were to be defeated and because the Imperial Japanese Navy had played a distinguished part in protecting allied shipping in the Mediterranean during the First World War. They paid dearly for their forgetfulness, for by the beginning of 1945 only a thin trickle of supplies was reaching Japan from Indochina. 'The war against shipping was perhaps the most decisive single factor in the collapse of the Japanese economy and the logistic support of Japanese military and naval power.'[45]

Two years after the publication of the report of the US Strategic Bombing Survey, Jerome Cohen, who had served in Japan as a language officer for the authors of the report and was now professor of economics in New York, concluded his study of the Japanese economy by claiming that the 'ever-enveloping American blockade of Japan, by shutting off essential supplies of industrial raw materials, brought Japanese war production to a virtual standstill before the main weight of the strategic air attack was delivered, and thereby made it impossible for Japan to continue the war'. Similarly, in 1988 an article in Britain's leading naval journal, *The Naval Review*, stressed the extraordinary way in which the Japanese began the Second World War with a merchant marine that was far below their peacetime requirements: 'It is no less difficult to understand why the allies did not strike at the Achilles' heel – their shipping – with the deliberate intent of crippling their activities as rapidly as practicable and in the most economical manner. However, they did not. Nevertheless, ultimately, the Japanese were forced to surrender through lack of shipping.'[46]

Since the members of the US Strategic Bombing Survey, a distinguished US economist and a British naval officer could come to exactly the same conclusions about Japan's centre of gravity as Paul Einzig had done in 1943, it is necessary to explain why the strategy was not taken up and worth speculating on what its effects would have been. First of all, it has to be said that holding the ring around Japan, concentrating on demolishing its merchant marine and defeating the Germans in Europe was more desirable from Britain's point of view in 1943 than from America's. British capacity to wage offensive campaigns against the Japanese in 1942 was negligible so any such efforts would depend entirely on the United States. But Britain did not want the US to concentrate its forces in the Pacific; on the contrary, it hoped to convince Washington that Germany had to be defeated before Japan.[47]

National leaders played a major part in deciding allied strategy. Immediately after the Japanese attack on Pearl Harbor, Churchill had sailed for the United States. On the way he wrote to Roosevelt about the strategy he believed should be followed. In the Pacific he assumed that the allies would initially be on the defensive but that stubborn resistance in Singapore, the Philippines and elsewhere would strain Japanese communications. Before the USA could recover naval superiority in the area, an event that he envisaged as materializing already in 1942, 'attack upon Japanese sea communications by United States and Dutch submarines and other vessels constitutes a grievous danger to the enemy.' In 1943 he believed that the allies could begin offensives to drive the Japanese back to their own islands, offensives that would include incendiary attacks on Japanese cities.[48] Thus, the prime minister saw from the start that submarines could be useful in the Pacific – his battleship was after all having to zigzag across the Atlantic to avoid U-boats – but he was too pugnacious to leave offensives against Japan to submarines, unless of necessity. Moreover, Roosevelt had to deal with an

American navy under Nimitz that wanted to fight its way as quickly as possible towards the Japanese homeland, with an American army under MacArthur determined to avenge the Philippines and with an American army air force that wanted bases within range of Japan from which to pound the Japanese homeland. All these put pressure on the administration to attack the Japanese by land, sea and air, rather than to follow a subtle strategy of throttling enemy trade.[49]

Public opinion polls in the USA and Britain show that there was a yawning gap between the perceptions of the two publics. It would, thus, have been risky for British leaders to be any more pressing about playing down the Pacific war because this would simply have been seen as the British again asking the Americans to do their fighting for them. In May 1942 just under a quarter of Americans believed that Britain was the ally doing least to win the war, while 40 per cent believed that their own country was doing the most. By July of the same year Gallup found that only 6 per cent of Americans believed that Britain was trying harder than the other allies to win the war. In sharp contrast, Gallup found that 42 per cent of Britons believed in April 1943 that their own country had done most to win the war, though 50 per cent said that the Russians' contribution was greatest. Only 3 per cent felt that the United States was trying the hardest. They justified their ranking by claiming that the Russians were suffering the most and that Britain had 'stood alone' before the Russians and Americans were attacked. Gallup's analysis suggests that there was a good deal of resentment on both sides of the Atlantic. Roosevelt and Churchill had to be cautious about exacerbating the situation by ignoring pent-up American fury over Pearl Harbor.[50]

On their side, the Japanese did not expect the US Navy to use submarines on any scale against their shipping because they thought, from Anglo–US pressure at disarmament conferences for the abolition of submarines, that the Americans were prejudiced against undersea warfare. They were right but not right enough to save their merchant fleet. Naval officers were well aware that German U-boat warfare had brought Britain to the verge of defeat in 1917. But the conventional wisdom in the interwar period was that the submarines had been defeated by the introduction of convoys and that the threat they presented had been further reduced by 'asdic' sonar devices. It was only as the Second World War intensified that the limitations of the sonar systems were revealed and that convoys proved insufficient on their own to protect merchant ships from more efficient submarines and the 'wolf pack' tactics of surfaced submarines.[51] German submarines were defeated in the battles of the Atlantic by the allies' ever advancing ASW technology, deployment of great numbers of convoy escorts and maritime patrol aircraft, high grade intelligence, the scientific study of the data on loss of merchant ships and the most efficient uses of the resources available.

But Japanese officers had been brought up on the Mahanian ideal of the great naval battle, on the 'Tsushima pattern' demonstrated at the end of the Russo–Japanese war and, like their Anglo–American counterparts, they preferred offensive to defensive battles.[52] The result was a reluctance to build enough convoy escorts. They also failed completely to introduce the sort of systematic analysis of naval matters that R. V. Jones, P. M. S Blackett and other scientists were introducing in the West.[53] Thus the Japanese wasted their merchant ships by sending them from one port to another in ballast and by the end of the war 2345 merchant ships, displacing 8.6 million tons, had been lost.[54] Far more publicity was given in the West to the great naval battles of the Coral Sea and Midway but the submarine force, 2 per cent of the US Navy's effort, accounted for 55 per cent of Japan's maritime losses, including one battleship, eight aircraft carriers and eleven cruisers. The submarine force was by far and away the most cost-effective element in the US Navy.[55]

At the start of the war, if submarines were too lightly dismissed by both the Japanese and the allies, so both sides underestimated Japanese vulnerability. According to Jerome Cohen, most US estimates put Japanese oil stocks at 75 to 80 million barrels. The actual figure was 43 millions. The USA believed that Japan had bauxite stocks of half a million tons, although the real figure was only half as great. Iron ore reserves had actually been decreasing in the years before the war and the Japanese were far less efficient at mobilizing resources and husbanding them to best effect than Einzig and others had expected.[56] Consequently, according to Cohen, 'generally, we failed to appreciate Japan's vulnerability to blockade and the extreme degree of her dependence on imported raw materials. Our margin of error grew greater as the war progressed.' As late as November 1944 the US foreign economic administration believed that Japan had ample raw materials. But, thanks to the submarine campaign, this was far from the case. Unmolested, the Japanese could have produced 15.2 million metric tons of steel, but they were only able to manufacture 6.5 million metric tons. At the end of the war the US Navy was astonished by its own achievements against Japanese industry.[57] By January 1943 US submarines had sunk 139 ships of 550,000 tons, but they would have destroyed far more if their torpedoes had been anything like as effective as their Japanese equivalents.[58] These faults began to be remedied as superior boats were introduced and better commanders appointed from August 1943 onwards. In the following month the Japanese lost 172,000 tons, rising to 265,000 tons in November and to a peak of 321,000 tons in October 1944.[59]

If such devastation had been envisaged from the beginning, Einzig's advice had been followed and the allies had fought a largely defensive war in the Pacific except under the sea, then the Imperial Japanese Navy would have had to swallow some of its big-ship prejudices, introduce more effective convoys and build vastly more convoy escorts.[60] Japan would still have had to maintain sufficient carriers and battleships to block a possible US naval advance. Battleship construction was a ferocious consumer of steel. The three Yamato-class battleships together displaced 200,000 tons, which was the equivalent of 235 coastal defence vessels of the type needed in the campaign to protect merchant shipping. Japanese supply lines were greatly overextended and they passed through a number of 'choke-points' which would have made them vulnerable, even if the Imperial Japanese Navy had done far more to protect shipping from submarine attack.

A campaign that focused on Japanese merchant ships would still have involved terrible loss of life. Some 52 US submarines were lost in the Pacific war. Just over 3500 submariners were killed, a loss rate of 22 per cent, which, it has been said, was the highest for any arm of the US forces.[61] The US Navy was so concerned about these losses that there was some friction between London and Washington over the publication of reports on allied successes against German U-boats. The US Navy believed these might be studied by the Japanese to increase their efficacy.[62] Losses were even more appalling among Japanese merchant seamen. Of the 122,000 men in the Japanese merchant marine at the start of the war, 27,000 were killed and 89,000 wounded.[63] Intensified warfare against Japanese ships would have increased these figures and would also inadvertently have killed more Russian, Chinese and Malay seamen (and sometimes women) than was in fact the case. Submarine warfare against merchant shipping is warfare without legal and conventional limitations. Some submarine commanders so depersonalized their enemies that they were willing to machine-gun enemy soldiers in the water, although it has to be said that others found attacks on unprotected fishing boats so sickening that they eventually desisted.[64]

But, if intensified submarine warfare had brought the war to an end before the allied bombing raids on Japan killed over 300,000 civilians, it might still have been less destructive and inhumane. The crucial question is whether this was, indeed, imaginable. It is notable that a Royal Navy officer writing in 1988 should assume that Japan had to surrender, in any case, because of its maritime losses – and of course this sort of claim has figured widely among the arguments of those who suggest that the atomic bomb attacks were 'unnecessary'.[65] Comments of this type often fail to distinguish between a defeated Japan and one that would actually surrender. Much of the supporting evidence has, in any event, been derived from the interviews conducted by the US Strategic Bombing Survey, Barton J. Bernstein has pointed out that the postwar interviews with former Japanese leaders on which this claim was based were vague and inconclusive.[66] Moreover, merchant shipping losses and the possible suffering of the Japanese people as a result, seem to have played no greater part in the surrender than warship losses, defeats on the islands and in Burma, the entry of the Soviet Union into the war and the conventional and nuclear bombing raids. If anything, there seems to be a distinction between senior military officers who stressed the importance of military defeats and civilians who emphasized civilian suffering. Power was in the hands of the military.

It appears unlikely that the Japanese would have surrendered for a long time in the face of a submarine blockade alone. Their armies would have been cut off in China, Southeast Asia and the Pacific islands, and the people in Japan and in those Japanese territories who were not self-sufficient would have slowly starved. An official Japanese report had suggested in 1938 that 80 per cent of Korean peasants only survived the spring by eating weeds, roots and bark from the trees.[67] Any further reduction in living standards would have led to mass starvation. Yet, given their ethos, patriotism and bravery, the Japanese might well have decided to starve rather than surrender, taking the colonial peoples with them; just as many Japanese soldiers starved in Burma and elsewhere. The caloric intake of the Japanese was far lower than that of European peoples and by 1943 it was 12 per cent lower than the minimum requirement. Prices soared across the empire; by 1945 the cost of eggs had increased 45 times in Rangoon and 100 times in Shanghai. Banana prices had risen 4000 per cent in Bangkok.[68] The whole of Asia was reverting to a subsistence and (very often) near-starvation economy. We also know far more today about the resistance of dictatorships to economic blockade than Einzig had known in 1943. It is difficult to believe that the Japanese leaders would have demanded less of their people than the Iraqi leaders demanded in the 1990s or that the Japanese people would have been less willing than the Iraqis to respond.[69] In sum, it is hard to be certain that casualties among prisoners of war, Asian peoples and the Japanese themselves would have been diminished by Einzig's 'alternative strategy'.

The economic, political and military spheres often have logics or dynamics of their own. Einzig had produced a logical economic analysis of Japan's prospects in 1943 that was more accurate in some ways than those written by the US intelligence community; but military dynamics and the general public demanded great battles. It may be that allied political and military leaders were not as prejudiced or ill-informed as they appear at first sight in choosing to ignore Japan's economic vulnerability. In retrospect, historians may argue that Japan was defeated before the atomic bombs were dropped and before the conventional bombing intensified. If defeat means the inability to take the offensive, the isolation of the component parts of the Japanese Empire and permanent blockade, then Japan was indeed defeated, just as Iraq was in the 1990s. But if defeat means surrender by the government followed by occupation, then the conclusion is much more obscure. Einzig saw that there was no rational economic reason for Japan to expand in the 1930s, yet he failed to see that rationality might play as small a part in the decision to surrender.

Nevertheless, Einzig's suggestions certainly deserved far more examination than they received in 1943. If he was wrong, he was wrong for very good economic reasons. His book remains an historical curiosity. It may have been much less commercially successful than other books, such as John Morris's *Traveller from Tokyo*, but in strategic terms it was far more original.[70] It was very rare in 1943 for non-military men to offer strategic advice. The former *Times* correspondent in Japan, Hugh Byas, had published a book on Japan and its vulnerability in April 1942 that concluded with a chapter on 'How we can Defeat Japan'. Yet Byas offered no original ideas, concluding lamely: 'Speculation is speculation. Arm-chair strategy is arm-chair strategy. The plan for victory will be worked out by the United States General Staffs in combination with those of their British and Dutch allies.'[71] There was another civilian commentator whose contemporary examination of Japanese power was published in 1942 – Simon Harcourt-Smith, a British diplomat who had served in Beijing and in the Far Eastern Department of the Foreign Office. His *Japanese Frenzy* had much more to say about the inadequacies of British military preparations than Einzig's book. Harcourt-Smith warned that the Pacific war would be fought without quarter and that Japan was as redoubtable an enemy as Germany. But he took the wholly erroneous view that 'even if we were in a position to exert it, no blockade would seriously inconvenience Japan any longer.' Strategically, his work was far less original than Einzig's and his main claim to be remembered is in the clarity with which he saw the deficiencies in the British Empire: 'We must no longer fight in the East as strangers among sullen populations. We must show the world that in the bad old sense we are no longer imperialists.'[72]

Encouraged by their contacts in Whitehall, Harcourt-Smith and Einzig were both unusual in their willingness to intrude into the military sphere. It was much less characteristic of Einzig that he subsequently made so little of his book and did not even mention it in his autobiography. Admittedly, he was the author of more than 60 books and so he could not dilate on all of them, and maybe he was disappointed by the lack of reviews and the poor sales that *The Japanese New Order in Asia* achieved.[73] It is surely odd that he should not mention a book that was so perceptive about allied strategy, but then most of the memoirs by allied leaders failed to mention the commerce warfare against Japan. If they talk about submarines, it is in the context of the defensive Battle of the Atlantic, not the offensive war in the Pacific.[74] Thus this battle is today far better remembered in the West than the more decisive Battle of the Pacific, of which Einzig was a lonely British prophet. Such indifference may help to explain Einzig's amnesia about his book after the war; certainly, it underlines the originality of his proposals in 1943.

Chapter 7

BRITAIN AND THE RECOVERY OF JAPAN POST-1945

Peter Lowe

Amid the devastation in Japan in August 1945, as the Pacific war came to an end, the revival of the country seemed a very distant goal, unlikely to be attained for many years.[1] The United States was primarily responsible for the defeat of Japan and it was to be expected that American policy-makers would be decisive in determining the future of the country. However, British ministers and officials did not anticipate the extent to which Britain would be marginalized: Ernest Bevin, the new foreign secretary, thought there would be scope for influencing the political, economic and social initiatives arising from the allied occupation.[2]

In 1945–46 it transpired that neither President Harry S. Truman nor the proconsul in Tokyo, General Douglas MacArthur, desired Britain to have a significant part in deciding the destiny of the vanquished foe.[3] Britain and the United States shared certain common aims but they also diverged on other issues. They were in agreement on the following:

- demilitarization must proceed rapidly since it was important for the Commonwealth, notably Australia and New Zealand;
- democratization of Japanese institutions was needed, although British officials were less sanguine than some of their American counterparts on the extent of transformation;
- stability had to be accomplished through resolving rural unrest, extending the franchise to women and cultivating political parties dedicated to Western concepts of constitutionalism;

- the monarchy should be retained, as should Emperor Hirohito, but it must be purged of its intimate association with 'state Shinto'.

They diverged in their approaches to the rebuilding of Japan in the middle and later stages of the occupation when the British held that the economy was being rekindled rather too rapidly and that American enthusiasm for rearmament was advancing too fast.

Britain was represented in Tokyo by its liaison mission. For most of the occupation this was headed by Alvary Gascoigne, a military man turned diplomat who had known Shigeru Yoshida since the early 1920s.[4] Gascoigne was a shrewd operator and was successful in establishing a cordial relationship with MacArthur until it was undermined by the repercussions of the Korean war in 1950–51. Gascoigne assumed his post in 1946, by which time the principal characteristics of the occupation had been established. He knew that there would be only limited room for influencing American policy and this would best be achieved through discussing matters with MacArthur, at least while MacArthur enjoyed considerable freedom to direct policy in Tokyo. Gascoigne's military experience in the Great War doubtless persuaded MacArthur to pay more attention to him than would otherwise have been the case; moreover, and indispensably, Gascoigne was a good listener. MacArthur sometimes required British support, particularly when Washington intervened conspicuously, thus curbing his freedom of manoeuvre. The British respected MacArthur's ability and achievements and believed that he met the challenges of governing Japan effectively. There was no fundamental divergence between the British and the Supreme Commander of Allied Powers (SCAP) before the outbreak of the Korean war in June 1950.

In the economic sphere Britain supported reducing the power of the zaibatsu financial conglomerates and introducing greater competition. American policy was perceived as erratic;[5] MacArthur was slow in embarking on radical reform of the zaibatsu and when he did move, in 1947–48, it was seen as linked with MacArthur's presidential ambition in the 1948 elections.[6] This was stimulated by references within MacArthur's 'court' to his interest in gaining the Republican Party's nomination as the campaigning season unfolded. Somewhat improbably MacArthur was accused of pursuing 'socialistic' policies in encouraging trade unions and in curbing the power of big business. British officials did not regard MacArthur as a socialist but they felt that he was sometimes over-sanguine and that economics were not his forte.[7] British concern focused on areas where British firms had encountered sharp Japanese competition before the Pacific war and where it was feared that British recovery would be undermined by Japanese competition. The principal areas of anxiety comprised textiles, potteries and shipping. This has to be set in the context of the economic aims of the Labour government headed by Clement Attlee which assumed office following the general election in July 1945. Labour was committed to ambitious, far-reaching economic and social reforms that hinged on developing a viable full-employment economy.[8] The horrors of degrading long-term unemployment haunted the Labour ministers and it was feared that a significant Japanese revival would affect employment adversely. Employers and trade unions combined to remind the government that their interests must be protected. I shall now consider these industries in turn.

The textile industry in Lancashire led the world in the great industrial revolution from the latter part of the eighteenth century. In a counter-blast at the new economic historians who regarded the eclipse of Lancashire textiles as 'the most terrible retreat in the history of industry', Douglas Farnie has observed: 'What is surely most important is not the contraction of that industry but the long duration of its primacy. The decline of the Lancashire cotton industry remains the least significant feature of its long history: its influence changed the world forever.'[9]

Coming from Manchester University, I have sympathy with this defiant statement but I am addressing the latter part of the long era referred to by Farnie. Problems developed in Lancashire before the Great War and explained why a minority of mill owners were attracted by Joseph Chamberlain's advocacy of tariff reform.[10] Decline was accentuated in the 1920s with the economic depression. The last cotton mills to be constructed in Lancashire opened in 1926 at a time when man-made fibres began to threaten markets.[11] Japanese competition in China had resulted in the loss of the market for 'piece goods' from Lancashire in 1917. The disappearance of the old elite of foreign merchants in Manchester after 1914 handicapped exports.[12] Trade unions became very powerful in the nineteenth century to the extent that their general secretaries secured membership of the Manchester Chamber of Commerce from 1887.[13] Japanese competition intensified during the Great War; Lancashire's response was inadequate and market trends were not grasped clearly. Management and unions were responsible for discouraging initiative and reorganization.[14]

Japanese firms were castigated for employing 'sweated labour', a common allegation and one that influenced two successive foreign secretaries during the occupation – Ernest Bevin and Herbert Morrison.[15] In fact, Japanese success resulted from the efficiency with which their firms were run and the application of scientific management. Sir Walter

Preston, chairman of Platt Brothers of Oldham, recognized Japanese business prowess in the mid-1930s, but this was atypical.[16] From 1935 onwards Japan displaced Britain as the main supplier of cotton cloth to India and Burma. John Maynard Keynes argued that rationalization was imperative in Lancashire and he despaired at the attitude of the majority of company directors. Already in 1926 he inclined towards the removal of the bulk of the industry's 6000 directors: in 1944 Keynes sardonically lamented that German bombers had not destroyed factories 'at an hour when the directors were sitting there and no one else'.[17]

The Foreign Office reviewed Japanese economic prospects in March 1948. The aim, as established by the Far Eastern Commission, should be to restore the standard of living to that obtaining between 1930 and 1934. Reparations should comprise industrial assets, shipping, gold deposits and other external assets. As regards textiles, the Foreign Office did not advocate imposing restrictions but Japanese wages and working practices should conform with fair commercial criteria – 'We want good wages and working conditions in the Japanese factories and the elimination of sharp commercial practices.'[18] Sir Raymond Streat, chairman of the Cotton Board, was closely involved with the effort to restructure Britain's cotton industry so that a greater contribution could be made to the export drive. He urged further rationalization, increased investment and the removal of restrictive practices by trade unions. Streat had devoted his career to Lancashire and was a well-known personality in the Manchester Chamber of Commerce. He worked sedulously to promote cotton both in Manchester and through his liaison with government. He visited Japan, met General MacArthur and experienced MacArthur's preference for monologues (one-sided). He was duly impressed with the general's grasp of the topic. MacArthur held that the Japanese economy must be stimulated and that Britain should not be too apprehensive of Japanese competition. Any difficulties that arose should be resolved via mutual discussion involving the American, British and Japanese industries. MacArthur emphasized that he would not restrict Japanese revival.[19] SCAP and the Japanese government regarded textiles as of considerable importance for the short- to medium-term growth of the economy. Textiles constituted Japan's principal export between 1946 and 1960, averaging 60 per cent of production. The reorganization of Japanese textiles after 1946 embraced decentralization of cost control and the application of techniques of quality control over exports.[20]

The commencement of serious negotiations for a Japanese peace treaty in 1950 accentuated anxiety in Lancashire because it was realized that

Japan would soon regain sovereignty and that Japanese governments, unfettered by SCAP, might encourage more rapid expansion of textiles. A Foreign Office official attended a dinner party hosted by the Board of Trade for the textiles fibres advisory committee on 3 July 1951, by which time negotiations with Japan had largely been completed. He reported the fear in Lancashire that Japanese competition would intensify and that the peace treaty would do nothing to mitigate the situation. Employers perceived 'sweated labour' as a problem and recommended that the Japanese government should be given an appropriate warning.[21] The new foreign secretary, Herbert Morrison, conveyed such a warning to the Japanese prime minister, Shigeru Yoshida , when the two men met in San Francisco for formal signature of the peace treaty in September 1951: 'There was anxiety in Great Britain lest prewar conditions of sweated labour and competition were revived. In the interests of the people of Japan and of relations between Japan and Britain it was essential that this should not happen.'[22] Labour, Conservative and Liberal MPs raised questions about the issue in the House of Commons.[23] Although the cotton industry enjoyed a brief 'Indian summer' in the late 1940s, the apprehension of the damage that would ensue from renewed Japanese competition was borne out during the 1950s.[24] The numerous attempts to restore Lancashire's fortunes were seen to be futile during the sharp decline in the 1960s and 1970s.

Representations from the Staffordshire potteries were vigorous and again advanced by manufacturers, trade unions and MPs. The two Labour MPs for Stoke-on-Trent were vociferous and ensured that ministers and diplomats did not lose sight of their claims in the midst of the greater clamour created by cotton interests. The government was less concerned that potteries would be undermined than it was with the protests from textile and shipping interests, but political realities meant that suitable representations had to be made in Tokyo.[25]

As far as shipping and shipbuilding were concerned, economic and strategic factors overlapped. An underlying sub-theme in Foreign Office minutes was that Japanese nationalism would revive within a decade or so of the close of the occupation. Australia and New Zealand were worried over a future Japanese threat. Too generous an approach to shipping could prove dangerous and the American obsession with communism could produce an underestimation of a future threat from Japan. Herbert Morrison stressed shipping and shipbuilding in the course of exchanges with the American representative, John Foster Dulles, during the latter's visit to London in June 1951, and these was followed by further communication during the concluding stages of negotiating the peace treaty. Shipping interests viewed Japanese ambitions in much the same light as their counterparts in textiles and the potteries. Japanese shipping had been subsidized for many years and many held that unfair advantages were conferred by government.[26] Japanese construction expanded considerably during the Great War of 1914–18 and the potential came to be appreciated more fully in Britain. By 1950 Japanese yards had recovered from wartime damage and completed 547,000 tons, the highest figure since 1919.[27] Japanese expansion has to be viewed in the context of the swift growth of world shipbuilding capacity with tonnages increasing tenfold within 25 years.[28]

British ministers believed in 1951 that the Americans were pursuing a permissive attitude on spare capacity in Japan because of the preoccupation with the cold war. Statistics produced by the British were challenged by the Americans. In June 1951 British officials estimated existing Japanese capacity at 810,000 tons. John M. Allison, Dulles's chief aide in the State Department, supported a Japanese estimate of 676,000 tons. The argument hinged in part upon the inclusion or exclusion of yards not then in production.[29] Allison indicated that Japanese yards were operating at between 70 and 80 per cent with output ranging between 400,000 and 500,000 tons a year. It was stated that Japan would probably possess approximately 1,549,000 tons of ocean-going ships. Rapid growth was envisaged as essential down to the mid-1950s. British officials adhered to the view that Japanese growth would exceed that suggested in Japanese estimates submitted to Allison. The British argued that Japan's capacity could be held at the figure of 400,000 tons a year. Australia and New Zealand supported the British but India, Pakistan and Ceylon dissented.[30]

The cabinet discussed the position on 1 August 1951. The minister of transport fully supported the serious reservations expressed by Morrison regarding Japanese potential. More general anxiety was forthcoming over a broader pattern of intensified competition from Japan. At the same time the force of counter-arguments was recognized, which included the impact of population growth and the desirability of encouraging democracy to flourish through adopting an understanding attitude.[31]

The challenge for British shipping lay in its inability to compete effectively. Yards had not been modernized and investment was not targeted. British management became too bureaucratic after the Great War and trade unions maintained restrictive practices.[32] As with the cotton industry, the fears within Whitehall were confirmed in the course of the 1950s: by 1958 Japan was producing approximately one-third more tonnage than Britain and, by 1970, 8.5 times as much.[33] The traditional

British industries were incapable of competing successfully. Anxiety over shipping was wider in scope than with textiles and the potteries because of its strategic dimension.

However, Australia and New Zealand were placated by the American decision to underwrite their defence in the ANZUS treaty, and the fact that the 'new Commonwealth' was more sympathetic to Japan had to be kept in mind.[34] The negotiations over a Japanese peace treaty in 1950–51 demonstrated the differing emphases of the United States and Britain. The Attlee government agreed with General MacArthur that the allied occupation should not be extended unduly, since animosity would be kindled through failure to appreciate the strong desire to regain sovereignty. The Labour government wavered in its resolution only once, briefly in March 1951.[35] The perspectives of the American and British governments diverged significantly where the future of Japan was concerned. The United States regarded Japan as a cornerstone of Western strategy in Asia in blocking the advance of communism. Secretary of State John Foster Dulles wished to encourage Japanese rearmament to an extent deemed unwise by Prime Minister Shigeru Yoshida, who did not want to assist the return of old-style militarism.[36] The Truman administration had changed direction in 1947–48: MacArthur's freedom was now restricted through growing intervention from Washington and much of it was inspired by economic motives. American taxpayers did not want Japan's economy to be depressed so that they would be forced to come to its support. Moreover, the future stability of Japan, and its cooperation with the West, depended on economic progress.

This pointed towards the conclusion of a generous peace treaty. Of course, Japan would forfeit its colonial possessions but Dulles was not receptive to the argument that Japan should pay higher reparations and lose its gold deposits. Dulles was not influenced by the desire to impose undue retribution. Japan had been punished sufficiently for Pearl Harbor. The British approach was different. The surrender of Singapore in February 1942 and its concomitants weighed heavily in the British outlook, as did the memories of the inhumane treatment of POWs and civilian internees.[37]

Such mistreatment was referred to during cabinet deliberations in 1951 and was underlined during questions and debates in the House of Commons. Ministers and officials recalled prewar competition and did not relish the prospect of formidable competition to come. Civil servants revealed more understanding of diplomatic reality than did cabinet ministers. Some members of the cabinet thought that the United States could be pushed into adopting a tougher approach to the peace treaty.

The principal advocate of a harsher line was the chancellor of the exchequer, Hugh Gaitskell. He spoke trenchantly at a meeting with Dulles held on 6 June 1951. On this occasion Gaitskell stressed the continuing resentment at the savage treatment of POWs and the strength of public opinion. The British people would not comprehend Japan receiving a more magnanimous settlement than Germany. Dulles responded firmly, underlining the cost of the occupation and the deep commitment of the United States to ensuring its success. If any country had a right to claim Japanese gold, it would be the United States, but such a course would not be pursued because the priority was to ensure that Japan possessed a stable economy when the occupation terminated. Dulles also reminded Gaitskell that Japan had lost all of its colonial territories. Gaitskell commented that he would prefer the United States to take the Japanese gold deposits rather than Japan receiving them.[38]

The sole concession made by Dulles concerned the Congo Basin treaties. This was offered as a token gesture. Japanese rights originated in a treaty signed in 1885 and were extended to Japan as one of the victors at the Paris peace conference in 1919. If Japan retained these rights, as contemplated by Dulles in the earlier stages of negotiations, Japan would be able to export cheap cotton goods to Africa, thus weakening the Lancashire industry. The president of the Board of Trade, Sir Hartley Shawcross, explained to Dulles that Britain was not trying to eliminate Japan from competition in this African market but rather wished to limit the volume of Japanese exports. He linked the issue with the balance of payments and rearmament in Britain, explaining that British textile exports should be increased by 40 per cent over the preceding year so as to rectify the failure of other exports to achieve the recommended figure.[39] Since he compelled British ministers to accept American wishes in other respects, Dulles clearly concluded that one or two crumbs of comfort had to be offered. Thus, the cabinet was informed on 14 June 1951 that Dulles now accepted that Japan should forfeit its rights under the Congo Basin treaties.[40] Gaitskell and Morrison recognized that it was unfeasible to press the question of gold deposits further and accepted the American decision.[41]

The San Francisco conference proceeded more smoothly than expected. The Soviet Union advanced half-hearted criticisms and regretted the absence of the People's Republic of China. However, Andrei Gromyko, the Soviet delegate, did not disturb the proceedings unduly. Dean Acheson, the American secretary of state, presided firmly and the treaty was signed. It was one of the few triumphs for the Truman administration's policies in eastern Asia and, ironically, a Republican was responsible for this success. The British ambassador-designate to Japan, Sir Esler Dening, assessed economic relations shortly before the end of the occupation. He appreciated that the Board of Trade was unsympathetic to Japan and knew it did not envisage most favoured nation (MFN) terms being extended to it. Dening anticipated that Japanese competition would soon become serious in certain areas. It is instructive to reflect on Dening's list - British industries about to experience the chill wind were rayon, textiles, toys, electrical accessories and appliances, cameras, pottery and enamelware. Dening warned that the consequences in these areas for employment would be serious.[42]

While his list included the familiar items of textiles and pottery; electrical goods and cameras pointed more to the future. It was significant that he emphasized the approach of the Board of Trade. This pointed towards the negative British policy pursued subsequently in the 1950s. Britain was much slower to come to terms with Japanese economic revival than the United States. This is attributable to several factors. Britain was largely marginalized during the occupation and this led it to take up a more biased position than it might otherwise have done. The shadow of Singapore, 1942, affected Britain's view as did the process of coming to terms with its diminished status in the world.

Sir Hugh Cortazzi has reflected on Anglo-Japanese relations in the light of his lengthy connections with Japan.[43] He noted that, typically, Britain and some other states invoked article 35 permitting the withholding of MFN treatment when the Japanese acceded to the General Agreement on Tariffs and Trade (GATT) in 1955.[44] This obstacle was removed in 1962 with the conclusion of a treaty of commerce and navigation. The pattern of trade changed significantly in the 1960s. This is well conveyed in Cortazzi's succinct assessment: instead of tinned salmon and mandarin oranges, textiles, pottery and toys the Japanese began to expand their exports of more sophisticated items. The Japanese electronic and machinery industries were growing fast, and the shipbuilding and steel industries were particularly successful. Many British ship owners ordered ships from Japan and British shipbuilders sent to Japan a mission including a trade union representative to see how the Japanese managed to produce ships so cheaply and efficiently. British Steel also sent a mission to learn about Japanese methods of steel production. Some British exporters began to wake up to the opportunities in the Japanese market, but there was only limited recognition at this time of the threat that the Japanese drive to increase their exports of sophisticated consumer goods would pose to foreign manufacturers in the next decade.[45]

Disputes over electrical goods, motorcycles and cars characterized the ensuing decade and a half before better relations followed in the latter part of Margaret Thatcher's premiership when Japanese investment in Britain acquired greater momentum.[46] During the 1990s Japan became Britain's third largest direct foreign investor and a major trade partner outside the European Union.[47]

Let us conclude. The British government and public opinion wished to restrict Japanese economic revival after 1945. This was the consequence of the bitter conflict of 1941–45 and of recollections of the serious nature of Japanese competition in the interwar period. The astonishing progress made in the Japanese economy from the later 1950s was not anticipated but Japan's ability to compete intensely was recognized, hence the representations made by the members of traditional British industries. If British leaders had been free to shape the Japanese peace treaty as they wished, it can be stated with assurance that it would not have been concluded on terms as generous as those applied by John Foster Dulles.

However, American pressure was so marked that ministers in the Attlee government and civil servants modified decisions accordingly, although the former acted more reluctantly than the latter. This is best understood in the context of British decline. Japan had contributed very significantly to the humiliating diminution of British prestige and to the more rapid disappearance of the British Empire in Asia. Labour ministers were striving to restore the economy, boost exports and carry through a highly ambitious domestic reform programme. Japan had inflicted much pain in the past and, at least in the economic sphere, was likely to do so again in the future. American tenacity prevented the inclusion of restrictive clauses in the peace treaty. Instead, the British were left eyeing Japan warily and voicing anxiety in querulous tones. The Americans were more farsighted and the forecasts made by General MacArthur and John Foster Dulles were more accurate than those emerging contemporaneously from Whitehall. However, the United States was also to experience the heat of Japanese competition with reactions coming from threatened industries not dissimilar to those seen in Britain decades before. Japanese luck itself ran out in the 1990s as the close relationship between politics, business and finance, often cited earlier as one of the reasons for the success of the economy, was now perceived as contributing to stagnation and irresolution. Ironically, the British economy was widely described as advancing successfully at the beginning of the twenty-first century. It is unusual for a historian to end on a note of optimism regarding British economic performance, so I shall make the most of this opportunity and conclude at this juncture.

Chapter 8

SHIPPING AND SHIPBUILDING

John Weste

Sons of the sea, all English born

As Peter Lowe pointed out in the last chapter, defeat and occupation by the allied powers in August 1945 eliminated, however temporarily, Japan as a serious rival to Britain's economic position and trading links with the Asian region. That Japan ended the Second World War with 2,000,000 tonnes of merchant shipping, little of which was actually sea worthy, as opposed to the 6,000,000 tonnes with which it began demonstrated the extent of ocean-going Japan's fall. Nonetheless, the strain of prolonged conflict also told heavily on Great Britain. Certainly, a still powerful military and a recaptured empire held a promise of future resources, trade and global might. The capacity to mediate Anglo-Japanese trade through the Southeast Asian colonies and Australasia remained.[1] Nonetheless, as the 1950s progressed, this approach was increasingly weakened through colonial independence movements, internal conflict within the remaining Commonwealth and a growing conviction among the British metropolitan elite that prosperity and security lay instead in strong ties with the capitals of Western Europe and Washington. Equally, colonial possessions and the Commonwealth could not protect the home islands themselves from the impact of direct Japanese competition. Further, however, London sought to frame its economic and diplomatic relations with Japan in the postwar era; it was Washington, intent upon an economically vibrant Japan in alliance with the capitalist bloc, that now held the greater sway as the dominant Western power in East Asia and the Pacific.

For Britain and Japan, the shipping sector, both in terms of building, and the conveyance of goods and passengers, was held to be crucial to future economic prosperity. Britain's traditional position as a leading shipbuilding nation was not one to be surrendered readily: between the years 1948 and 1950, for example, Great Britain held 35 per cent of the world's export market.[2] The international provision of services through the shipping of trade on British-owned vessels was also highly lucrative. Industry dreaded a Japanese resurgence, feared its competitive capacity and lobbied the British government and bureaucracy for support. It is important to observe, too, that such fears were not mere reflections of wartime hatred, but did indeed carry on from the prewar period where the contribution of Japanese competition to the decline of British shipping in Asia was held to be all but incalculable. Of particular concern at the time were the India–Japan and Japan–Australia lines.[3]

It is also of equal importance to confirm, however, that such fears did not necessarily translate into a blanket British opposition to the re-emergence of Japanese trade and manufacturing: the government, the civil service, industry and colonial officials were by no means united. As early as October 1946, the president of the Board of Trade, Sir Stafford Cripps, stated that Japan must be left 'internationally solvent' as the alternative of 'permanent foreign support' was clearly way beyond Britain's capacities.[4] In May 1948, Foreign Secretary Ernest Bevin warned against leaving Japan and its 'ninety millions of people ... in a cesspool of poverty'.[5] Later that July, Bevin emphasized his point by refusing to receive a Lancashire delegation demanding that restrictions be imposed on Japanese spindles. In a letter to Harold Wilson, the then president of the Board of Trade, he explained that 'On the grounds of economic principle, political possibility and administrative expediency, HM government have always maintained that no proposal for restricting the development of Japanese consumption goods industries should be put forward.'[6] Of course, the above does not suggest that Japan was necessarily held in any great affection either. Recollections of prewar competition, wartime atrocities and postwar concerns were powerful: Anthony Eden, foreign secretary in the later Conservative government represented well this dichotomy; he acknowledged that the Japanese 'count for a great deal and will count for more', but also claimed that as a people they were hardly likeable.[7]

The possibility of an unpleasant aspect to the Japanese national character had long since been seized upon by British industry and Eden's words offered little comfort. In May 1951, the council of the Chamber of Shipping could do little but confirm that 'shipowners would have to face increasing competition from Germany and Japan and that all that could be hoped for was that the British government would see fair play.'[8] Admitting its essential inability to deny Japan, but still adamant upon lambasting Japanese competition, industry tended to focus more on the nature of Japanese competition than on the sheer fact of its actual existence. In this context, the notion of gentlemanly conduct in trade, and a distinctively British duty to enforce it, came to the fore. As the 1955 annual report of the Chamber of Shipping of the United Kingdom declared, 'the aspirations of Japan to play a prominent part in world trade are understandable. But it is idle for her to think that she will be readily accepted back into the comity of nations so long as she continues to pursue an aggressive trade policy.'[9]

With regards to support from Whitehall, Anglo-Japanese relations in the shipping sector do cast some light on how various sections of the civil service viewed economic rivalry with Japan. For obvious reasons, the Foreign Office (FO) held a dominant role in London and in Japan through its United Kingdom Liaison Mission (UKLM) in Tokyo.[10] In matters of an economic nature, the Board of Trade might also be expected to occupy a key position. However, in the case of the shipbuilding and shipping sectors, the Ministry of Transport (MT) also emerges as a body with definite interests, both in London and in Tokyo, in Anglo-Japanese economic and trading relations and American occupation policy for Japan. As did the more prominent government agencies, MT also sought to influence and inform official thinking with regards to British policy for occupied Japan and the latter's economic re-emergence in the subsequent decade.

That this issue remained of core importance to Great Britain is of no doubt. By 1956, for the first peacetime year since 1920, a foreign nation launched more merchant ships than the UK. That it was Japan hardly softened the blow. Two years later, West Germany claimed second position and so, in little over a decade since the end of the war, the UK had fallen into third place behind its two wartime enemies. Of whomever the sons of the sea were born, it was quite clear they were no longer singularly electing to 'sail British'.

'The price we have to pay for not being able to do the job ourselves':[11] Japanese merchant shipping, shipbuilding and Great Britain

The gradual return of Japanese shipping to world commerce was relatively quick and by the late 1940s, a presence had been re-established in the Middle East and in Southeast Asia, which reflected natural Japanese commercial desires but equally keen official American support. The Occupation was a considerable financial burden on the United States and, if the use of Japanese vessels over foreign lowered costs, then there was an obvious advantage to be had. As cold war tensions, marked by the 1949 communist victory in the Chinese civil war and the June 1950 outbreak of war in the Korean peninsula, grew, American policy emphasized a relatively prosperous Japanese economy. Overly tight controls and subsequent economic doldrums, it was feared, would turn the Japanese away from the Western allies to the communists. Moreover, the potential links between Southeast Asia as a source of raw materials and a market for Japanese manufactures and products had also been identified as a means to stabilize the region and thus further protect against communist penetration.[12]

By late 1946 the British had noticed a practice, disturbingly recognized as almost 'natural and normal', of Japanese shipping, with the support of the American occupation authorities (Supreme Commander of Allied Powers or SCAP), returning to the lines between Japan and Korea, China and Formosa, where British firms also sought to regain their former position. Moreover, where Japanese vessels were unavailable, SCAP's Economic and Scientific Section (ESS) advocated using Japanese crews on US ships carrying Japanese trade to decrease Japanese foreign currency expenditure. While it was 'most desirable that everything should be done to arrest at an early stage this tendency', UKLM staff were also forced to observe it was one 'the Japanese know to exploit' and that anyway British shipping could hardly fill all the gaps.[13] Indeed, the trend proved irresistible and, precisely one year later, MT reported that Japanese vessels were carrying cement to India and returning laden with coal.[14] In a similar manner, Japanese tankers began a shuttle service to the Persian Gulf in 1948 and over 1949, again with SCAP encouragement, Japanese shipping was lifting bulk purchases of rice from Siam, and iron ore from the Philippines and Malaya.[15] This time it was for MT to comment that it was 'not anxious to see the Japanese flag back in ocean trade'.[16]

Such statements did not reflect a mere automatic distaste at the return of a former bitter rival and enemy: by early 1949, MT representatives in East Asia had identified the core fact that the Japanese market was important to British shipping. Compared with the relative chaos in northeast Asia, Japan, 'however bureaucratic the hierarchy of administration', had a stable economy and considerable overseas trade.[17] Indeed, freight to and from Japan had come to represent the single largest item of earnings of British ships north of Singapore and the British flag carried the largest share of goods moved in and out of Japan in the normal course of trade. For example, in December 1948, of the 127 dry cargo ships calling with inbound cargo to Japan, 43 ships (carrying 208,000 tons) were

British; 39 were American (168,000 tons); the next closest rivals were the Chinese with a mere 12 vessels (69,000 tons). Similarly, for outbound trade, Britain led with 20 ships (29,000 tons), the USA came second with 12 (14,000), with the Dutch and Norwegians coming equal third with five ships (at 15,000 and 7000 tons respectively).[18] Such trade was clearly valuable and well worth government support to sustain.[19]

Likewise, with the shipbuilding sector, British observers regularly returned dispatches to London confirming determined moves towards redevelopment, again with open support from SCAP, and the latent potential of Japan to threaten core UK industrial concerns in the long run. MT officials in Japan toured Japanese shipyards and confirmed their generally sound condition despite wartime damage. Original occupation plans designated 20 Japanese commercial and five military dockyards as reparations, with only one major yard to be left intact at Nagasaki. Nonetheless, the British were also aware that increasingly shipyards were being removed from reparation lists, such as the Mitsubishi yards at Kobe and Yokohama, and that others soon would be.[20] While such a trend can be held to exemplify one further aspect of the reverse course in Occupation policy, Japan was the one site in East Asia that fortuitously combined both an immediate technical capacity and major trade routes for allied shipping. The Japanese further indirectly gained from American military retention of their shipyards: Mitsubishi's Kobe yard was re-equipped with 'up-to-date plant of every description and the work done there ... compares well with that done in the United States'.[21] Modern techniques learnt from the US military could be readily applied later to civilian and commercial manufacture.

The year 1949 further marked the return of Japan to shipbuilding with the first signing of a contract for large vessels. Enquiries rapidly followed from the Brazilian, Indian and Pakistani governments and, to make clear the global nature of Japanese commercial ambitions, Canadian and Scandinavian firms had also entered into discussions for low-cost shipbuilding in Japan. J. V. Clyne, chairman of the Canadian Maritime Commission, passed on these worrying trends to MT, London, but was equally cognizant of SCAP's support for the Japanese because exports of ships were valuable sources of foreign currency.[22] Projecting the future remained difficult with uncertainties abounding. Nonetheless, by 1950 MT had estimated that of the 1.7 million tonnage of shipping in Japanese ownership a mere 300,000 tons of dry cargo vessels were active with the remainder either unfit for service or small coasting and river craft. Assuming all things equal, a production figure of 4,000,000 tons by 1959 was considered achievable.[23]

Friends and allies: the United States and the British Commonwealth of Nations

Naturally, the revival of Japan's shipbuilding and shipping sectors did not occur in a vacuum. Equally, British fears and ambitions were played out in the context of crucial relations both with the United States (in Washington and Tokyo), and the remaining colonial territories and the emerging Commonwealth. American dominance is clear because, despite extreme frustration and even anger with American policy as enacted in Japan, Britain was forced to adopt a conciliatory position and accept conditions not necessarily to its benefit. The Commonwealth offered certain advantages, whether in terms of potential leverage *vis-à-vis* Japan and the United States or as an arena where at least some aspects of Anglo–Japanese economic competition could be deflected and dealt with indirectly. Such gains also came at a cost because both the USA and Japan remained suspicious that British influence in the former empire was detrimental to free trade, including that of Japan's. Steadfast British opposition to Japanese entry into GATT (until 1955) in the face of fierce American pressure symbolized concerns on all sides.

On 15 August 1947, Japan was declared once again open to private business, yet, as *The Economist*, pithily observed, the dastardly obstacles, including a plethora of forms, currency conversion issues and the like would be 'as many as the dragons confronting the hopeful knight-errant in a medieval romance'.[24] Jests aside, the November 1946 experience of the British vessel SS *Cape Howe*, which called at Miike to load coal for Hong Kong, had already proven the damage such barriers represented to legitimate British trade and the vital need for determined on-site representatives to support UK business. After arrival, the ship's master wired UKLM to request funds to procure provisions, but was told the mission had no yen funds and to approach the local American military mission instead (60 miles away by tram for which the master had no money for a ticket). Upon arrival, the military mission turned him down on the grounds that they had no written authority from Tokyo to dispense funds. In the meantime, as the master was presumably feigning deafness to the irritation of ticket sellers on the Japanese public transport system, the crew had no money in port, had run out of cigarettes and were forced to sell their clothes on the black market. Perhaps it was their subsequent nudity that in turn encouraged the 12 cases of venereal disease, for which medical attention also proved incredibly difficult to obtain. Understandably, the master wrote furiously to the British government protesting that UKLM had placed 'British vessels and crews in a position that should not be tolerated especially before the eyes of a defeated nation. It was all rather degrading.'[25]

Both FO and MT made reference to this case and, by early 1947, with an approximate 20 British ships projected to use Japanese ports on a monthly basis to deliver salt and phosphates, the need for official UK representation was 'a matter of considerable urgency'.[26] While at one level a straight-forward matter, the stationing of HMG officials in Japan proved to be extremely tiresome and, at a microcosm, amply demonstrated SCAP's determination to control the occupation and the level of difficulty faced by any nation that sought to dilute this control. Initially, MT aimed to send 12 representatives to Japan, but was soon dismayed to learn that SCAP favoured a scheme whereby two men only would be permitted. Further, these two men were not to consider themselves as purely British representatives, but would have to carry out general shipping duties on behalf of US military command. Such an arrangement was most unsatisfactory, with MT fearing its employees would be virtually under SCAP's direction and 'may be hampered in the main purpose for which their appointment is sought'.[27] The sheer logistics of arranging billets in Japan also proved to be formidable. MT observed that most of the private property, such as the Messrs Butterfield & Swire offices in Yokohama, had been requisitioned by SCAP by right of military occupation, with little interest shown in its speedy return to the prewar owners. Indeed, such was the shortage of accommodation and office space that the British felt the need to station a ship for the long term in Japan to service such requirements.[28]

Beyond such housekeeping concerns, other areas also attracted the ire of MT, particularly its belief that certain American practices for shipping goods in and out of Japan discriminated against established prewar shipping interests, namely the British. Fury over the US War Department's decision that where its funds were used for the bulk purchase of foodstuffs for Japan and Korea, carriage, where possible, was to be confined to US flag vessels was one example. Even more infuriating to the MT was the revelation, contrary to the assurances of American officials in Japan, that Everett's Oriental Line, purportedly a non-American line with its headquarters in the Philippines, was to be treated as American for such purposes.[29] Further unofficial enquiries, for example about why GARIOA (Government Appropriation for Relief in Occupied Areas)-purchased bulk cargos were limited to US bottoms rather than Japanese ships, which would at least save the American taxpayer money, were deflected with a variety of answers, including that the unions would not wear it and that US laws would not allow the entry of Japanese vessels.[30] By mid-1947, MT tolerance had evaporated, declaring that it had 'for some time past been very patient with the

American Soldiers' disregard of fair play in shipping practice', and that US War Department policy was contrary to recent international shipping discussions and 'inconsistent and improper'.[31] The FO was requested to instruct its Washington embassy to make representations to the USA protesting against such discrimination where it transpired that the directive to use US bottoms for War Department supplies was based on a law passed in 1904.

Beyond the relatively narrow confines of Japan and the Anglo-American relationship, it was the Commonwealth, especially its Australian and Southeast Asian members, that further established the external framework for Anglo-Japanese rivalry in the shipping sector. American weight behind Japan was crucial, but equally so was London's attitude towards a reinvigorated Japanese trading presence in Southeast Asia.[32] It should also be emphasized that again blanket opposition did not characterize this attitude. In very general terms business and colonial officials opposed the Japanese return, but Whitehall and Westminster, albeit with some distaste and concern, were generally supportive. Japanese trade could contribute to improving local economies and thus help fulfil UK long-term plans for regional security; moreover, Japan could also help to plug the business and financial gaps that British firms left as the trend towards non-imperial markets grew. In this sense, acknowledging a Japanese presence in Southeast Asia reflected the complexities of British decolonization as much as a cold war inspired need to cooperate with the USA.

As a case in point, in early 1950 SCAP approached UKLM requesting permission for Japanese vessels to load 112,000 tons of ore at Dangun in British Malaya over September that year. The British reasons for complying with this request were multiple and only one reflected worry over American and Japanese grumblings about 'restrictions presently imposed by several governments upon Japanese shipping'.[33] Indeed, it was held that accepting the request was a competitive advantage: it would absorb Japanese tonnage into a bulk trade relatively unattractive to British tramp shipping. In addition, total exclusion would only artificially increase the concentration of Japanese competition elsewhere, quite likely to ports where Great Britain had no control; far better, then, that competition be minimized by spreading Japanese incursions as broadly as possible and, where convenient, under local British supervision.[34] This latter point informed a mid-1950 HMG request to the Southeast Asian colonies to accept that Japanese shipping be cleared for as wide a range of trade as possible to spread it as thinly as practicable. The wording of the request openly acknowledged it was based on the interests of British shipping and that Commonwealth security and economic interests were only indirectly involved. The colonial response was generally gratifying, though the Japanese were to be restricted: crews would not be allowed ashore and Special Branch agents would need to guard against the infiltration of Japanese communists.[35]

The Japan–Australia shipping lines, a point of bitter rivalry and contention from before the war, also serve to emphasize the role of the Commonwealth in Anglo–Japanese shipping rivalry. A major postwar Australian export to Japan was wool and the Japan/Australia Conference, originally consisting of five European–Australian lines, expanded in 1952 to include Nippon Yusen Kaisha (NYK) and Osaka Shosen Kaisha (OSK), in order to oversee orderly trade and a balanced Japanese presence. By a two-year agreement, the Japanese were granted a monthly sailing and 20 per cent of the northward-bound wool. This supposedly cosy arrangement was rudely shattered in mid-1953 when the Japan Australia Line (in reality a joint service of NYK, OSK and Mitsui) demanded admission. Distressing 'intricate oriental negotiations' followed, by which NYK, OSK and the Japan Australia Line each received nine sailings per annum, 14 per cent of the northward bound wool and a 5 per cent reduction in freight rate. The Japanese were acknowledged to hold a strong position inasmuch as they were important customers of Australian wool, but nonetheless their actions were seen as a virtual assault 'and we may need to invoke the assistance of both the Australian and the Home governments, if the British side is not going to be slowly strangled'.[36]

Such arrangements had attracted the interests of the 'British side' since the proposed inclusion of NYK and OSK in the Japan Australia Line. The home nation, which readily identified itself as British because it perhaps still pleased the former dominion, had a difficult line to tread. On the one hand, London was not eager to interfere directly in commercial shipping questions on the grounds that the conference system, negotiated privately between the commercial lines concerned, was the best means of guaranteeing orderly shipping at a stable cost. Australia was requested to hold back, but nonetheless to watch closely, given Japan's dubious prewar reputation, and to resist stoutly any pressure to ship by Japanese vessels as a condition of sales to Japan.[37] On the other hand, however, London was equally aware that many Commonwealth nations discriminated against Japan to the advantage of the UK; reductions on British economic discrimination against Japan might encourage others to do likewise, much to the detriment of the home islands.[38] Slightly earlier Anglo–Australian discussions on the nature of Canberra's control over

Japanese shipping adopted a compromise: the Australian government should make it clear that any readiness to see the 'Japanese coming back into trade with the Australians depended upon the Japs coming in an "orderly" manner'.[39] The former empire remained vital to British attempts to mediate Japanese trade and to dissipate concentrated competition.

'Japan, like Britain, is a maritime country'[40]

Japanese (or even Japanese and West Germany combined) competition alone did not undermine the British shipping sector: domestic weaknesses, ranging from disruptive strikes and demarcation disputes to the clear failure of managers to make the necessary capital investments, counted for a great deal too. Perhaps it was blindness to this latter point, combined with the constant focus on the potential threat from Japan, that led the FO to conclude somewhat inaccurately that, when facing the Japanese, the UK 'would have to rely on the good sense of the Americans to realize the importance to our economy of the UK shipbuilding industry'.[41] Japanese competition was, however, simply one aspect to the decline of British shipbuilding.

Nonetheless, the British shipbuilding industry lacked the capacity to reverse its rival's return, particularly given the American support the Japanese revival enjoyed. Equally, neither the shipping industries, nor indeed the British government, intended to surrender abjectly this crucial industry and Britain's leading place as a maritime nation. Japanese competition would have to be accepted, but its nature could be challenged. Here industry and government could unite: Japan's return should be gradual and fair so that prewar wicked practices (of the Japanese, of course) would not re-emerge in the post war. The Japanese required re-education and European-style trade unions.[42]

The period of the 1945–52 occupation also seemed to provide Britain with the chance, indeed perhaps its only opportunity, to guide Japan into fair rather than foul play, given that peace treaty negotiations made clear that restrictions on the Japanese shipping industries were unacceptable. Reminding Japan of its international duties and, indirectly through them, its obligation to behave if acceptance into the global community of nations were at all desired, was one such tactic. MT, for example, regularly emphasized that the principles of the 'Fairplay Shipping Code', as promoted by the convention of the Intergovernmental Maritime Consultative Organization (IMCO), could be helpful in this context. If Japan learnt to cooperate before independence was returned then the greater the odds that the habit would last into the future.[43]

Quite apart from the abstruse matter of fair play and ethical codes of commercial behaviour, the Occupation also seemed to provide the best time for Britain to attempt to safeguard its future with the more tangible matter of guiding Japanese shipping into its future trade routes. Rather than seek to control Japanese shipping absolutely, it was HMG that expressed displeasure at the return by SCAP on 1 April 1950 of Japanese vessels to private owners on the grounds that decontrol had not gone far enough: shipowners still had to apply to SCAP for clearance for each trade in which they wished to participate. SCAP should instead throw world trade open to Japan in order to spread its shipping as far as possible to ensure that as it grew its impact would be less injurious than if narrowly confined.[44] If Britain were to hurt, then all nations should hurt equally, again in the spirit of fair play.

Nonetheless, the British shipbuilding and shipping industries' views on Japanese competition often seemed to rate more as 'helpful' than crucial. Westminster retained its opinion that Japan should be permitted to retain peaceable trade and industry: British industry must survive through being more competitive and efficient. On the whole, Whitehall also followed this line: in 1949 MT wrote to UKLM reminding it of the July 1948 principle that any limitation on the range of trade open to Japanese tonnage would be contrary to HMG's world shipping policy.[45] More specifically, 'Japan's position as the principal trading nation in the Far East necessitates a mercantile marine [and] it is most desirable that Japanese ships should have their reasonable share from the start.'[46]

External concerns, namely the pre-eminence of the United States, also helped to frame British policy. The Americans were opposed to undue restrictions on this sector of the Japanese economy and suspicious of any perceived British revival of prewar protectionism. At best, HMG could only attempt to limit the size of Japanese merchant vessels on security grounds, yet this view was not shared by the Department of State, and a concrete British proposal for such languished in the Far Eastern Commission.[47] These constraints were important yet also overlook areas of British strength, namely the Commonwealth and Britain's leading position in Southeast Asia, at least over the first half of the 1950s. The ability to deflect and mediate Japanese competition through the former British Empire was a great, even if short-term, advantage.

The postwar re-emergence of Japan's shipping industries and the nature of the challenges they posed to Great Britain are as much diplomatic as economic history. British decline and American pre-eminence is clear. Equally, imperial habits did not fade instantly, and the presence of the remaining colonies and the Commonwealth suggested that Britain retained its potential to project global influence and to combat threats against core British interests, even from the other side of the planet. That this resource was to prove limited, fragmented and no stepladder up which Britain could clamber to be of the same height as the two superpowers was not necessarily clear in the late 1940s and the early 1950s. Finally, it is also evident that Japan's gradual move from isolation to global integration over the 1950s, whether diplomatic or economic, mattered to Great Britain. American strength in Japan cannot be overlooked, and Britain could not overturn it, but it is also only one aspect of the Western response to Japan's postwar revival.

Chapter 9

ANGLO-JAPANESE ECONOMIC RELATIONS SINCE THE 1970S

Hideya Taida

I have worked at Marubeni, a leading Japanese *sōgō shōsha* (general trading firm), for 40 years. Since 1977 I have been posted to London twice for a total of ten years. It is fair to say that London has become my second home. In Tokyo I was engaged in the international corporate planning and international corporate strategy areas for nearly a quarter of a century in all, with the UK included in this work.

In dramatic contrast to the tone of the last two chapters, I think that during this period economic relations between Japan and the UK were quite different from those between Japan and the USA, or Japan and other countries in Europe. I felt that a mutually cooperative relationship was formed during this time, mostly due to the unique working approach the UK took towards Japan. If one looks at Japan's history, I believe one could say that this is a rare case of a good relationship at the time.

At the beginning of the twentieth century Japan and Great Britain were engaged in an alliance in which Great Britain played a huge role in Japan's development. After the Second World War, American influence on Japan was most prominent. However, from the 1970s onwards, despite a very important relationship as the world's number one and number two economies, economic friction has occurred repeatedly between Japan and the USA. In economic terms, Japanese–US relations are much more extensive than Japanese–UK ones. But in other areas, such as cultural and person-to-person exchanges, and in the fact that we are both island nations sharing many common characteristics and similar perceptions, the importance of the Japan–UK relationship is well recognized. In fact, it has been through the efforts of many of those contributing to this book that this relationship has been built into such a fine one.

In this chapter I talk about my personal experiences over the last 25 years as a businessman and about Japan–UK economic relations. In my view the key to establishing good relations between states is in building trust between individual human beings as their foundation.

At the beginning of the 1970s Japan became internationally competitive, which was evident from the lopsided trade balances it began to record as a result of exports in such fields as electrical appliances, steel products and most areas of machinery, especially automobiles. This saw the beginning of the trade friction problem, which was particularly acute between the USA and Japan and eventually became highly politicized. And, although economic relations between Japan and Europe were not on quite the same scale as those between the USA and Japan, the structure of the problem was the same.

In 1973 the Japanese government sent its first 'import promotion mission' to Great Britain. Initially, there were some complaints in Japan that it was 'strange for the prospective buyer of the products to go out and conduct marketing activities for them rather than the seller of those products'. However, this mission was an attempt by the Japanese government to rectify, to some extent, Japan's trade imbalance, even though it was politically a somewhat difficult thing to do. The leader of this mission was the then executive vice president of Marubeni, Mr Matsuo, who also served for over 25 years as chairman of the British Market Council. The participants in this mission were from various industry groups in Japan, the main members being from trading companies and department stores. The outcome of this mission was that the 'UK should not expect a surge in exports to Japan right away but rather should look at the possibilities and opportunities for future exports'. On their return to Japan, the main members of this mission established the 'British Market Council' to follow up on the mission. In fact, though, rather than actually following up, the gatherings became more of a reunion of the members of that trip to the UK.

In the autumn of 1976, the chairman of Keidanren, Mr Dokō, led a mission of business executives to various regions in Europe and encountered strong resistance and protest over Japan's export offensive there. This was quite a shock and caught Mr Dokō by surprise and, on returning to Japan, he emphasized to the government the need for Japanese business and the government to address this structural problem. A debate on whether or not to implement export controls ensued. However, rather than suppress exports a consensus on a plan to increase imports to balance trade took root in both business and government circles. An import target promotion campaign to find various ways to promote imports to Japan was launched. As a result, the Ministry of International Trade and Industry (MITI) announced its support for this voluntary group and as a by-product asked the British Market Council to form a UK import promotion body within the organization. In 1978 an executive director was appointed and UK import promotion activities were officially started.

In the autumn of 1979, again, the then president of Marubeni, Mr Matsuo, led a second, but this time more serious, import promotion mission to the UK, sponsored by MITI. This was a very representative and large-scale mission totalling 150 members in all. The mission was active in making the rounds in the UK and offering serious advice to UK businesses on what possibilities there were for exporting to Japan and how they could carry this out. This was at the time of the Callaghan government. The UK side officially announced that a buying mission had come from Japan and that a number of contracts had been signed during their visit and that there would still be more export opportunities to come. However, through this mission it was also recognized by both sides that this one visit would be insufficient to increase British exports to Japan greatly and that continued efforts by each side would be necessary. The UK, for its part, promised to make every effort to promote exports to Japan. This was very significant as an outcome at the time.

In addition to the Japanese government's import promotion policy, serious thought was now being given towards promoting Japanese investments in the UK. At this time, the Thatcher government had just come to power and the number of unemployed in Great Britain had reached more than three million. The UK had already been active in seeking foreign investment, especially through regional development corporations in each region of the country. The unemployment situation had the effect of accelerating the British government's ongoing quest to attract foreign businesses and secure foreign investment. As a result of the UK's positive initiatives, more than 40 per cent of all Japanese investment in Europe went to the UK. Upon witnessing the UK's success in attracting Japanese investment, many other European countries later began actively to pursue Japanese investment, too. However, due to the UK's strong efforts early on, Great Britain was able to take advantage of its head start and remained the focus of Japanese investments in Europe up until recently.

In 1980 Sony began producing televisions in Wales and nearly all Japanese electronic appliance manufacturers came soon after. The Japanese automobile industry followed with Nissan, at the time the number one selling Japanese car in the UK, finally constructing a factory. It had taken a number of years, mostly because of strong opposition from domestic Japanese labour unions. In Nissan's case, the UK government's aggressive stance toward investment, culminating in Margaret Thatcher's urgent personal request for Nissan to set up a factory in the UK, clinched the decision. Nissan's factory finally opened in Sunderland in 1986, with Prime Minister Thatcher there to cut the ribbon.

The Plaza Accord led to the sudden and rapid appreciation of the yen. Up until then, Japanese companies' moves, factory transplants and other investments overseas were aimed mainly at becoming 'insiders' to strengthen their regional position for fear of being left out. In the background there was the regional consolidation of the European Community, which was known as 'Fortress Europe' at the time. The skyrocketing yen changed all that by weakening Japan's export competitiveness. This spurred and accelerated Japan's foreign direct investment (FDI), that is to say the transfer of Japanese manufacturing facilities overseas. From 1985 onwards, not only sizeable Japanese companies but also small and medium-size enterprises began to move overseas. After Nissan located a plant in the UK, the call went out for a number of its parts makers and suppliers in Japan to join them. By 1989 the number of Japanese manufacturers in the UK had increased to 103 companies. Other Japanese concerns then recognized the merit of operating in an English-speaking environment and of the proactive foreign direct investment policies of the UK government. They expanded their investment in the UK and eventually the number of Japanese manufacturing companies there reached about 280 at their peak in 1999–2000.

By 1988 the UK's trade deficit with Japan had still not been eliminated, so the UK government put forward a new landmark export promotion plan. It wanted to shift the focal point of the trade situation from that of a problem to that of an opportunity. In 1987 the British government announced a plan to double UK exports to Japan within three years, and it launched the 'Opportunity Japan Campaign' to expand exports by focusing on the opportunities available in the Japanese market to British exporters. During this period, while the USA and many European countries were united in strongly denouncing Japan's trade imbalances, the British government alone took a cooperative stance, which of course Japan's public and private sectors greatly appreciated.

Due to Britain's attitude the Japanese government, especially the likes of MITI and the Japan External Trade Organization (JETRO), actively promoted missions from the UK during this time. The British Market Council also created a task force, of which I was chairman, specifically to promote the Opportunity Japan Campaign. The result of all this was a 32 per cent increase in British exports to Japan in 1989 and a further 14.1 per cent rise in 1990. It goes without saying that all those involved on both sides were very pleased with these achievements. Following on the success of the Opportunity Japan Campaign the British government came forward with a new effort called the Priority Japan Campaign. This campaign now reflected the great importance of the Japanese market to British companies and the high priority they were now placing on it. The main pillars of this campaign were:

- promoting exports to Japan;
- promoting direct investment to Japan; and
- technology transfer from Japan.

Unfortunately, this campaign coincided with the bursting of Japan's economic bubble, so that initially it failed to meet expectations and improve on the previous years' performance. However, in the third year of the new campaign, with a number of missions to Japan having come and gone, exports to Japan rose 19 per cent over the previous 12 months.

The mutual cooperation and shared goals of these campaigns mirrored the attitude and efforts of the British side in sharp contrast to many other countries like France, which were critical of Japan's trade imbalances and took a confrontational position implementing import quotas for Japanese products. Again, needless to say, the UK's approach in all of this was welcomed not only by the Japanese government but by the Japanese business world as well. In fact, the influence of these campaigns by the UK on other countries in Europe has been enormous as many of them began to use the British model in their approach to Japan.

After having gone through various stages the 'Priority Japan Campaign' was continued in spirit in the new 'Action Japan Campaign'. The distinctive feature of this campaign was the strong interest and clear strategy on the UK side in targeting 13 specific sectors in some very important fields in Japan. What is especially worthy of note about this campaign, though, was not that it targeted products in specific sectors of specific fields, but that it called for UK-Japanese cooperation in projects in third countries. The trade imbalance had for a long period been the most pressing problem between Japan and the UK. However, over the years the use of UK-made machinery and cooperation with British engineering firms by Japanese trading companies in large projects in Asia, the Middle East and Africa had been growing substantially. This activity had not been included in figures for Japan and now the UK had begun to recognize this in its export promotion.

As background to this, compared with Japanese business enterprises, European firms' response to Asia's remarkable economic development had been rather slow and inadequate. Therefore, to make advances into Asia, European companies began to seek tie-ups with Japanese firms as an effective way of entering the Asian market. I believe the UK was far ahead of the game in this regard. This was partially a result of the UK's own vision and initiative, but also of the fact that London had become a centre for many Japanese financial institutions and subsidiary companies, including the *sōgō shōsha,* which used London as its base of operations to cover Europe and Africa.

During this time I was in the midst of my second posting to London (1993–97). There I was a member of the Japanese Chamber of Commerce in London and participated on a task force that included JETRO and the Japanese embassy in the UK in support of the 'Action Japan Campaign', specifically as chairman of the 'Third Country Project Cooperation Committee'. You can see the depth of the support for this and the other campaigns. It did not just operate in Japan or within the Japanese government but included people like me, Japanese expatriate businessmen who were cooperating with the UK government in the UK.

This brings me to just a few of the reasons why these campaigns were so cooperative and went so well:

- The UK approach was so positive and cooperative in nature that the Japanese government had to respond to it. (In fact it was so successful that the Japanese government recommended it as a model for other countries to follow in terms of cooperation with Japan.)
- At the same time the UK named as its trade minister Mr Richard (now Sir Richard) Needham, a very well known figure in Japan. Mr Needham had a deep understanding of Japan and Japanese business strategy and was very active in the UK–Japan 2000 Group as a founding member. Furthermore, Mr Needham had strong relations and connections not only with Japan but with Korea, Malaysia, India and other Asian countries as well. He served in this position for quite some time and had a powerful impact on economic relations.
- The chairman of the campaign on the UK side was the chairman of Unilever, Sir Michael Perry. Not only was Sir Michael well versed on

> Japanese affairs, having had expatriate working experience in Japan, but he was a distinguished manager and executive as well. It was this balance of seasoned judgement in business and knowledge of the other side that led to a feeling of trust between both the UK and Japanese sides.

It was generally understood that not only government policy, but also the execution of policy by the core people involved was central to the success of this campaign and the other UK–Japan campaigns as well. In this regard, the UK knew the importance of having the right core people in place. Furthermore, it was important to accumulate a wealth of trust over a long period of time; after all, 'Rome was not built in a day.'

In all of this I would just like to add that nothing has quite equalled the continued and superb support of the British embassy in Japan. The efforts of all the embassy people, from the ambassadors down to the line staff, and especially the heads of the commercial and economic departments, have been invaluable in my view. I doubt if you will find an embassy as passionate about maintaining contact and working with Japanese business as the British embassy. For example, in 1993, the then ambassador to Japan, Sir John Boyd, hosted a reception marking the twentieth anniversary of the British Market Council at his official residence. It was held in appreciation of not only the many people who have contributed to the success of these campaigns, but to the deep mutual trust that has developed between our two countries through these activities. And, recently at the embassy, two of the Japanese staff were awarded the MBE (Member of the Order of the British Empire) from the Queen for their long years of service, and I think all the Japanese attending were deeply moved by the event and appreciative of the symbolic meaning of this gesture.

Now, getting back briefly to the 'Action Japan Campaign', I would like to mention that from 1993 to 1996 exports from the UK to Japan had been targeted to rise from 2.65 billion sterling to 3.5 billion, though they in fact reached a high of 3.75 billion sterling in 1995.

In May 1997 the Labour Party, led by Tony Blair, came to power in the UK. Although various export promotion policies were reviewed at this time, it was decided to continue the export promotion campaign in Japan and to use the same name because of the Japanese market's great importance to the UK. The new government moved very quickly after it was installed and named a new trade minister, Margaret Beckett, who visited Japan within just a couple of weeks of her appointment and, in a message to Japan's economic community, remarked that even though the

UK had a Labour government, in the light of the importance of the relationship, it would not change policies towards Japan. This was appreciated and met with a very favourable reaction from the economic and business community in Japan. The 'New Action Japan Campaign' identified nine items in priority sectors. In addition to some of the fields that were emphasized before, high technology and direct investment in Japan were incorporated into the plan to differentiate it from the previous campaign. As is quite evident, British industry had come to recognize the value of being in the Japanese market to strengthen its own competitiveness in the global market.

In April 2001 the UK launched a standardized type of trade campaign in various countries, including Japan. The Japan campaign is called the 'Trade Partners UK–Japan Campaign'. This campaign is being carried out through British Trade International (BTI) in a plan aimed at new developments in the twenty-first century. It targets export promotion and direct investment in Japan in competitive sectors in ten fields. We are very pleased that Sir David Wright, a former British ambassador to Japan, is now playing a key role in this as chief executive of the BTI. In the last two or three years of the twentieth century British investment in Japan leapt, mainly in the field of telecommunications; up until the early 1990s the focus had been on Japanese investment in the UK. However, that concentration has now shifted in the opposite direction, and I believe this is a desirable trend for both countries.

The era of direct investment from Japan in the UK through technology transfers, which helped increase employment in the UK, basically ended in the first half of the 1990s. Japanese manufacturing investment has already worked its way through the UK economy and now a new investment relationship between the UK and Japan is required. As the UK's economy is in fairly good condition with a low unemployment rate, the need for investment to guarantee employment is no longer pressing. In this regard the climate on the British side has completely changed. Furthermore, with the pound highly valued compared with the currencies of continental Europe, the UK is relatively low on the priority list for investment in new manufacturing bases by Japanese companies. Also, with the high pound and the fact that the UK has not yet decided whether or not to adopt the Euro, Japanese companies in the UK began to worry about their production activities there in the second half of the 1990s.

Given this framework, there has been little choice for them but to close down and shrink production facilities in the UK and move some of these to locations like Poland where costs are much lower. However, there is some new movement at a different level by Japanese companies. Rather, than bring in technology (mostly production technology) to the UK, Japanese companies are now using British technology and setting up R&D centres in the UK to position themselves for the future. This is especially evident with pharmaceutical and high-tech companies as they increase their presence in the UK.

In addition, up until recently, in their advance overseas, Japanese companies have relied mostly on Japanese people to manage their operations. However, Japanese companies are now recognizing that the key to successfully developing their businesses overseas is to make full use of talented local human resources in the running of their operations. I believe the true test for Japanese companies entering the twenty-first century is whether, in this era of globalization, they can truly globalize their management. In this regard, increased investment in Japan by foreign companies will also become important in helping Japan in the globalization process. And, for their part, I think British companies have come to recognize that success in business in Japan is a passport to success in the global marketplace.

Finally, I truly hope that the strong trust built up in the economic relationship between our two countries over the last quarter of the twentieth century continues to develop and flourish in the twenty-first century.

Chapter 10

MILITARY AND ECONOMIC POWER: COMPLEMENTING EACH OTHER'S NATIONAL STRENGTH

Reinhard Drifte

There has been much more substantive security cooperation between Britain and Japan over the last few years than for a very long time. Before then the bilateral security relationship consisted mainly of a dialogue on security issues that was of interest to both sides. However, in the wake of the global changes after 11 September 2001 and in the light of the more proactive Japanese foreign and security policy, opportunities for security-relevant cooperation, which range geographically from the Middle East to Africa, have expanded and are increasingly being taken up.

Both countries realize that the concept of security has to be enlarged to prevent military conflict or at least to deal with existing conflicts in a more comprehensive way and that one should try to address their origins as well as their symptoms. The growing security relationship also reflects Britain's desire to maintain its international role, which is symbolized by its permanent UN Security Council membership and its close relationship with the USA. This international status makes Britain an ideal partner for Japan with its growing international involvement. Finally, both countries realize that against a background of mounting demands for action on questions of security, bilateral cooperation can supplement scarce resources and strengthen multilateralism.

In this chapter I look first at the fundamentals of UK–Japan security cooperation and use the examples of cooperation on Korea and Iraq to illustrate what has been achieved. I also show how the EU's evolving

Common Foreign and Security Policy has been a shaping factor. Saying that the opportunities and motives for more substantive security cooperation between the two countries are expanding should not blind us to the many limitations and obstacles that both sides are still facing, and in some cases will always have to accept. Understanding these constraints is important in order not to overburden the deepening cooperation with unrealistic expectations. Britain is anchored in the EU and in the transatlantic framework, whereas Japan looks first to its alliance with the USA and the Asian region. The security environment for both countries is very different, and so is the perception of security problems. The UK is a self-assured military power and has a very different approach to security as a long-time colonial power in the past and permanent member of the UN Security Council today. For Japan, security issues are only now leaving the realm of taboo and military power is viewed with great suspicion, even in the case of UN-sanctioned peacekeeping operations (PKOs). Japan is therefore more comfortable with addressing human security challenges than with straight-forward military problems, and it prefers to act with the huge material resources of a great civilian power. Different political styles and cultural approaches compound these circumstances.

Given these differences, motivations for bilateral security cooperation also vary. As the second largest economic power and a trading power depending on a never-ending expansion of markets and suppliers, Japan is increasingly realizing its vital interest in peace and stability in every corner of the world, and that it has to do more to protect these interests. Its American security partner in the first instance, but also many countries and organizations, demand from Japan greater international burden sharing. At the same time Japan's leaders want more recognition from the international community and this is, for example, expressed in the government's desire for a permanent UN Security Council seat.[1] Achieving international recognition in turn helps the government domestically to get support for playing a bigger role internationally and to respond more positively to international calls for more burden sharing. Playing a more extensive international role also prevents Japan being internationally isolated despite its geographic location and special political and economic position in Asia. To achieve these goals and to reduce its overall dependence on the USA, working together with other powers is beneficial for Japan. This is particularly the case with Britain because of historic ties, the scope of economic cooperation, and particularly Britain's international standing and role as a permanent UN Security Council member. As Britain is a close ally of the USA, cooperation with Japan in a sensitive area like security is less likely to attract the suspicion of the American partner, while at the same time it is easier than cooperation with the USA in view of the latter's tendency towards unilateralism.

The UK's motivations are equally strong. Expanding security cooperation with Japan is seen to be in Britain's interest because working together with the world's second largest economic power and Overseas Development Administration (ODA) donor further enhances and sustains the country's international position. As a country that has lost considerable power compared with other states that have risen since 1945, working together with Japan helps to maximize dwindling power resources in an ever harsher international environment. Cooperation with Japan also expands Britain's geographic reach and influence, and reduces the perception that the UK relies too much on the USA. Both countries are also very complementary in so far as Britain can provide a wider experience and greater manpower resources, whereas Japan's human resources are stretched. In view of Japan's economic crisis and high budget deficit in the 1990s, its original material abundance has declined, which accentuates the importance of burden-sharing and utilizing the allies' complementarity.

The Anglo–American invasion of Iraq in March 2003 faced Japan with a rather delicate dilemma and the ensuing developments symbolize the limitations of the UK–Japan security cooperation. It all started with a strong Japanese endorsement: given the memory of its experience during the last Gulf War, when Japan was perceived as having failed its American ally despite a record monetary contribution, on 4 April 2003 Prime Minister Koizumi Junichiro declared his government's support for the war and the post conflict rehabilitation of Iraq. This policy was enunciated in five principles:

- Iraq's sovereignty and territorial integrity should be maintained;
- Iraq's governing regime should be decided by the Iraqi people;
- there should be sufficient involvement of the United Nations in the reconstruction effort;
- Japan will engage in reconstruction assistance in a seamless manner without any interruption; and
- Japan will secure the participation of non-governmental organizations (NGOs) and other entities in order to form an all-Japan team.

These principles are sufficiently vague, notably the one on the role of the UN, to allow Japan to start immediately to send aid to Iraq as well as to agree with the UK on the sensitive issue of the UN's involvement. At the end of March 2003 Japan promised a $100 million non-project grant to Jordan, on 31 March the Air Self Defence Force transported 160 tents to Jordan, and on the 9 April Japan promised $100 million in aid to Iraq. Soon after the end of the war the Japanese government sent officials to the Office of Reconstruction and Humanitarian Assistance (ORHA), which became known later as the Coalition Provisional Authority (CPA). Japan stressed the link between the resolution of the Israel–Palestine issue and the stabilization of Iraq, and it supplied additional help to the Palestine Autonomous Region while also insisting on the enactment of the so-called road map. All this provided a good foundation for UK–Japan cooperation on Iraq, which has been cemented by close contacts between the two governments since March 2003 as well as visits by Japan's Foreign Minister Kawaguchi and Prime Minister Koizumi in April and May respectively. As a concrete initial result of UK–Japan cooperation, Japan gave a $2.5 million emergency grant to the United Nations Development Programme (UNDP) for a project to dredge Iraq's Umm Qasr port, which is in the UK zone of occupation. Tokyo finalized a law that allowed up to 1000 SDF soldiers to be sent to Iraq. In December 2003 the first air self-defence forces team arrived in the region followed in January 2004 by the first ground (GSDF) team; the latter was initially involved in humanitarian tasks but has since then provided reconstruction assistance in the area around Basra, which is also the UK zone of Samawah. Japan would have felt much more isolated had it had only the USA with which to work together. The UK is naturally also relieved to have political as well as economic support on an issue that has been extremely divisive for the EU and the transatlantic relationship.

However, it was much easier for Japan to offer political and economic support than to provide any kind of SDF involvement. Within the Japanese political context, economic and political help was surprisingly fast, but in view of allied expectations Japan's delay on the latter showed the limitations of Japan's security cooperation with any country. The allied invasion was as contentious in Japan as it was in Britain. Differences in political institutions and style allowed the British government to provide ground troops, whereas Japan merely initiated a series of investigations in Iraq. The Japanese government has been extremely concerned about the possibility of casualties, particularly after the killing of two Japanese diplomats in November 2003 and two journalists in April 2004. These incidents have severely limited even the SDF's reconstruction assistance. Since 1 May 2005, security in Samawah has been provided jointly by UK and Australian troops. The GSDF contingent formally joined the Multinational Force–Iraq (MNF-I) in June 2004 after the formation of the Iraqi transitional government. From that time they became part of the formal coalition structure. The Air Self Defence Force provides transport to the coalition but from a base in Kuwait.

In this context one has also to mention Japan's refuelling of British naval vessels, along with US warships, in the Indian Ocean as Japan's contribution to the 'fight against terrorism' (in addition to the commitment of $500 million to the reconstruction of Afghanistan). This free-of-charge refuelling operation began in January 2002 and expanded in 2003 to include the naval vessels of other Western countries supporting 'Operation Enduring Freedom'. According to an MOU between the UK and Japan, the Japanese navy could transfer up to 950 cubic metres per month to the Royal Navy. By May 2005 the Maritime Self-Defence Forces (MSDF) had transferred a total of 400,000 kilolitres. The UK government gave permission for the five Japanese ships of the MSDF to use the British territory of Diego Garcia during command handovers. The island serves as the anti-terror coalition's main logistic base in the Indian Ocean. In Afghanistan itself the Japanese ODA continues to fund construction work on the Kandahar–Herat highway as well as on building schools and hospitals.

The greatest incentive for Prime Minister Koizumi to support the USA and UK over Iraq was the renewed nuclear crisis on the Korean peninsula. As the USA is Japan's only military alliance partner and as Tokyo has serious constraints on its own military deterrent, Tokyo is always on the horns of a dilemma: if it does not support the USA to an extent judged sufficient by the American leadership, it risks abandonment. On the other hand, if such support goes too far, it risks entrapment into US designs and alienation from its Asian neighbours. Japan's political and humanitarian support for the allied efforts in Iraq is therefore an insurance not only that the USA but also major countries like Britain will come to Tokyo's help in addressing the current serious nuclear crisis on the Korean peninsula.

In a surprise move, Prime Minister Koizumi tried to create a breakthrough in the stalled negotiations with North Korea on normalizing relations when he visited Pyongyang for a day on 19 September 2002 and again in May 2004. The revelations about a second North Korean nuclear programme and the North Korean mishandling of abduction issues dating from the 1970s and 1980s immediately blew away US as well as domestic support for any further steps by Japan. The USA has taken a very hardline position on North Korea, refusing any bilateral negotiations before North Korea has undertaken unilateral nuclear disarmament. Japan therefore hopes that other countries could exert direct or indirect (via Beijing) pressure on Pyongyang to accept multilateral talks and nuclear disarmament. As a permanent UN Security Council member and close ally of the USA, Japan expects the UK to contribute to these efforts through the UN, the EU and the Group of Eight (G8). However, Japan and South Korea (which, as the most directly affected country, has a more accommodating approach to Pyongyang) want such support to respect their paramount interests, which are not totally congruent with those of the USA. Both countries also wish for support for their involvement in multilateral talks, which finally took place for the first time in summer 2003 and have been intermittently extended since then. The UK and Japan are members of the Proliferation Security Initiative (PSI), which was established in 2003 at US instigation. This aims to interdict North Korean and other countries' exports of weapons of mass destruction and their delivery vehicles as well as North Korea's trade in drugs and counterfeit bank notes. The UK's involvement in this initiative is important because of its military capabilities, but also to avoid Japan's isolation and to prevent the USA from too unilateralist moves, such as the interdiction of North Korean ships on the open sea. However, the member states of the PSI are not all in agreement on the scope of PSI activities and a too forceful procedure by Britain may worry Japan.

The UK, as a member state of the EU that has supported the Korean Peninsula Energy Development Organization (KEDO) since 1998, has also been involved in defusing tensions on the Korean peninsula. This body was charged with building two light-water reactors in North Korea. Until they were complete, it was also to supply North Korea with heavy fuel oil as a quid pro quo for Pyongyang to abandon its nuclear weapons programme. When KEDO was launched in 1995, at the request of the USA and Japan, the UK immediately made a national contribution of $1 million. This was before the EU, under the European Atomic Energy Community (EURATOM) treaty regulations, became a member of the KEDO executive board in 1997. Until then the board had only consisted of South Korea, the USA and Japan. While the UK has not made any national KEDO contributions since 1995, some EU member states like Finland, France, Italy and Greece have been doing so. Since KEDO involves not only the supply of heavy fuel oil but also arms control and nuclear non-proliferation measures, the EU Council of Foreign Ministers has demanded that it be involved through the EU presidency in case these issues are raised. This request was made by the UK and France as nuclear powers. The KEDO case is thus an illustration of the extent to which Britain's foreign policy and security is enhanced as well as constrained by its EU membership, which has an impact on individual items of UK–Japan security cooperation. Even though the EU's financial contribution to KEDO was relatively low, it is higher than what a single member state like Britain would have made.

As a result of North Korea's admission that it had a new nuclear programme in 2002, KEDO's operations came to a standstill when the organization stopped its regular heavy fuel oil deliveries to the north in December 2002. After a two-year suspension KEDO was finally dissolved in 2005.

Iraq, the 'war against terrorism' and action over the Korean peninsula are only the most recent and most visible areas of UK–Japan security cooperation. There has also been cooperation through the framework of the action agenda for cooperation in diplomacy, national security, conflict prevention and peace-keeping, which both sides signed in September 1999. The first case materialized in May 2002 when both sides decided to contribute to the 'Community Reintegration Programme: Phase 2 (CRP 2)' in Sierra Leone to help the country overcome the devastation brought about by civil war. The UK provided £8.7 million and Japan £1.5 million. This donation had been preceded by a joint fact-finding mission to Sierra Leone by Britain's Department for International Development (DFID) and Japan's Ministry of Foreign Affairs (MOFA) in October 2001.

There have also been contacts on peacekeeping operations between the defence authorities of both countries that go back to the 1990s. There are plans to expand cooperation and to put it on a more systematic footing. When Japan was involved in mine-sweeping in the Gulf in 1991, it was done under the supervision of and in coordination with the Royal Navy. There was also some cooperation on peacekeeping and peace-building in 1997 and 1998, and in November 2005 the UK held a cross-government seminar on PSO (Peace Support Operations) doctrine in Tokyo.

As we have seen in the case of KEDO, the EU's Common Foreign and Security Policy (CFSP) makes a considerable impact on the scope and direction of UK–Japan security cooperation. The evolving CFSP is driven by the ambitions of individual member states as well as by the efforts of the EU Commission to develop the CFSP to enhance its role as the engine of European cooperation. Allies and friendly states put pressure on the EU to make greater contributions to the maintenance of the international system. The US pressure on its European allies and on Japan to help in the anti-terrorist campaign is the most recent example, prompting allies to consider individual as well as multilateral contributions at a military, political and/or economic level. The EU framework is an essential tool through which Britain can enhance its foreign and security policy, although political and economic differences with its European partners somewhat reduce the existing potential.

The EU started to focus on Asia within the framework set out in the EU's 1994 Asia paper, *Towards a New Asia Strategy*, which was followed by several other policy papers focused on individual Asian countries. The 1995 policy paper, *Europe and Japan: The Next Steps*, dealing with EU–Japanese relations came first in the following year. The Asia paper stated that the 'Union needs as a matter of urgency to strengthen its economic presence in Asia in order to maintain its leading role in the world economy'.[2] As a result of its growing economic weight and the 'unparalleled political fluidity' in Asia, the region warrants much closer attention in order to maintain peace and stability, which is essential not only for the EU's economic interests in that region, but also to maintain the 'respect of international obligations and agreements on which the Union itself depends for its security, e.g. regarding nuclear non-proliferation'.[3] In an attempt to adapt the policy paper to the new developments and changes in both regions, the EU adopted an updated paper in 2001 that speaks of 'strengthening the EU's political and economic presence across the region, and raising this to a level commensurate with the growing global weight of an enlarged EU'.[4]

The EU–Japan relationship plays a very prominent role in implementing this enhanced EU strategy towards Asia. One of the main tools to achieve its goals is the strengthening of relations with key Asian players, which, of course, include Japan. The joint declaration between the European Community and Japan ('The Hague Declaration of 18 July 1991') sets forth common objectives such as the enhancement of policy consultation and coordination, including international security matters and cooperation with the countries of the Asia Pacific for the promotion of peace, stability and prosperity of the region. To celebrate the tenth anniversary of The Hague Declaration, both sides agreed at the ninth summit meeting in July 2000 to inaugurate a decade of Japan–EU cooperation from 2001 onwards. A new declaration with a concrete action plan and a regular progress review mechanism was launched on the occasion of the tenth summit meeting in Brussels in December 2001 (an action plan for EU–Japan cooperation). It aims at greater cooperation, which is to include harmonizing positions, concerted actions and joint declarations. Through this action plan, the relationship between Japan and the EU is to move from mere dialogue and exchange of opinions to closer policy coordination and concrete joint activities in the political and security, economic, legal and social fields. In addition, the EU plans a streamlined Regulatory Reform Dialogue to revive the Japanese economy through opening markets further and stimulating direct investment from the EU. The EU wants to form stronger alliances with Japan. Two examples are to cooperate in launching a new trade round, achieved in November 2001, and to implement the Kyoto Protocol, also achieved in Marrakech in the same month. The goals of the action plan are to:

- promote peace and security;
- strengthen the economic and trade partnership;
- cope with global and societal change; and
- bring together people and culture.

At the same summit in December 2001, Prime Minister Junichiro Koizumi and the EU Commission's President Romano Prodi also published an EU–Japan joint declaration on terrorism, which has become a regular exercise at high-level meetings since 11 September 2001. The main regional forums to discuss and address security issues in Asia that involve both the EU and Japan are the Asia–Europe Meeting (ASEM) and the ASEAN Regional Forum (ARF). Both the Commission and the presidency represent the EU in the ARF, which aims to improve regional security dialogue and to implement concrete measures through various inter-sessional meetings. The most important of these is the Inter-sessional Support Group on Confidence-building Measures, to which the EU can bring in its experience of the Organization for Security and Cooperation in Europe (OSCE).

The European experience is also passed on to Asia through the observer status in the OSCE granted to Japan, South Korea and now also Thailand. ASEM is the highest level meeting between Europe and Asia and the agenda of its summits every two years include security issues. For Japan, ARF and ASEM are important organizations through which to promote Asian cohesion and to balance China's rising influence over the region. European participation helps Japan to avoid the impression of wanting to play a too visible role and thus eases the political as well as economic burden.

From the experience summarized above, it is clear that the future of bilateral security cooperation between the UK and Japan lies in the PKO areas, in naval cooperation and in anti-terrorism, which are all becoming increasingly interlinked. The area of peacekeeping is broadening out, including more and more aspects of human security, in which Japan is particularly keen to work. Moreover, as the examples of Kosovo and the International Security Assistance Force (ISAF) in Afghanistan show, the link between peacekeeping and the UN is changing. The Iraqi case will demonstrate whether we are moving away from peacekeeping forces that no longer have a direct UN mandate or UN approval. Japan seems to be increasingly willing to accept such a situation as its new law for the deployment of the SDF in Iraq (albeit only for humanitarian assistance) indicates. This would not only enhance the opportunities (and need!) for greater cooperation between the UK and Japan, but also require certain elements of training for the SDF that the SDF itself cannot supply.

In July 2003 the British Ministry of Defence proposed two short-term training programmes to the Japanese defence authorities, but it was ironically the worsening of the Iraqi situation that caused the Japanese government to decline the invitation. Japan's growing PKO involvement would benefit if UK–Japan cooperation in this field could move away from *ad hoc* to more systematic cooperation. One example might be a 'lessons learnt' unit for Japan, similar to the UK's Joint Doctrine and Concepts Centre in Shrivenham.

The naval area is also a promising route for cooperation, as we have seen with Japan's anti-terrorist contribution. Both Japan and the UK have been participating in the US-sponsored naval training exercise RIMPAC, which takes place every two years. One possibility would be UK participation in the exercises and training of Southeast Asian countries to fight piracy, which Japan started in 2000. Piracy has become a serious issue in the region because of the loosening control of political and military authority in some Southeast Asian countries, most notably Indonesia with its huge archipelago. The UK could reinforce this Japanese initiative in view of its abilities and its military links with Malaysia and Singapore. One particular problem to be addressed is the navy versus coast guard asymmetry: in the case of Japan, it is the coast guard and not the MSDF that is responsible for such tasks.

The war against terrorism has many different aspects. The Japanese ground force is now acquiring capabilities for these tasks and building up special operations units. If political sensitivities in Japan about 'collective defence' (not allowed according to the current government interpretation of Japan's constitution, even despite the Japan–US security treaty!) can be overcome, the UK could certainly contribute to these Japanese efforts on the basis of its capabilities.

Chapter 11

BILATERAL STABILITY, GLOBAL INSTABILITY: THE POLITICAL ECONOMY OF CONTEMPORARY ANGLO-JAPANESE ECONOMIC RELATIONS

Simon Lee

In the evolution of Anglo-Japanese economic relations, there has been a long tradition in which the political economies of both the United Kingdom and Japan have been affected by ideas, institutions and policies derived from the other country's 'best practice'. Admittedly, during the latter half of the nineteenth century, the progress of Japan's 'developmental', state-led industrialization owed more to continental European best practice and the neo-mercantilist political economy of Friedrich List and the German Historical School than to the neo-classical orthodoxy of Adam Smith and the Scottish Enlightenment.[1] This trend was particularly marked after 1881 when the teaching of political economy to future state officials at the National University of Tokyo was transferred from the faculty of arts, whose curriculum had drawn upon the liberal free trade principles of James Mill, to the faculty of law, where the curriculum focused on the more technocratic and nationalist German political economy.[2] Nevertheless, in practical terms, the English influence on Japanese modernization was enormous. As early as 1867 a loan as large as ¥3.75 million was raised by the City of London primarily for the purpose of constructing the Tokyo–Yokohama railway.[3] The equipment and technical advice supplied, for example, by

Platt Brothers of Manchester was instrumental in the development of the Japanese textile industry in the decades prior to the First World War.[4]

A century later, Japan's recent influence on the industrial modernization of British manufacturing has been perhaps even more pronounced. After a long period of relative economic decline, during which successive UK governments were exhorted to learn lessons from Japan[5] or to replicate in Whitehall some of the institutions and policies of the postwar Japanese developmental state,[6] the Conservative governments of the 1980s and 1990s sought salvation more directly from an industrial policy based on foreign direct investment (FDI) in the UK by Japanese corporations. Indeed, as Mr Taida pointed out above, from 1990 to 2000 the UK was the recipient of 53 per cent of Japanese investment in the European Union (EU).[7] At the same time, many UK firms embraced Japanese 'lean manufacturing techniques' in an attempt to retain their global competitiveness.

Given the historic importance of the exchange of ideas for the political economy of Anglo–Japanese economic relations, in this chapter I explore contemporary relations by focusing on the ideas that are now shaping the bilateral relationship between two of the Group of Eight (G8) industrialized economies. I contend that the greatest challenge, and indeed the principal threat, to Anglo–Japanese economic relations derives from the destabilizing effect of the neo-liberal orthodoxy of the 'Washington Consensus'.[8] A political economy of liberalization, privatization and deregulation has underpinned both the macroeconomic and microeconomic agenda advanced by the multilateral institutions during the past two decades. This agenda is shown to have failed to have delivered enduring economic growth for either the global economy or for major national economies, notably Japan. The conclusion drawn is that, as leading members of the multilateral institutions that govern global trade and development, Japan and the UK should now exploit the strength of their bilateral economic relations to challenge the neo-liberal hegemony governing global markets.

In November 2002, at an Anglo–Japanese Jiji Top Seminar, Baroness Elizabeth Symons, the British government's Foreign and Commonwealth Office minister, was able to mark the centenary of the Anglo–Japanese Alliance by remarking that '100 years on we are closer than ever – in politics, in business, in people-to-people links. We have a great deal in common.'[9] In truth, bilateral Anglo–Japanese economic relations have never been more stable and the two economies do share many political and commercial interests. In September 1999, the UK and Japanese governments had launched their 'Action Agenda 21' partnership, which included no fewer than 21 areas for practical bilateral cooperation. Reflecting the common challenges faced by Japan and the UK, these areas included cooperation for 'mutual prosperity' in the fields of 'economy, science and technology, health, social security, employment and government reform'. In particular, as two of the world's leading trading nations, with Tokyo and London serving as two of the three largest global financial centres, the UK and Japanese governments committed themselves to work together at the World Trade Organization (WTO) ministerial and Group of Seven finance ministers' meetings to promote reform and liberalization of trade, and the strengthening of the international financial system.[10]

In noting the strength and cordiality of bilateral Anglo-Japanese economic relations, due attention must also be paid to the fact that never has the political importance of this bilateral relationship been so heavily mediated by other structures of market governance - notably Japan and the UK's membership of the G8 industrialized economies, the International Monetary Fund (IMF), the WTO and the World Bank. Above all, the UK's membership of the EU, and the role played by the EU in multilateral institutions such as the WTO, has become an important strategic influence. Thus, while the exchange of goods and services between Japan and the UK has continued to be conducted on a bilateral basis, the principal institutional framework for Anglo-Japanese economic relations has been provided by the EU's relationship with Japan. Together, the EU member states and Japan now account for more than 40 per cent of global GDP.

As a member state of the EU, the UK's economic relations with Japan have taken place within the framework provided by the July 1991 European Community-Japan joint declaration on relations between the then European Community, its member states and Japan, which established both common principles and shared objectives in the political, economic, cultural and cooperative spheres. Annual EU-Japan summits have taken place since July 1991, the twelfth of which was held in Athens in May 2003. At the tenth summit in December 2001, Japan and the EU member states signed *Shaping Our Common Future: An Action Plan for EU-Japan Cooperation*, the second objective of which was to strengthen the economic and trade partnership by 'utilizing the dynamism of globalization for the benefit of all'.[11] Since 1994, the EU and Japan have also engaged in an annual Regulatory Reform Dialogue, a process that has seen both partners present each other with requests for deregulation of their respective economies. For example, at a meeting in Tokyo in

November 2003, Japan was presented with EU priority proposals for regulatory reform in Japan. These proposals included a range of measures 'to address structural and regulatory obstacles which at present inhibit business activity, entrepreneurial initiative and the competitiveness of the Japanese economy'.[12] They provided an important external bolster to Prime Minister Koizumi's own request, at the May 2003 EU–Japan bilateral summit, for more EU companies to invest in Japan, and supplemented the 10 July 2003 signing of an EU–Japan agreement on cooperation on anti-competitive activities. Since March 1996, Anglo-Japanese and broader EU–Japanese economic relations have been given a further institutional dimension by a series of Asia–Europe Meetings (ASEMs). This informal process of political dialogue has further enhanced economic cooperation, not least through the measures agreed upon at the fourth ASEM in September 2002, where, for example, ministers agreed that US measures were 'clearly inconsistent with WTO rules', namely that the sanctions against steel imports introduced by the Bush administration, should be ended.[13]

Despite participation by Japan and the United Kingdom in multilateral and supranational institutional negotiations, the most significant form of bilateral Anglo-Japanese economic relations has remained the contacts between the private sectors in each economy. The most tangible impact of Anglo-Japanese relations has been FDI by Japanese companies in manufacturing, research and development (R&D) and services in the UK. In 2002–3, despite a 20 per cent fall in global FDI flows, the UK was the beneficiary of a further 49 FDI projects by Japanese companies, raising the total of Japanese 'inward investors' to 958 companies. This followed on from the 60 new Japanese FDI projects in the UK in 2001–2.[14]

Not only has the number of Japanese FDI projects continued to flow, but the trend has been towards investments in higher added value activities, notably R&D and design. Despite this huge injection of capital and innovation, the UK has recorded a current account deficit every year since 1984, recording a deficit of £19 billion in 2002. In its transactions with Japan, the UK recorded a deficit of £2.9 billion in 2002, following deficits of £6 billion in 2000 and £4.8 billion in 2001.[15] However, but for Japan's FDI, especially in the UK's manufacturing industries, the UK's current account deficit would have been significantly worse. Most importantly, for the stability and cordiality of Anglo-Japanese economic relations, since the 1980s the UK has consistently regarded its trade deficit with Japan as a competitive challenge to enhance its own productivity and broader international competitiveness, rather than as a motive for protectionist measures. This experience is in sharp contrast to Japan's bilateral trade relationship with the United States where the latter's longstanding trade deficit has frequently been the source of demands for protectionism and a quantitative target-based approach to trade relations.[16]

The enduring stability of Anglo–Japanese economic relations now stands in vivid contrast to the instability, market volatility, investor uncertainty and faltering economic growth performance of the global economy that has marked the era of ideological hegemony by the neo-liberal orthodoxy of the 'Washington Consensus' agenda of liberalization, deregulation and privatization.[17] However stable and successful the bilateral UK–Japan relations, they have been unable to compensate for the broader volatility fostered by the greater licence accorded to liberalized markets. The prospects for the global economy remain uncertain because of the fundamental imbalances arising from the rapid (but unsustainable) growth in the US economy during 1993, its twin burgeoning balance of payments and fiscal deficits, and the relatively slow economic growth experienced by the European Union and Asian economies. Here the failures of the 'Washington Consensus' are writ large. The world's two largest economies, those of the USA and Japan, are predicted to have sustained budget deficits of 6 per cent and 7.4 per cent respectively during 2003.[18] In the case of the USA this constitutes a worrying volatility in fiscal policy given that it achieved a fiscal surplus of 1 per cent of GDP as recently as 2000. It also does not augur well for the stability of the dollar given that the USA is forecast to run a current account deficit of 4.7 per cent of GDP in 2004, following a 5.1 per cent deficit in 2003.[19]

This deterioration in growth performance and the increasing incidence of financial crises, not least in Asia in 1997, has been attributed to the damage caused by 'crony capitalism'.[20] Given that financial crises have afflicted developed and developing economies alike, including many, such as Russia and Argentina, whose markets have not been so markedly affected by the 'crony capitalism' of developmental states, this explanation for slower global growth has been shown to be erroneous. Indeed, the ideological assault on the postwar political economy of developmental states, notably Japan and South Korea, has been the product of a 'politics of resentment', which has reflected a 'Western conceptual inability to deal with the resistance of the Asian model of economic development to converge towards, and conform with, an Anglo-American form of capitalism'.[21] In an attempt to discredit the model of Asian industrialization, with its emphasis on the principle of 'directed' or subsidized credit to promote investment, an institutional nexus of primarily US-based vested interests, commonly known as the 'Wall Street–Treasury–IMF Complex'[22] has sought to assert the alleged superior developmental benefits to be derived from free capital mobility. But, as the aforementioned statistics for national economic performance suggest, the 'Washington Consensus' has misunderstood the causes of slower growth.

The real culprit for slower growth, both globally and in major markets such as Japan and the UK, has been the volatility, uncertainty and diminished investor confidence arising from insufficiently governed financial markets. As members of the G8, both Japan and the UK have been party to the G8's ineffective attempts to restore confidence in the capacity of the multilateral institutions to deliver sustained global growth. Thus, at Evian, France, in June 2003, Japan and the UK signed up to the G8 declaration that reiterated the G8's 'faith in and commitment to the multilateral trading system, which has contributed so much to international growth, stability and sustainable development for over fifty years'.[23] What that declaration failed to acknowledge was that stability and growth in trade and development for much of the G8's history had been achieved by a more decisive political leadership and government of the global economy, especially financial markets. The World Bank has claimed that 'the challenges confronting developing countries seeking to expand their international trade are primarily domestic'.[24] While major domestic challenges do indeed confront both developing and industrialized economies, not least Japan and the UK, the collapse of the Cancún WTO ministerial negotiations in September 2003, following the previous WTO ministerial failure at Doha in 2001, have demonstrated that shortcomings in global governance and the agenda of the multilateral institutions are acting as a constraint upon domestic economic performance and bilateral economic relationships.

The dividend for Japan and the UK from the slower global growth delivered by the policies of the neo-liberal orthodoxy has not been a positive one. In terms of overall international competitiveness, and at 56.3 per cent of the performance of the USA, the world's most competitive economy, Japan, was ranked only eleventh in the *World Competitiveness Scoreboard 2003*, a ranking broadly consistent with its performance during the previous four years. For its part, at 66.5 per cent of the US overall competitiveness performance, the UK was ranked seventh overall, a slight deterioration from its ranking of fifth or sixth during the previous four-year period.[25] In terms of GDP per worker productivity, the USA achieved productivity 30.8 per cent higher than the UK in 2002, while Japan's productivity was only 93.9 per cent of the

UK's.[26] Not surprisingly, neither the Japanese nor the UK economy has escaped unscathed from recent scrutiny of their respective domestic economic policies or performance. In the case of Japan, the OECD's December 2003 survey has identified 'a disappointing decade during which economic growth has averaged only 1 per cent a year'. Following the Koizumi government's re-election in November 2003, the OECD has urged it to pursue 'a broad-based policy that features structural reforms to improve resource allocation, revitalize business sector activity and restore the soundness of the banking sector'.[27]

This is therefore a particularly challenging juncture for the competitive advantage of the Japanese and United Kingdom economies. While the ideological, institutional and macroeconomic policy shortcomings of global governance have remained unresolved, attention has focused primarily on the challenges for microeconomic policy. The need for both Japan and the UK to bridge the productivity gap with the United States is evident. For the third quarter of 2003, the output per hour of the business sector in the USA rose by 8.6 per cent (on a seasonally adjusted annualized rate).[28] For the UK economy, since both unemployment and inflation remain at their lowest in several decades, the principal microeconomic challenge concerns the need to reduce the UK's large trade and current account deficits - not least with Japan. For the Japanese economy, the principal challenge remains to escape the current deflation, not least by taking greater competitive advantage of FDI. Indeed, the *World Investment Report 2003* has revealed that in 2002 the UK's FDI stock of inward investment stood at $638.6 billion (equivalent to 40.8 per cent of GDP) while its outward stock of FDI stood at $1033 billion (or 66.1 per cent of GDP).[29] By contrast, Japan's stock of inward FDI was only $59.6 billion (or 1.2 per cent of GDP) and its outward FDI stock $331.6 billion (equivalent to 8.3 per cent of GDP).[30] An important source of innovation, competition and investment remains largely untapped.

There is significant external and internal pressure on the Japanese and UK states to make the appropriate domestic economic policy choices to enable them to enhance their respective competitive advantages. Unfortunately, this is a particularly difficult juncture for making the economic policy choices that affect their bilateral relationship. Globalization has increased the pressure for a transformation in the role of the advanced industrialized state away from its previous incarnations as a social democratic welfare state in the UK, or an industrialization-driven developmental state in Japan, towards a 'competition state'. This transformation has in turn been accompanied by a parallel movement from industrial policy through competitiveness policy to enterprise policy, namely a shift in public policy 'away from policies that constrain the freedom of firms to contract and towards policies enabling the start-up and viability of knowledge-based entrepreneurial firms', not least because 'the comparative advantage of the high-cost countries in the OECD is increasingly based on knowledge-driven innovative activity'.[31]

At all levels of governance of the market, the fostering of entrepreneurship has been identified as the key to competitive advantage. The task of politics, and the attendant role for the state, has been narrowly defined as to build institutions for the market.[32] The primary purpose of politics has been to serve the interests of entrepreneurs, private enterprise and liberalized markets within a neo-classical orthodoxy on globalization, which holds that trade and development will accelerate and inequalities in income and wealth will narrow.[33] At the international level, in the final report of its growth project, the OECD has concluded that 'entrepreneurship has always been important, but its role stands out in the present time of innovative change.'[34]

The importance attached to making a successful transition, via 'competitiveness policy', from 'industrial policy' to 'enterprise policy' has inevitably placed the spotlight on the quality of the institutional and policy environment in Japan and the UK for fostering an entrepreneur-driven enterprise culture. In this regard, the *Global Entrepreneurship Monitor 2002* asserted that Japan had the worst overall performance among the major industrialized economies for fostering entrepreneurship, with only 1.81 per cent of its total labour force engaged in entrepreneurial activity in 2002 (a dramatic decline from 5.19 per cent in 2001). While the UK recorded a higher ranking of 5.37 per cent of its total labour force engaged in entrepreneurial activity, this was still barely half the US 10.51 per cent.[35] Policy in both Japan and the UK must take better account of the innovation-related information flows that occur through both market and non-market transactions, which can involve either tangible or intangible assets, and can involve not only private enterprises but also a network of public institutions, most notably 'business support agencies' and universities.[36]

The challenge now confronting both the Japanese and the UK economies is to make what Michael Porter has described as the transition to 'a new phase of economic development', namely an 'innovation-driven stage' where 'the ability to produce innovative products and services at the global technology frontier using the most advanced methods becomes the dominant source of competitive advantage'.[37] As a leading theorist of national competitive advantage, Porter has led audits of both the Japanese and British economies to evaluate the extent to which their respective policies, institutions and companies are capable of making this competitive transition. In the case of Japan, Porter's team has concluded that the Japanese state has pursued the wrong policies and Japanese companies the wrong corporate strategies. Much of the market-conforming intervention cited by Chalmers Johnson and other prominent 'Asian developmental state' theorists is held to have been almost entirely absent from the development of competitive industries in Japan. In short, 'the policies widely believed to explain Japan's success were far more prevalent in the nation's failures than its successes', with the consequence that the Japanese government model of competitiveness should be seen 'as a cause of failure, not the source of the Japanese miracle'.[38]

Porter's team has been equally scathing in its evaluation of the UK's international competitiveness and enterprise policies. Its damning conclusion is that the UK lags behind its major competitors in three key areas that determine productivity, namely skilled labour inputs, capital intensity and 'total factor productivity' (TFP). In terms of skilled labour inputs from its existing workforce, the UK lags behind the USA in terms of its share of high-skilled employees in the labour force but is slightly ahead in its share of low-skilled employees, while it also trails behind Germany and France in its share of 'intermediate-skilled employees'. In terms of capital intensity, the UK trails behind France by 60 per cent, Germany by 32 per cent, and the USA by 25 per cent in the statistical category of 'capital stock per hour worked'. In terms of TFP, namely that part of labour productivity that cannot be attributed directly to factor inputs, the UK lags behind the USA by about 50 per cent, France by 10 per cent, and is comparable to Germany.[39] Thus, the study in effect merely repeats the conclusions of a plethora of other reports that have documented the UK's relative economic decline during the twentieth century.[40]

The policy and institutional implications Porter and his team members laid down for both Japan and the UK are clear, but at the same time demanding if the success and stability of their bilateral economic relationship is to be maintained. Competitiveness 'increasingly relies on a country's appropriate structures of roles, institutions and processes to enable, organize, and drive efforts to improve business environments and clusters'.[41] The role of the state must be transformed from a framework of nationally driven policies and incentives to one where government plays 'a central role in convening and supporting competitiveness efforts, even though these efforts will tend to be led by the private sector or other institutions'. The role of the state is essential because 'without government involvement, initiatives lack legitimacy and they fail to address those competitiveness issues government policy can directly affect.'[42] It is clear that Porter and his colleagues are not advocating that the Japanese developmental state model must be abandoned wholeheartedly in favour of the 'Washington Consensus' policies favoured by the 'Wall Street–Treasury–IMF Complex'. On the contrary, certain key features of Japanese government policy that have enhanced productivity are deemed to merit retention, namely 'high standards in basic education, policies to encourage savings and investment, a stable macroeconomic policy, the collection and dissemination of extensive business information, and continuing upgrading of physical infrastructure'.[43] In short, the new role for the Japanese state 'is neither a diminished nor a less important one' but rather 'a different role, one better suited both to Japan's status as an advanced economy and to the realities of modern competition'.[44]

In the case of the UK, Porter's team has identified some equally important policy recommendations, with potentially far-reaching implications for the wider political economy of Anglo–Japanese economic relations. In short, as with its policy prescriptions for Japanese competitive advantage, Porter's team's recommendations for the UK constitute an important departure from the simplistic advocacy of further liberalization, deregulation and privatization, which have informed the strategies of the principal multilateral institutions over the past quarter century. Thus, it has been asserted that 'lower taxes, less regulation, and an even smaller role for the government are no longer the most critical elements for UK competitiveness'.[45] What is required instead is an upgrading in the productivity of UK companies through their competing on the basis of more unusual and innovative products and services. Among the prerequisites that must, in turn, be in place to deliver this upgrading is increased investment in the physical and human infrastructure.

The clear implications of the Porter team's studies of the Japanese and UK economies is that a different set of ideological assumptions about state–market relations are required for the reinvigoration of both domestic economies and the global economy. The incentives for the Japanese and UK governments to act together, within the G8, WTO, IMF, OECD and World Bank, to challenge the hegemony of the neo-liberal orthodoxy are manifest. An agenda of liberalization, deregulation and privatization has failed to deliver the rates of global and domestic economic growth achieved during the postwar decades of the Bretton Woods international economic order. From the perspective of Japan, the rise and eventual collapse of the speculative 'bubble economy', which was driven by new bank loans of $220 billion to the property sector and a further $75 billion of loans by housing loan corporations and other non-bank financial institutions between 1985 and 1990,[46] only arose following external pressure to liberalize and deregulate Japan's financial markets. The 13 subsequent years of faltering economic growth, deflation and escalating fiscal deficits, with gross government debt predicted now to rise from 154.6 per cent of GDP in 2003 to 167.2 per cent in 2005 (having been around 40 per cent in 1990),[47] have demonstrated the severe and damaging political and social consequences of the 'one-size-fits-all' policies that have given excessive licence to deregulated financial markets. If the world's second largest economy, with its massive economic resources, has been unable to sustain domestic prosperity within the framework of global governance provided by the 'Washington Consensus' for more than a decade, the developmental prospects for other, less prosperous economies would appear grave.

From the perspective of the UK, the domestic dividend from the pursuit of liberalization, deregulation and privatization has also been questionable. Admittedly, the UK has now enjoyed more than a decade of economic growth, but at average annual rates that have not departed significantly from the UK's long-term trend rate of growth of 2.25–2.50 per cent during decades of relative economic decline. Manufacturing investment has collapsed and the UK now regularly sustains record monthly trade and current account deficits. Furthermore, while public sector net debt has fallen from 44 per cent of GDP in 1996–97 to 30.9 per cent of GDP in 2002–3, those six years of temporary fiscal prudence are now to be followed by seven years of deteriorating public finances, commencing with a projected fiscal deficit of £37.4 billion in 2003–4. On the Blair government's own optimistic projections, public sector net debt is due to reach 35.5 per cent of GDP by 2008–9, following the addition of £200 billion to the national debt.[48]

The global economy is now facing a scenario where the world's two largest domestic economies, those of the USA and Japan, and another member of the G8, the UK, are alike confronted by massive private indebtedness among consumers, property-owners, banks and enterprises. The presence both of the lowest real interest rates for many decades and low global inflation, which constitute the so-called macroeconomic 'fundamentals' or 'basics', which the IMF, World Bank and other multilateral institutions have claimed are the prerequisites for sustained global economic recovery, have failed to deliver global growth very largely because of this burden of private debt. As a consequence, the most important contribution the Anglo-Japanese economic relationship can now make to the governance of the global economy is to mount an ideological challenge to the neo-liberal orthodoxy that has locked major industrialized and developing countries alike into an era of slow growth. This challenge should seek to exploit the key roles played by Japanese and British ministers in forums such as the G8, World Bank and IMF.

The framework to launch such an ideological challenge is already in place. The British government has already proposed a 'Modern Marshall Plan for the Developing World' to tackle global poverty through the creation of an International Finance Facility (IFF).[49] This 'new deal for the global economy' would provide an alternative to the opposite temptations of a retreat into protectionism and isolationism on the part of the USA and other major economies, and a recycling of *laissez-faire* ideas.[50] While the original Marshall Plan, or European Recovery Programme, had delivered $13 billion over four years, the Blair government has proposed that the IFF would deliver a doubling of annual official development assistance from $50 billion to $100 billion. With the parallel elimination of $350 billion of annual subsidies in the developed world, this would make it possible for the World Bank's millennium development goals to be achieved by 2015.[51]

For its part, the Japanese government has shown itself willing in the past to challenge the neo-liberal hegemony of the 'Washington Consensus' on several occasions. The first occasion was during the early 1990s when Japanese pressure for a recognition of the effectiveness of the Asian developmental state as a model of economic growth resulted in the World Bank's erroneous dismissal of the role of the state in East Asia as 'largely ineffective'.[52] The second was in September 1997 when, in the immediate aftermath of the onset of the Asian financial crisis, Japan had proposed the creation of an Asian Monetary Fund, to provide a $100 billion 'standby fund' for East Asian economies to combat disruptive speculative pressures on their national currencies.[53] A third was at the turn of the millennium when Japan nominated Eisuke Sakakibara, former vice minister of finance, as its candidate to become the next managing director of the IMF. This act was a protest against the previously closed nature of the selection process, which had seen the key roles at the World Bank and IMF carved up between Americans and Europeans, to the exclusion of Japan - despite its status as the world's second largest economy and largest creditor nation.[54] Japan urgently needs to rediscover this willingness to defend its interests and 'developmental state traditions' against the so-called neo-liberal orthodoxy.

If evidence were needed of the desirability both of challenging the relentless 'one-size-fits-all' pursuit of liberalization, deregulation and privatization, and reassessing the viability of the developmental state tradition of decisive governmental intervention to govern the market, it has been provided by South Korea and the IMF's own evaluation of the success of the Korean economy in recovering from the damage inflicted by the financial crisis of 1997–98. Real GDP growth in Korea has averaged 7.25 per cent during 1999–2002,[55] but this impressive growth performance has not arisen because of the pursuit of the limited but effective role for the state of 'building institutions for the market' advocated by the World Bank and the 'Washington Consensus'. On the contrary, Korea has applied the Asian developmental state tradition of vigorous government-led intervention and restructuring to its troubled banking and corporate sectors. As the IMF has itself acknowledged, since the onset of the financial crisis, the Korean state has increased its ownership of commercial banks from only three banks and 18 per cent of total banking assets to either majority or co-ownership of 18 banks and around 60 per cent of banking assets.[56] Rapid economic growth has been restored to the Korean economy, and unemployment has halved from 6.4 per cent of the workforce in 1999 to 3.1 per cent in 2003, because of the state's willingness to depart from the neo-liberal orthodoxy. There are important lessons for Japan from this successful conduct of economic policy, not least the likely political appeal to a sceptical Japanese electorate of an agenda more proximate to the one that delivered decades of economic growth.

In bilateral terms, Anglo–Japanese economic relations remain stable and cordial. Japan and the UK continue to work together in multilateral institutional arenas for their mutual self-interest. However, the stability of this bilateral relationship, and the capacity of Japan and the UK to resolve their respective macroeconomic problems, and to move to the next stage of international competitiveness, is threatened by the broader context of instability, volatility and uncertainty in global markets. As a consequence, the most urgent task confronting Japan and the UK is to provide together the political leadership to challenge the hegemony in the institutions of the global governance of the 'one-size-fits-all' neo-liberal orthodoxy of the 'Washington Consensus' that has brought about slower growth and greater volatility. And, since both the British and Japanese governments have shown themselves capable of challenging the neo-liberal orthodoxy, this task is neither a revolutionary proposal nor such a large leap in political imagination.

The World Bank itself has concluded in its report *East Asia: Recovery and Beyond*, that 'any attempt at a one-size-fits-all policy agenda is ill-advised'.[57] Furthermore, in its 1997 World Development Report, *The State in a Changing World*, the World Bank contended that 'For human welfare to be advanced, the state's capability - defined as the ability to undertake and promote collective actions efficiently - must be increased'. To this end, the state's role must be matched to its capability, which in turn must be raised by reinvigorating public institutions.[58] The challenge now for Japan and the UK is to build on the strength of their bilateral relationships to use their privileged positions within multilateral institutional forums like the World Bank, OECD and G8, and their regular chairmanship of influential bodies such as the International Monetary and Financial Committee of the IMF, to present an alternative agenda for the reinvigoration of public institutions, both in their domestic economies and in the arena of global governance. Such bold action should ensure that Anglo-Japanese economic relations can be conducted in an environment of greater external stability to complement the cordiality and effectiveness of the bilateral relationship.

Chapter 12

JAPAN AND THE UK AT THE G8 SUMMIT, 1975 TO 2006

Hugo Dobson

The highest level of diplomacy

The Group of Eight (G8) summit process provides both a historical snapshot of more than thirty years of international politics and also a framework by which to structure and make sense of these relations. Its longevity and utility have surpassed several better known international institutions and organizations, such as the League of Nations, and it continues to provide the only opportunity in the calendar of international diplomacy for the G8 leaders to meet.

The G8 first met as the G6 (France, Italy, Japan, United Kingdom, United States and West Germany) in November 1975 at the Château de Rambouillet in the Paris suburbs. French President Valéry Giscard d'Estaing and West German Chancellor Helmut Schmidt, the progenitors of the summit, sought to recreate at the prime ministerial or presidential level the behind the scenes, friendly but frank atmosphere of the meetings of the leading finance ministers (known as the 'library group' because the meetings took place in the White House library) they had attended when both served as finance ministers of their respective countries. Although intended as an impromptu, never to be repeated and informal meeting in reaction to both the 1973 oil crisis and the collapse of the Bretton Woods' system of fixed exchange rates, the utility of this forum led to a second conference in San Juan, Puerto Rico in June 1976 at which Canada was invited to form the G7. Representatives of the European Community (EC), later to become the European Union (EU), participated from the 1977 London summit onwards, and Russia formally joined from the 1998 Birmingham summit to create the G8 we know today. Alongside an expanded membership, the remit of discussion has developed beyond economic issues to embrace the most pressing political, social and security issues of the day.

The G8 differs greatly from the other organizations and institutions that have been created to provide global governance, such as the United Nations (UN), the International Monetary Fund and the World Bank. It is therefore important to understand the nature of the G8 summit process as the vagueness that surrounds it has led to general ignorance, over-expectation and inevitable disappointment. For example, at one extreme, it is regarded as having come 'to occupy centre stage in the continuing struggle to create order out of anarchy in the world's economic and political life'.[1] At the other extreme, it has been dismissed as little more than a 'ritualized photo opportunity'.[2]

The G8 has none of the usual trappings of an international organization – no headquarters, no dedicated staff, no budget, no flag and no formal mechanisms to enforce its decisions. Rather, it is an informal forum that emphasizes the role of the individual and the ability of these individuals to create an atmosphere of cooperation that, it is hoped, will foster international policy coordination. The G8's utility lies in its ability to address issues in an iterative fashion while maintaining the flexibility to respond to changes in the international system and to add pressing issues to its agenda at the eleventh hour. After each summit, the G8 delegates the task of implementing its decisions to other institutions and organizations. In the words of the late Michael Hodges of the London School of Economics, 'The G7/8 is a forum, rather than an institution. It is useful as a closed international club of capitalist governments trying to raise consciousness, set an agenda, create networks, prod other institutions to do things that they should be doing, and, in some cases, to help create institutions that are suited to a particular task.'[3] Despite this unique position, it is only recently that the G8 has received sustained academic attention, largely thanks to the G8 Research Group at Toronto University and the associated 'G8 and Global Governance' series published by Ashgate. Nevertheless, country-comparative studies between G8 members remain largely an unexplored area in this emerging field of 'G8 studies'. In this chapter I attempt to fill this lacuna by focusing on two founding members of the G8: Japan and the UK. To this end, I will first of all establish the positions of both governments within the G8 and their respective patterns of behaviour, highlighting the most salient similarities and differences. Thereafter, I will explore areas of cooperation and conflict between the two governments from 1975 to the present day. Finally, I will highlight future challenges that the G8 summit process will have to confront and the respective efforts and roles of Japan and the UK in finding effective solutions.[4]

Japan and the UK at the summit

A number of roles played by Japan at the 31 summits held since 1975 can be discerned.[5] First, the G8 allows Japan to promote itself as a responsible member of international society, proud of its founding position within the G8 and eager to host successful summits. Japan is in fact the most consistent host of successful summits.[6] This contrasts with the position of latecomer and outsider that Japan shoulders in organizations such as the UN. Second, as the only non-Western member of the G8 and, encouraged by its neighbours, Japan has embraced the role of the representative of Asia bringing issues of regional concern to the attention of the European and North American leaders. For example, Ryūtarō Hashimoto inputted a number of Asian issues into the agenda of the 1998 Birmingham summit and was also expected to fund many of the G8's responses.[7] Third, and connected to the previous role, Japan has served as a bridge between East and West. This was evident when Japan sought to mediate the West's reaction to the 1989 Tiananmen Square massacre. Finally, both through the summit and the bilateral meetings that take place on its edges, the Japanese government has sought to manage and reinforce its bilateral relationship with the USA, central to its international relations. Added to these roles specific to Japan, the prime minister of the day shares an interest with other G8 leaders in the summit as a means of boosting his popularity at home and chances of re-election.[8]

However, Japan is often regarded as a passive actor at the summit table; the corner at which its leader sits has been dubbed the 'silent corner'.[9] This is partly the result of inconsistency in personnel. Attendance at the summit reflects the differing political systems of each participant – US presidents, for example, will attend either four or eight summits, depending on how many terms of office they serve and whether or not they are impeached. Japanese prime ministers suffer from a relatively short lifespan and are most similar to their Italian counterparts in the average number of summits attended. In total, 14 Japanese leaders have attended the annual summits and this means that a Japanese prime minister attends on average two summits (see Table 12.1, p. 157). Thus, the Japanese prime minister has failed to achieve any consistency in his attendance at a forum that depends heavily on individuals and personalities. Nakasone Yasuhiro broke the mould and for a long time was the most durable Japanese leader by attending five summits (1983 to

1987). It took 20 years for Koizumi Junichirō to surpass this record by attending six (2001 to 2006). Clearly, Nakasone and Koizumi stand out as exceptions and it is also these two prime ministers who have been most warmly welcomed by fellow G8 leaders. On his return from the 1983 Williamsburg summit it was reported that 'Nakasone did break with the cautious policy followed by his predecessors ... [and managed] to elevate Japan's position by several notches by being regarded anew as "one of the gang".'[10] Equally, at his debut at the 2001 Genoa summit, Koizumi 'proved a livelier summit participant than most Japanese leaders'.[11] However, and notwithstanding the efforts of these two men to become international statesmen, the Japanese prime minister has generally been less durable than his Western counterparts and cannot compare with Helmut Kohl, who attended 16 summits (1983 to 1998), or François Mitterrand, who attended 14 (1981 to 1994).

Like Japan, the UK is a founding member of the G8. UK governments, despite the UK's relative postwar decline, have regarded it as both symbolic of their position in the world and a useful forum for international policy coordination. Thus, it has been asserted that the Foreign and Commonwealth Office maintains 'an entirely pragmatic opinion of the G8'.[12] The UK can also boast a solid record of summit performance comparable to other summit nations, a tradition of hosting relatively successful summits and one of the highest levels of compliance with G8 pledges. In addition, the UK has carved out a role for itself as innovator at the summit with the goal of improving the way in which it functions. Finally, and similar to Japan, it has found itself torn at times between its regional identity (as a member of the European project) and its 'special relationship' with the USA over divisive issues such as combating climate change. Yet, in contrast to Japan, the UK's position within the G8 is seen to be a central one, as reflected in its invitation and Japan's non-invitation to the January 1979 four-power Guadeloupe meeting to discuss security issues. Similarly, on the eve of the 1980 Venice summit, it became known that France, West Germany, the UK and the USA had been conducting secret ambassadorial-level meetings in Washington, which served to create the sense of a two-tier summit process that, like the Guadeloupe meeting, excluded Canada, Italy and Japan.[13]

UK prime ministers have tended to play a more vocal and active role in summit discussions than their Japanese counterparts. On the one hand, this may be a result of the personality of the prime minister of the day. For example, Margaret Thatcher is the longest-serving UK prime minister in the summit process and was known as a forceful defender of UK national interests and an ideological supporter of the USA during the

1980s. What is more, at the 2005 Gleneagles summit, Tony Blair became the first UK prime minister to host two summits and was partly responsible for putting debt relief so saliently on this summit's agenda. On the other hand, a higher degree of stability in representation at the summit may have engendered a more active role for the UK prime minister. In contrast to the 14 Japanese prime ministers, only five UK prime ministers have attended the summit in total (see Table 12.1, p. 157). This has given the UK a consistency in personnel that is necessary to create the interpersonal relationships that are central to the successful working of a concert mechanism like the G8 summit. Insofar as Japan–UK relations are concerned, only two durable relationships have emerged in summit history: Nakasone–Thatcher and Koizumi–Blair, both sets of prime ministers that are often likened to each other.

Although relations with the USA have traditionally dominated the international relations of both Japan and the UK, the summit has provided an opportunity for the two governments to interact directly both on the edges of summit proceedings and at the actual summit table. This interaction has resulted in both cooperation and conflict.

Cooperation

During its 31-year history, the G8 summit has been utilized to foster Japan–UK cooperation across a number of economic and political issues, as well as to promote general understanding between the two peoples.

Economic issues

The discussion of macroeconomic issues was the *raison d'être* for the creation of the G8 and to this end Japan and the UK have regularly addressed a range of multilateral and bilateral economic issues through the annual summit. For example, when Japan hosted the 1986 Tokyo summit, Foreign Minister Abe Shintarō met his counterpart Geoffrey Howe before the summit began to discuss bilateral trade issues, the high taxes levied on imported Scottish whisky, and the Maekawa report on deregulation and structural reform in Japan.[14] On the final day of this summit, Nakasone met Thatcher before her departure that evening to discuss the value of the yen and the trade imbalance between the two countries.[15] On the opening day of the 1997 Denver summit, Hashimoto met German Chancellor Helmut Kohl and UK Prime Minister Tony Blair to discuss a range of bilateral issues and the possible impact of European monetary union.[16] Finally, on the day before the 2002 Kananaskis summit began, Koizumi met a number of leaders on a bilateral basis, including Blair, to discuss the progress of Japan's structural reforms.[17]

Table 12.1: Japanese and UK prime ministers' attendance at the G8 summit, 1975 to 2005

Summit venue and year	*Japanese Prime Minister*	*UK Prime Minister*
Rambouillet 1975	Miki Takeo	Harold Wilson
San Juan 1976		James Callaghan
London 1977	Fukuda Takeo	
Bonn 1978		
Tokyo 1979	Ōhira Masayoshi	Margaret Thatcher
Venice 1980	Absent*	
Ottawa 1981	Suzuki Zenkō	
Versailles 1982		
Williamsburg 1983	Nakasone Yasuhiro	
London 1984		
Bonn 1985		
Tokyo 1986		
Venice 1987		
Toronto 1988	Takeshita Noboru	
Paris 1989	Uno Sōsuke	
Houston 1990	Kaifu Toshiki	
London 1991		John Major
Munich 1992	Miyazawa Kiichi	
Tokyo 1993		
Naples 1994	Murayama Tomiichi	
Halifax 1995		
Lyon 1996	Ryūtarō Hashimoto	
Denver 1997		Tony Blair
Birmingham 1998		
Cologne 1999	Obuchi Keizō	
Okinawa 2000	Mori Yoshirō	
Genoa 2001	Koizumi Junicihirō	
Kananaskis 2002		
Evian 2003		
Sea Island 2004		
Gleneagles 2005		
St Petersburg 2006		

* Ōhira Masayoshi died ten days before the 1980 Venice summit. Foreign Minister Ōkita Saburō took his place in the leaders' summit discussions.

Political issues

Despite the original intention of the summit, political issues have come to dominate the G8's agenda and, interestingly, the Japanese delegation has not shied away from this trend and has found areas of cooperation with the UK. For example, at the 1984 London summit, Nakasone emphasized building on the forceful statements issued at the previous year's summit in Williamsburg as regards Western solidarity, nuclear disarmament talks with the Soviet Union and regional conflict resolution. He was also eager to have the other leaders discuss terrorism, an issue on which he was supported by Thatcher.[18] At the 1990 Houston summit, Kaifu Toshiki had a meeting with Thatcher on the day before the summit officially began and managed to draw out a tacit understanding for Japan's resumption of loans to China after the Tiananmen Square massacre.[19] The following year, at the 1991 London summit, Kaifu met John Major for the first time before the summit began and during their two-hour meeting it was agreed that both Japan and the UK would only extend considerable aid to the Soviet Union if Gorbachev could demonstrate an effective programme that moved towards a free-market economy and democracy – something about which both leaders expressed scepticism. On the final day of this summit, it was also announced that Japan and the UK would submit a joint arms register proposal to the UN.[20] During a meeting in London on the afternoon of 4 July while *en route* to the 1992 Munich summit, Miyazawa received the support of Major in his capacity as UK prime minister on the Northern Territories' issue but not in his position as president of the EC Council of Ministers.[21] Finally, on the eve of the 2000 Okinawa summit, Mori Yoshirō and Blair discussed a working holiday programme for 18 to 25 year olds. Blair also expressed support for the discussion of reforming the UN Security Council and the inclusion of Japan.[22]

Social events

As mentioned above, the G8 summit has been accused of being nothing more than a photo opportunity. This impression has probably been fostered by a number of social events that have been arranged on the edges of the summit and are seemingly unrelated to international policy coordination. A host of similar events have been organized over the years with the goal of enhancing Japan–UK ties and understanding both on a governmental and societal level. For example, the 1978 London summit proved to be a nostalgic trip for Fukuda Takeo as he had been dispatched to London in the 1930s as a finance ministry bureaucrat and attended the 1933 World Economic Conference. Fukuda took time out of the summit discussions to visit his former lodgings. After the 1984 London summit, Nakasone gave a speech at the International Institute for Strategic Studies and met the Shōwa emperor's grandson who was studying at Oxford University. The afternoon meetings on the second day of the 1998 Birmingham summit were cut short so that Blair could watch the English Football Association Cup final in which his favourite team Newcastle United were playing. Hashimoto went so far as to join Blair in sending the team a handwritten good luck message.

Likewise, when UK leaders have visited Japan to attend summit meetings, similar events have been organized. Thatcher was the focus of cosmetic company Kanebo's advertising campaign during the 1979 Tokyo summit. On the first day of the 2000 Okinawa summit, Blair visited the town of Chatan where in 1840 the shipwrecked crew of the British ship *Indian Oaks* was helped by the local people.[23]

Conflict

However, Japan–UK interaction at the summit has not always been as cordial, particularly over economic issues.

Economic issues

Japan's position at the 1978 London summit emphasized the maintenance of global free trade in anticipation of other summit nations, especially the UK and USA, calling on Japan to curb exports and increase imports through 'economic adjustments' – a synonym for voluntary export restraints (VERs) – to the principles of free trade.[24] The European participants were keen to use the summit to encourage Japan to purchase more EU goods and the USA was eager to see Japan adopt VERs in its export of shoes and electronic goods to the USA – either way, the anticipated impression of the summit was one of it being used as 'a convenient battering ram' against Japan.[25] After the summit meetings were concluded, Fukuda met Callaghan to discuss the imbalance in trade between the two nations and the threat to UK shipbuilding posed by the pricing policy of Japanese shipbuilders.[26]

Trade issues continued to dominate the 1981 Ottawa summit and the Japanese government again feared the worst, but much to its relief it came away from the summit with any differences of opinion with its summit partners deleted from the final Ottawa communiqué in line with its wishes, despite strong criticism in private meetings, especially from Thatcher.[27] During the discussion of economic issues at the 1987 Venice summit, Nakasone used a tried and tested strategy to pre-empt any 'Japan bashing' by announcing, to the applause of the other summiteers, a pre-summit economic package and stressing his commitment to stimulating domestic demand. However, Thatcher expressed scepticism about whether Japan could increase its foreign imports.[28]

Political issues

As regards political issues, Uno Sōsuke met Thatcher on the afternoon before the 1989 Paris summit began and the latter raised the issue of the Tiananmen Square massacre and demanded that the summit issue a strong condemnation - something the Japanese government was reluctant to do.[29] Their meeting was also anticipated in the Japanese press in terms of how a female leader would react to meeting a Japanese prime minister recently tarnished by a sex scandal. However, probably the most controversial issue at this summit was the Falklands War between the UK and Argentina. The impact of this conflict was captured in a *Yomiuri Shinbun* cartoon that depicted the conflict as the dynamite waiting to blow up the summit meeting.[30] The summit officially began with a banquet hosted by Mitterrand at which discussions focused on the conflict. Thatcher expressed both criticisms of, and disappointment with, the lack of support from the Japanese government at the UN in dealing with the conflict.[31] Suzuki Zenkō countered these criticisms by drawing the summit's attention to pressing issues in Asia, centring on Japan's relations with China and ASEAN and stressing Japan's contribution to regional and global peace and security.[32]

Japan found itself in a difficult position again at the 2001 Genoa summit during discussions on environmental issues and ratification of the Kyoto Protocol. The administration of President George W. Bush had decided not to participate in the agreement, whereas Europe wished to implement the protocol as rapidly as possible, with or without the USA. The Japanese government's position on this issue was that Japan would not ratify the agreement without US participation, and it thereby found itself stuck between two polar opposite viewpoints.[33]

Summitry

As regards the successful functioning of the summit, although the Japanese government, as will be demonstrated below, has supported and adopted various UK initiatives, the two have found themselves at loggerheads on occasions. For example, the release of the final 15-point joint declaration at the end of the 1975 Rambouillet summit was a practice initially opposed by France and the UK but supported by Germany, Japan and the USA.[34] As part of the process of creating a G8 (discussed below), Japan has been warier than the UK of embracing the

Soviet Union. This process began with the issue of whether or not to invite Gorbachev to the 1991 London summit. Western G8 members regarded it as conditional on the Soviet Union's recognition of human rights and self-determination in the Baltic states, whereas in Japan opposition was strong owing to the unresolved bilateral territorial dispute and Kaifu regarded it as premature and inappropriate.[35] However, a proposal to invite Gorbachev to an unofficial, post-summit briefing, at which he would be able to outline his economic reform programme and, as a proviso, no concrete aid pledges would be forthcoming, was regarded by both sides as acceptable.[36]

Future challenges

In recent years the G8 summit process has found itself facing a number of criticisms that focus attention on issues that have haunted it since its inception: inefficiency and illegitimacy. The G8 nations have responded over recent years through a process of internal reform and outreach to a range of other actors. Japan and the UK have both played a part in advancing these initiatives.

Shaping the summit

In addition to the goal of ensuring a successful summit, Japanese prime ministers have sought on occasions to improve its efficiency. It was the Japanese government's intention at the 1993 Tokyo summit to respond to Major's calls for a simplification of the summit process and reduction of the peripheral 'festivities' associated with it, thereby creating more time for informal and frank discussion between leaders. As one official of Japan's Ministry of Foreign Affairs (MOFA) put it, 'our policy is to promote more substantial discussions among the leaders, a move away from a political show.'[37] Especially in the light of the recession in Japan at the time, a downsizing of the summit made sense. Ten years later, a free discussion was conducted during a working dinner on the second day of the 2003 Evian summit – a format originally proposed by Koizumi, singled out and praised by Chirac, but somewhat deflated by the non-attendance of Bush and Blair.[38] However, the Japanese government's extravagant hosting of the summit has at times served to increase the peripheral 'festivities' and damage the perception of the G8, even calling its necessity into question. Okinawa proved to be the most expensively hosted summit (US$ 750 million) and possibly the most overblown in terms of carnival atmosphere and opportunistic promotion of related merchandise. Oxfam spokesman Phil Twyford summed up the feelings of disgust: 'For US$ 750 million, they could have put 12 million children into school and repay the debt of Tanzania for three years. It is really an insult.'[39]

The UK, despite initial failure, has been more vocal and successful in its attempts to reform the summit process. Harold Wilson claimed at the very first summit that there was a glut of international bodies concerned with the issues discussed at the summit and that the system needed to be streamlined. But this suggestion was not taken up immediately thereafter.[40] Two decades later, Major also sought unsuccessfully to make the summit less ceremonial, return it to its simple roots, limit the size of delegations so that the leaders could meet alone, and keep the summit agenda and summit declarations as short as possible.[41] It was not until the 1998 Birmingham summit that Blair was able to realize many of Major's goals by separating the meetings of the summit leaders from the foreign and finance ministerial meetings in an effort to make the summit less formal and more conducive to substantive discussion. The agenda at Birmingham was also limited to three main items and summit declarations were also considerably shorter than they had been in previous years. However, some of these reforms came under threat as a result of the broader, unfocused themes and the increasing number of declarations issued at the 2003 Evian summit and 2004 Sea Island summit.[42]

As regards the issue of G8 membership, Birmingham was a watershed in that it was the first summit to recognize the incorporation of Russia and use the title of G8. Although the UK encouraged Russian membership of the G8, the Japanese government found it to be a more problematic issue owing to the poor state of bilateral relations and lack of progress in signing a peace treaty and resolving the Northern Territories dispute. By contrast, the Japanese government has been more comfortable in its traditional role as Asia's representative, and at the 1993 Tokyo summit it sought to accommodate Indonesian President Suharto's wish to be invited. However, Foreign Minister Douglas Hurd expressed reluctance towards this initiative in talks with Miyazawa.[43] In the end, Suharto met Clinton on the edges of the summit. As regards China's possible future participation, both Japan and the UK are wary of expanding the G8 to create a G9. The UK government has been largely reticent on the subject but has expressed doubts about whether China adheres to the same democratic principles as the G8 nations. The Japanese government is willing to contemplate inviting China as a participant (an option Obuchi explored in preparation for the 2000 Okinawa summit and Chirac realized at the 2003 Evian summit) but regards China as a potential rival to its coveted role as Asia's representative and as a result opposes extending full membership.

Embracing civil society

At first glance, it may appear that civil society's impact on this meeting of presidents and prime ministers orchestrated by bureaucrats would be minimal. This is a resonant accusation and the G8 has responded by attempting to embrace the non-governmental organizations (NGOs) that constitute civil society. Since the 1995 Halifax summit (when NGOs were mentioned for the first time), this trend has been evident in G8 statements, which have encouraged the development of an active civil society and thereafter, year after year, the G8 has regularly made positive references to civil society in its documentation.[44] However, Japan and the UK have responded in very different ways to calls to accommodate civil society's role in the summit process.

At Birmingham, the highpoint of NGO activity was a 'human chain' of 70,000 people organized by Jubilee 2000, an umbrella group representing a range of NGOs campaigning for debt relief, around the Birmingham convention centre where some of the G8 summit meetings had taken place (although the leaders were elsewhere on the day of the demonstration). In addition, a meeting was held with UK development secretary Clare Short, and Blair issued a separate document entitled *Response by the Presidency on Behalf of the G8 to the Jubilee 2000 Petition*, which acknowledged the efforts of Jubilee 2000: 'Your presence here is a truly impressive testimony to the solidarity of people in our own countries with those in the world's poorest and most indebted. It is also a public acknowledgement of the crucial importance of the question of debt.'[45]

In response to such campaigns, the UK has spearheaded the issue of debt relief at the G8 summits and has been willing to embrace civil society groups. Blair, in particular, has gone out of his way to engage with the celebrity campaigners associated with Jubilee 2000 and the drop the debt campaign, such as rock stars Sir Bob Geldof and Bono. Before the 2003 Evian summit, the three met for a breakfast meeting to discuss debt relief and the upcoming summit. Blair has also sought to convince the USA of the worth of the Jubilee 2000 campaign and placed the issue of debt relief firmly on the agenda of the 2005 Gleneagles summit almost to the exclusion of other issues.

Following the UK example, the Japanese government selected for the first time a regional venue for the 2000 summit - Okinawa - and demonstrated a willingness to facilitate the participation of NGOs. To this end, the government created the post of director-general for civil society participation and the Japanese sherpa Nogami Yoshiji met representatives of a number of NGOs such as Save the Children,

Christian Aid and Amnesty International. On the morning of 21 July, the first day of the summit, Mori met the representatives of a number of NGOs who were calling for the cancellation of African debt, action on infectious diseases and a reduction in the US military presence in Okinawa. Representatives of Jubilee 2000 targeted Okinawa and handed Mori a petition of more than 17 million signatures calling for debt cancellation. Despite Mori being a prime minister infamous for his slips of tongue, the Japanese government hailed this as the first time a summit host had met NGO representatives, although this was a false claim because dialogue meetings had been held at Birmingham and Cologne.[46] Nevertheless, NGOs were involved in the follow-up to the summit, including the creation of two taskforces to address the 'digital divide' and renewable energy, and a programme to combat infectious diseases. The most tangible action the Japanese government took was the construction of a centre for NGOs in Nago. This gave to the 44 NGOs and 300 activists who registered a physical work space, a base of operations and the offer of computers, telephones and photocopiers. This was symbolic of the first time a host nation had recognized the importance of NGOs by creating for them a physical space in which they could conduct their operations. This was greeted with enthusiasm by one activist of Médecins Sans Frontières: 'I think the Japanese government made an effort to make this space for the NGOs and the chance to meet Prime Minister Mori. The equipment is great and people here are very helpful.'[47]

However, the Japanese government has been ultimately less successful than the UK government in engaging with civil society. Its intentions have been questioned and a traditional disdain for civil society has been highlighted. For example, in the run-up to the 2000 Okinawa summit, Jubilee 2000 organized a letter-writing campaign within Japan and formed a human chain around the Finance Ministry. In reaction, the Japanese government stated firmly that it would not cancel debt and that because Japan was not a Christian country the Jubilee 2000 campaign could not be understood.[48] In fact, holding the summit in Okinawa – a remote and easily policed island chain – could in itself be regarded as a measure to limit the influence of civil society groups like Jubilee 2000. As regards the official G8 meetings, the first day resulted in a vague statement on debt relief, which NGO representatives greeted with disappointment. Ann Pettifor of Jubilee 2000 was quoted as saying: 'We are totally dismayed by this statement. The world's leaders have retreated to this remote island of Okinawa and have turned their backs on the poor, ignoring a call that is morally right, economically right and supported by millions around the world.'[49] Although receiving plenty of media attention for their causes, NGOs represented by Jubilee 2000 were disappointed by the G8's failure to address the debt problem, dubbing Okinawa the 'squandered summit'.[50] What is more, the NGO centre was under used, possibly because it was some distance from the international media centre (a 15–20 minute walk in the oppressive summer heat of Okinawa) from which NGOs were barred, cost ¥10,000 (US$ 91) per NGO to use, and involved procedures like submitting individual photographs and registering details such as address and height, suggesting surveillance and possible co-option by the Japanese government. Representatives of Jubilee 2000 and the Okinawa Environmental Network were highly critical of the poor facilities provided in the NGO centre and the overly strict supervision by MOFA.

Conclusions

The G8 summit has provided one of many forums in which the bilateral Japan–UK relationship has been managed on both the governmental and societal level, not only in the economic sphere – the summit's original remit – but also very much in the political sphere. As the G8 is an institution that emphasizes the role of the executive head, the success/failure and style of both countries' participation in the summit process has been partly conditional on the personality of the individual prime minister. As a result, through the inclusion of the issue of debt relief, Blair was able to stamp his personal seal on the three-day G8 summit held in July 2005 at Gleneagles in Scotland.

Japan's turn to host the G8 summit will come in 2008 and an educated guess based on the previous summit venue of Okinawa and the trend towards hosting summits away from the capital would point to Hokkaidō as the most likely venue. However, the only certainty by then is that Koizumi will no longer be representing Japan. Whether he will be replaced by an equally popular and assertive summit attendee and how this will affect Japan's performance and its relations with the UK is a question for the future.

Chapter 13

THE PRESSURE OF THE PAST ON THE ANGLO-JAPANESE RELATIONSHIP

Nobuko Margaret Kosuge

> Although geographically far apart, our two countries are similar in many ways. ... I am also glad to see some of our Japanese friends here today. I know that they pride themselves on knowing Britain and its ways sometimes even better than the British do themselves. But in the same spirit of bridging the cultural divide, let me begin by throwing some light on one of those cultural differences which may puzzle even those who are familiar with British ways.
>
> (Excerpt from speech by Foreign Secretary Robin Cook to the FT conference 'Japan Now', London, 29 June 2000)

Today it is thought that to resolve international business and commercial problems amicably it is necessary to promote types of 'dialogue' that are based on specific 'rules', which, in turn, reflect a mutual regard for 'culture'. Just as almost everybody will agree with the proposition that political and economic relations have many interactive aspects, it seems obvious to most people who study the question that 'trade problems' often arise in part because of differences in culture and sets of values. I shall address certain aspects of Japan–UK political and economic relations in the postwar period from the point of view that the two peoples had very different perspectives on their relationship. This is of great importance when we try to analyse certain problems and contradictions about how Japanese and Britons regarded their mutual relations during the latter half of the twentieth century.[1]

What the words 'Japan–UK relations' or 'Anglo–Japanese relations' bring to mind in the postwar years has tended to be rather different depending on whether one is a citizen of the UK or of Japan. Generally speaking, postwar Japanese people cherish a certain rather hard to define family-like feeling towards the people of the United Kingdom, who similarly live on an island and, like the Japanese, have a monarchy with a long history and tradition. And, because of this familial feeling, the Japanese have tended to feel a sense of 'trust', again often hard to define in concrete terms. These feelings of familiarity and trust towards the British, arising from what the Japanese have seen as similarities between the two countries, have played a central role in the way the Japanese have built up their image of postwar Japan–UK relations.

Some Japanese have even been tempted to give priority to images of Britain as a fellow one-time imperialist state that could be seen as an historical accomplice in the overseas imperialism of years past. This sort of image is linked, even today, to that of the 'honeymoon age' of the Anglo–Japanese alliance (1902–22), which some see as a sort of touchstone to which relations between the two countries might well, even today, hearken back. On the other hand, the topography of postwar British images of Japan has tended to be framed by two bitter past experiences, namely the Japanese trade and business practices in the 1930s that ultimately contributed to the failure of prewar bilateral relations, and the iniquitous betrayal of humanitarian principles that was seen in the mistreatment of British prisoners by Japanese army personnel during the war.[2]

In 1990 Louis Allen argued that it was the second of these that had the most impact on the British, for he claimed that, at a time when the Japanese were enjoying economic prosperity, economic frictions were not central to Anglo–Japanese relations. Allen warned that because of the bitter past, the British people were liable to continue to reconstruct a stereotype of the Japanese as 'cold-blooded and cruel'.[3] Certainly, the mistreatment by the Japanese of British POWs and civilian internees during the Second World War has caused strains in Anglo–Japanese relations, and the war memories have sometimes kept the British public at a 'psychological distance' from Japan.[4]

Yet, as Peter Lowe points out above, economic experiences weighed heavily and negatively on Anglo–Japanese relations, which was made clear by Britain's attitudes and priorities surrounding the postwar occupation of Japan (1945–52). Similarly, Yōichi Kibata notes that Britain took relatively little interest in Japan's societal reconstruction in the postwar period, and instead concentrated primarily on economic issues.[5] Britain was an exception in that British public opinion exhibited less interest in the occupation or peace treaty than it did in the threat posed by economic competition from Japanese industries. This formerly defensive position had softened somewhat by 1947, but as Japan demilitarized the British textile industry again became increasingly suspicious and wary of imminent economic rivalry with Japan. By 1949 Britain's textile industry had gone so far as to express the view that some Japanese military industries should be revived, and it was strongly opposed to occupied Japan's entry to the international treaty on wheat. This opposition was designed to prevent Japan's entry into the General Agreement on Tariffs and Trade (GATT).[6] Japan's successful adherence to the international treaty on wheat could set a precedent, facilitating Japan's participation in GATT before its conclusion of a peace treaty - or so influential members of Britain's textile industry feared. The draft of the peace treaty made by several British ministries led by the British Foreign Office in the spring of 1951 revealed a continuing strong opposition to Japan's entry into GATT on the part of the Ministry of Trade. In the same draft, the authors deleted, at the ministry's request, the sections endorsing Japan's entry into the UN and other international institutions. To be sure, this sort of protectionist policy advocated by the British industrial sector did not go uncriticized in Britain. Nonetheless, such a protectionist stance was in stark contrast to, and clashed with, the non-discriminatory *laissez-faire* policies endorsed by the United States, which among other things expressed moral qualms about privileges and profits tied to 'colonialism'.

While the main, direct reason for Britain's opposition to Japan's entry into GATT was the impossible prospect of both securing new export markets for the British Commonwealth and protecting British industries under the new international economic regime, another reason - the liability of 'the past', as a pretext or otherwise - loomed in the background. Ironically, Britain had endorsed a completely opposite position earlier when it welcomed Meiji Japan's entry into the international economic system in the late nineteenth century. At the outset of the twentieth century, Britain showed considerable pride in introducing Japan to the international community as its new Asian partner - the Japan that had treated enemy POWs in a commendable fashion in the Russo-Japanese war of 1904–5. By contrast, in the post-Second World War period, Britain was in the position of trying to guard international institutions such as GATT against Japan.

When examining the impact of 'the past' on postwar Anglo-Japanese economic relations, one must heed the mounting precedence of 'perception' over current reality. In postwar Britain, various economic discourses on Japan touched on the Anglo-Japanese trade wars of the 1930s and the Japanese army's infringements of international law during the Second World War. Particularly, the bitter legacy from the war became the historical basis - under circumstances in which the majority of UK citizens really knew very little about Japan - for the sorts of biases and stereotypes through which Japan was identified as a 'menace' and the Japanese as 'cruel and inhuman aliens'. As John Weste points out, while the lack of any Japanese military threat has made it relatively easier to focus on economic relations and the development of Anglo-Japanese business partnerships, the threat from the white collar of the *sarariman* (salary man) replaced the leggings of the Imperial Army, and the calculator replaced the threat from the rifle in the 1950s, particularly in Britain, and this view was further reinforced through the 1960s and into the 1980s.[7] Indeed, reflected by 'the historical basis', perceptions of unfair competition and economic rivalry were pervasive in Britain after the 1970s, spurred on by Japanese economic competition and not necessarily much reduced, at least initially, by Japanese investments.[8]

In Japan, little attention was given to the issue of 'Western, white' allied prisoners until the end of the 1980s. 'Anglo-Japanese reconciliation' was not always a well-accepted subject and, indeed, even at the end of the 1990s, a relative lack of interest was shown in British war prisoners compared with other related historical matters concerning Asian neighbours like China. Many Japanese were still obsessed with their premature 'post-colonial' points of views: they tended to feel that if they confessed to past wrong doings, reciprocal confessions would be made by the British.

In 1954, as Prime Minister Yoshida Shigeru was preparing to make a visit to the UK, a British businessman with whom he was on familiar terms came to see him and, 'as a friend's opinion', told him that his view of Japan-UK relations dated from 'the days of the Anglo-Japanese Alliance and [was] therefore a little stale'. Yoshida was then advised by his friend that it would be good to take along on his trip some Japanese who had recently worked in Britain. Following this friend's advice, Yoshida took Kōichirō Asakai, who had recently served as Japan's plenipotentiary minister in London. Yoshida gave a speech before a session of the Inter-Parliamentary Union (IPU) at the invitation of the British parliament, which was hosting the IPU that year. He called for British-Japanese collaboration against the communist threat and also recalled the earlier days of cooperation under the Anglo-Japanese Alliance. In his memoirs, Asakai recalls that, immediately upon finishing this 20-minute address:

> One after the other, about ten aggressively critical comments and questions – quite different in tone from Yoshida's just stated discussion of Japan–UK cooperation – flew up from the floor. We heard, for example things like: 'If communism is so frightening, why do you not improve Japanese labour conditions?' or 'Workers in Japan's textile industry are being made to work under inhuman conditions', or 'When do you plan to take care of the problem of compensating British war prisoners?' In attendance there were several parliamentarians known to be both well acquainted with and well disposed towards Japan, but perhaps they felt under some special pressure due to the general atmosphere in the hall and there were no verbal gestures of support for Japan. And perhaps it was not to be unexpected that even Yoshida-san lost some of his composure and sullenly refused to look his interlocutors in the face. Finally he became truly angered – and turned aside, saying to me: 'You make some appropriate reply to these impolite questions.'[9]

It was Prime Minister Churchill who managed to bring Yoshida's good spirits back and 'fully restored his amicable feelings toward Britain'. A day or two after the IPU event, Churchill hosted an evening banquet at 10 Downing Street at which Yoshida was the honoured guest. He spoke in a relaxed way about such things as the 'cohesiveness' of English trade unions and reminisced about the old days of the Anglo-Japanese Alliance. Prime Minister Yoshida was 'definitely delighted, and immediately discarded the unpleasant feelings which had eventuated from his address before the parliamentarians'.[10]

Behind the backward-looking nostalgia many people in Japan, including Yoshida, have felt for the 'honeymoon period' of the old Anglo-Japanese Alliance, one can detect some convoluted sentiments of latent anxiety – the anxiety a defeated country with few natural resources might experience in the postwar environment given the weakness of its negotiating position in bilateral relationships and its feeble 'ability to retaliate' in the event of being subjected to unfair treatment by another nation. For the whole period between the end of the war and the end of the twentieth century, Japanese people have felt and expressed amity towards Britain that is unparalleled in the way they regard any of the other former enemy nations.

The postwar Japanese substantially revised, generally for the better, their prewar and wartime images of the United States, but this was greatly helped along by the fact that the United States, in the postwar period, took the initiative in altering – admittedly in part because of what was thought to be strategic necessity – its former attitudes towards Japan.[11] This one-time enemy nation, separated from Japan by the expanse of the Pacific Ocean, systematically undertook to overcome, within the matrix of the 'American dream' and the cold war, the aversion and fear that had earlier been directed towards Japan. Nonetheless, throughout the period up to the present most Japanese have been unable to consider their pre-eminent American alliance partner as having a pattern of society or political organization to which they could comfortably liken themselves in the future.

Looking at the various countries of Europe, the Japanese have been quite sensitive to the 'Japan fear syndrome' that has lurked in many European minds. Here, the 'fellow defeated nation' Germany, which relatively early on wished to recognize Japan's entry into GATT and which, in the eyes of two astute Japanese observers, 'was unusual in not having prejudices towards Japan', should be taken as an exception. The country most strongly opposed to Japan entering GATT was France, but France did not do much 'real damage'. The real problem was that Britain, which should have been Japan's most important partner in trade with Europe, 'seemed to have, with respect to Japan, a skewed way of thinking – and had not forgotten wartime animosities – and so was hard to deal with'.[12]

Emperor Hirohito's state visit to the UK in October 1971 turned out to be an ominous example for the Japanese. At the time of the imperial visit, Lord Mountbatten behaved quite differently from Churchill, who had known how to please people from Japan; Mountbatten removed his scheduled meeting with the Emperor from his list of engagements.[13] Some newspapers reported that this act won him huge acclaim and raised his status among the general public.[14] The *Daily Express* went so far as to allege in its editorial that the imperial visit was neatly tied up with a Japanese 'new economic policy ... to seek to make Western Europe a substitute market for America,' and was 'an insult to the living and the dead who suffered from a regime over which he has presided', slating Hirohito as the 'Super-God' who lost his divinity and is now the 'Super-Salesman'.[15] The *Guardian* commented after the imperial visit:

> Many members of the Far Eastern Prisoners of War Associations would have found it easier to make their final reconciliation with the present Emperor's successor. It is even debatable, however, whether reconciliation is the right term. Hitler's Germany was a greater menace to the civilized world than Tōjō's Japan, but in the history of Europe it is even now, so soon after the event, beginning

> to look like an aberration. Previous links with Germany could, after an interval, be taken up again, and admiration for the good things that German had bestowed on Europe could be allowed to return. Moreover, Germany has shown remorse. Japan has changed direction, but is there any sadness about the barbarities it penetrated during the military occupation of much of Asia?[16]

The newspaper continued:

> Reconciliation, an idea which for Europe is heavily endowed with 2000 years of significance, may, to a Japanese, be inappropriate. Cultural differences, as any British businessman in Tokyo will testify, are important in any dealing with the Japanese. Japan, under the American occupation, has made great attempts to understand Western values while not necessarily accepting them. There has been less occasion for the West to try to understand Japan, although [its] qualities ... have turned that country in so short a time into one of the most formidable industrial nations.[17]

Somebody - who was never identified - uprooted a memorial tree that Emperor Hirohito had planted during the imperial visit to Britain. However, a letter from Manchester to the editor of the *Asahi Evening News* explained that many British people shared a 'sense of disgrace and shame at the senseless and insulting act of chopping down a tree planted as an expression for friendship'.[18]

Even while it is true that after the 1970s many in Britain felt a certain hesitation about seeing Japan as a special partner or trustworthy collaborator, the sentiment gradually grew that Japan must be 'better understood'. Japan was physically and psychologically distant, and its language and social behaviour were quite different from ours. Thus, if one were to hope for successful personal contacts between the people of the two countries, some unusual effort would be required, of rather a different kind from our relations with the people of America or other countries of Europe. In 1973 a report from the Fabian Society on the British Labour Party's policy towards Japan argued that what was now important was to refrain from needlessly provoking in Japan feelings of alienation or discrimination and, in ways that would not be taken amiss, to show a great deal of sincere interest - especially at a time when the Japanese could be expected to feel frustration and a sense of isolation as a result of the so-called 'Nixon shocks' - in constructing normal Japan-Europe economic relations.[19]

Nonetheless, during the period when Japan's direct investments in Britain were getting well under way, many British people still tended to have negative feelings towards the Japanese because of the 'bitter past', despite the beginnings of widespread and unalloyed interest in Japan and more frequent discussion of the importance of spreading mutual knowledge, including critical assessments of one another's lands.[20] And it was only after the beginning of the 1970s that the Japanese gradually began to notice how their feelings towards Britain had been rather uncritical and often a case of 'unrequited love', or that substantial numbers of Japanese began to realize how, 'even more so than in France', it was especially in Britain where there might be great contrasts in the way Japan was perceived as between 'the ordinary masses' of people – whose feelings towards Japan could appear somehow bent out of shape or apt to be 'overly biased' – and the better educated stratum of society.[21]

Turning back on the Emperor's trip to European countries in 1971, while the Foreign Office reasoned that the Anglo–Japanese partnership had been improving steadily over the years and an imperial visit would set the seal on such progress,[22] what it disclosed in reality was something that the Japanese public had forgotten: their monarch was, in the foreigners' eyes, inescapably associated with war memories and questions of war guilt.

Publicizing the Emperor's own personal experiences of the leisurely visit of several weeks he had made to Britain when he was Crown Prince in 1921 and his personal respect for the British constitution served to create in Japan (and in America) the image of a 'peace-loving, constitution-observing emperor' whose wish for peace had earlier often been hampered by the jingoists and chauvinists who surrounded him. The shared elements of constitutional monarchy were often used domestically as a vehicle for spreading the Emperor's new postwar image. The Japanese public was encouraged to believe that the continuation of a very ceremonial monarchy in their postwar democracy was an entirely natural process deriving from an ancient history, as in Britain. However, the postwar image of the Emperor became confused in Japan after his visit to Europe in 1971 and his encounters with 'ordinary' European citizens. It is even possible to say that subsequent debates by some Japanese intellectuals on the Emperor's 'war responsibility' and Emperor Hirohito's own response in the mid-1970s were initially motivated by what happened during the visits to Europe, and particularly to Britain, in 1971.

Later, when Emperor Hirohito lay in bed during his final illness, there were dozens of critical statements in the British (and other countries') mass media about the dying emperor. This was especially true of the British tabloid newspapers, which frequently referred to what took place during the war.[23] As far as these tabloid articles were concerned, this criticism was unexpected by a Japanese public that had embraced a romantic myth of its own monarch: Britain and Japan, although geographically far apart, were psychologically close because of their various similarities, the most essential and transcendental among these being the existence of constitutional monarchies 'with the longest historical traditions' in both countries. What the tabloids refused to acknowledge was this image that the Japanese public held of themselves. They ignored the way the Japanese monarchy had been encouraged by the US occupation authorities to recast itself into the same mould as the British monarchy.[24]

In 1988–89, it seemed likely that the British tabloid comments on Emperor Hirohito would have the same effect. In reality, the voices from Europe had a rather different impact on the Japanese public. Many Japanese had been embarrassed by the excesses of the Japanese mass media, which went on disseminating information about Emperor Hirohito's state of health almost every minute. It is true, too, that critical voices from Asian countries against this totalitarian-like phenomenon in the Japanese media were making more Japanese think about Japan's past aggressions and the oppression earlier inflicted upon neighbours. Yet, for those who felt that both Britain and Japan had been 'guilty' of their respective colonial rules over Asian nations, the British tabloid comments, the most sensational among the foreign commentary of the period leading up to and after the emperor's death, now seemed blind to Britain's own past. The movement in Japan to look squarely at the history of the perpetration of harm on others, which may be said to have reached a certain peak in the late 1980s and 1990s, tended to be largely carried forward by the momentum of feelings of surprise and anger towards revelations about specific types of shocking wartime misdeeds like the issue of the so-called '*jugun ianfu*' (women mainly from Korea and other Asian countries who were forced into sexual slavery to service Japanese soldiers), while the consciousness of large numbers of Japanese regarding the overall context of the war itself continued to be vague. In approaching the task of squarely facing up to past Japanese misdeeds that caused harm to others, there was also a tendency to see the misdeeds as similar to criminal actions that could be found in the past histories of the European and American allies. Therefore, many of those who have had the keenest interest in elucidating Japan's responsibilities for perpetrating harm on others in the past have put much effort into looking at the issue in global terms.

On the other hand, to those Japanese who had embraced romantic ideas about royal 'similarity', the tabloid articles were an eye-opening encounter with the British 'masses' at the very end of the Shōwa period. A Japanese journalist in London lamented that the statements made by the *Sun* and *Daily Star* were 'too exaggerated and sensational to be translated into the Japanese language'. The feelings expressed by many British ex-POWs as well as the street demonstrations irritated those Japanese whose complacent image of 'Igrisu' (England, and by extension the UK) had been largely influenced by a set of royal myths and articles from publications like *The Times*.

Five weeks before the Emperor's death in 1989, in the House of Commons more than 200 MPs supported a motion for reparations payable to ex-POWs of the Japanese. The motion stressed that 'Anglo-Japanese relations will not fully blossom until the wrongs done during the Second World War to Allied prisoners are fully accepted by the Japanese government and due reparation made.'[25] In the following years, through various parliamentary debates, the British government was often urged to support the compensation claimants, and finally, in the years 1994–98, non-governmental actors from the Netherlands, Britain, the USA, Australia and New Zealand initiated class-action lawsuits against the Japanese government. The claimants strongly appealed to their governments to demand from Tokyo a sincere, heartfelt apology for the wrongs done during the war. As far as compensation was concerned, the attitude taken by the British government was similar to the Japanese, who were reluctant to pay further reparations to the war victims. The authorities continued to state that the question of compensation had been legally settled by Articles 14 and 16 of the 1951 peace treaty.

For the Japanese diplomats who would be paving a path for reconciliation with British ex-POWs, what was most fortunate was that they could expect some advice and even voluntary cooperation from private sources. Already in 1984 a private veterans exchange visit had been organized between the Burma Campaign Fellowship Group, London (the forerunner of the Burma Campaign Society), and some volunteers from the All Japan Burma Veterans Association (AJBVA), Tokyo. The Japanese ex-soldiers sensed that their former enemies 'had never quite forgiven' their own government 'for not acknowledging VJ day in the way in which they acknowledged VE day'.[26] They tried to demonstrate their 'welcome' towards the British, who some felt had 'animosity to Japan hinted at on their faces'.[27] Shūchirō Yoshino, the vice-chairman of the AJBVA, related that in 1989 approximately 1000 Japanese Burma veterans participated in the Tokyo reception to welcome 11 British visitors to

Japan. According to Yoshino, inside the reception hall, an enormous handclap showed appreciation for the British guests, who were immediately besieged by all the Japanese attendants. 'Then I realized how our royal families feel when they are coming out among the public,' one of the British visitors reflected later on his pilgrimage to Japan.

Still, the failure to establish a private foundation financed by Japanese companies seemed to be evidence of a lack of concern by ordinary Japanese about the British ex-POW issue. A possible project was initially discussed between the British and Japanese prime ministers, John Major and Morihiro Hosokawa, in September 1993 when the former visited Japan. Major informed Hosokawa that he was examining whether non-governmental measures would assist in solving the problem and, based on the latter's agreement, Sir Kit McMahon, former deputy governor of the Bank of England, was appointed chairman of a committee to establish a foundation that might provide practical help to British ex-POWs. However, when McMahon visited Tokyo in November 1994 to test reactions, what became clear was that the Japanese private sector was uniformly negative to the project the British government had proposed. McMahon could only conclude that this kind of approach was unlikely to succeed.[28]

Voices demanding an apology and compensation from the Japanese were getting more vigorous. In 1995, the fiftieth anniversary of the end of the war, public opinion in Britain seemed to be severely critical of Japan and its nationals in this regard. In London, some younger Japanese travellers, without direct experience or even knowledge of the past between their country and Britain, may have been delighted with the fireworks shot off to celebrate the victory of half a century ago; yet some Japanese living in Britain felt obliged to guard their self-control in public.[29]

Meanwhile, Tomiichi Murayama, then prime minister, issued a statement expressing deep remorse and apology to the victims of the Japanese, including the former POWs of the Western allies. As part of an effort to 'face up to the facts of history', he had already announced in 1994 a ten-year, £650 million reconciliation programme called 'The Peace and Friendship Initiative', which would include exchange visits, historical research and scholarships for grandchildren of people killed or imprisoned during the war to attend Japanese schools. The main focus of the initiative was Asian neighbours, but the Western allies were also invited to take part, and £800,000 was offered for Britain in 1998. Sir Alistair Goodlad, a government minister, emphasized just after the fiftieth anniversary of VE Day that the initiative should not be dismissed because it 'provides evidence that the Japanese government are sensitive to the need to respond to the strong feelings in the country'.[30]

It was after the fiftieth anniversary of the war's end that the British government came out with a policy of encouraging 'all initiatives which promote reconciliation and recognize the sacrifices made by former prisoners of war'.[31] Tokyo reminded the British that the war criminals had already been executed or punished by the war crimes courts after the war, and expressed 'a strong desire to promote reconciliation with former prisoners of war', but reiterated that the government was not prepared to reopen the peace treaty.

In May 1998, Emperor Akihito's state visit to Britain took place. The state visit should have been the highlight of the various achievements of Anglo–Japanese reconciliation made by the governments as well as those privately involved in reconciliation over the last decades. The Royal British Legion showed its concern for the reconciliation initiatives that Hashimoto offered, and Hashimoto's apology published in the *Sun* was welcomed by Prime Minister Blair as 'a sign of a blossoming friendship between Britain and its former enemy', while the prime minister also stressed Britain's trade and tourism earnings from Japan, and the Anglo–Japanese economic 'partnership worth billions'.[32] Others refused the 'reconciliation package' as a 'pathetic insult'. Blair told ex-prisoners of the Japanese that they had the right to demonstrate their protest against the Emperor in a 'dignified way' and reminded them of the huge economic links between Japan and Britain. Hundreds of ex-prisoners and their relatives turned their backs in protest to the parade welcoming the emperor.

The Japanese mass media quietly reported what happened in London during the Emperor's visit. In the words of one Japanese newspaper editorial, 'Reconciliation and mutual understanding will take time, and there will probably be cases of protest demonstrations by persons who cannot make a clean break with the past. However, the significance of any protests and the significance of the visit are quite different in importance.' The editorial concluded as follows:

> We should not avoid personal exchanges with Britain, or any country, where all kinds of thinking are freely expressed, but should rather feel that, precisely because of the fact that its national character is such, it is meaningful to deepen friendship and goodwill. Furthermore, Britain not only has strong economic ties with Japan but is a country which, as shown by its efforts to resolve the dispute in Northern Ireland, has a tradition of trying to

> resolve complex and entangled problems through reason and a forward-looking attitude. There may possibly be instances where the royal couple will be somewhat at a loss, but let us hope from our hearts that we shall see them, to the greatest extent possible, bestow the fruits of goodwill through their contacts with large numbers of people.[33]

Some Japanese intellectuals still argued that the Japanese government should give priority to winning over Asian neighbours to friendship and mutual trust with Japan, and that the current Anglo-Japanese reconciliation movement lacked such an 'Asian viewpoint'.[34] However, this issue has in fact become a core theme in the way Japanese view the war and, as a Japanese newspaper precisely pointed out, if one might say that efforts to achieve Anglo-Japanese reconciliation have been relatively successful, that is largely because the British have tried to resolve the problem 'through reason and a forward-looking attitude', not blinded by the bitterness of the past. The efforts for reconciliation made by some British veterans and former POWs of the Japanese were the consequence of such efforts to compromise and stop any chain reaction leading to further arguments.

Not long after Emperor Hirohito's state visit, the British ambassador to Japan, Stephen Gomersall, stated that the POW issue belonged to the past and had no significant impact on Anglo- Japanese relations. Interviewed by a journalist he said that 'for most British people, Japan means employment opportunities and big businesses. They regard Japan as an attractive high-tech country. While anticipating further advances in the field of economy and investment, bilateral economic relations will be strengthened in the meantime by the opening up of both countries' markets.'[35]

Thus, the prisoner of war issue was for most people a matter of the past. England's younger generation was definitely more interested in Toyota and Sony products than in the Burma–Thailand Railway. And for Japan's younger generation the soccer World Cup games were a greater and more exciting event than Emperor Akihito's visit to Great Britain in May 1998.[36] These younger members of both island countries were sure to be able to foster mutual friendship in ways vastly different from the formalized reconciliation procedures and activities of the war veterans. Examples of former war prisoners, lonely and alienated, roaming the streets in search of products not made in Japan were by now a thing of 'the past'.

Yet, just as Louis Allen warned, the 'bitter past' might, even in the future, become a breeding ground for producing or resuscitating negative British stereotypes of people in or from Japan. As the British come to have a stronger interest in Japan, it might be inevitable that more will recall - even if not from personal memory - the 'bitter past'. Certainly, we must not take the Durham University professor's warning lightly. In the future, no less than today, this 'bitter past' may be seen by the British people as a sort of inauspicious subplot within the story of the 'miraculous economic development' that a defeated country with a quite 'different' culture attained during the second half of the twentieth century. At the same time, we also remember that a careless interpretation of the 'bitter past' could, whether in Japan or in Britain, help give rise to political forces that might believe in the 'truth' only of a parochial and one-sided reading of history and, as such, could apply a brake to mutually advantageous exchanges in the fields of economics and culture.

We should continue, in both Japan and the United Kingdom, to prepare the soil from which a wide-ranging, steady and unadulterated interest in 'the other', together with the sense of trust that will come from taking the measure of one another's countries and societies in perceptive and creative ways, can be constantly nurtured. However bitter many things in the past have been, it is in fact precisely because of this past that what is most important today is to educate a younger generation of citizens who will be able to cultivate and guide to maturity what we must hope will be some very much sweeter fruits of the future.

NOTES

Chapter 1. Korekiyo Takahashi and Japan's Victory in the Russo–Japanese War, 1904–5 by *Richard J. Smethurst*

1. Gotō Shin'ichi (1977) *Takahashi Korekiyo: Nihon no Keinzu* (Takahashi Korekiyo: Japan's Keynes), Tokyo: Nihon Keizai Shinbunsha.
2. See R. Smethurst (1998) 'The self-taught bureaucrat: Takahashi Korekiyo and economic policy during the Great Depression', in J. Singleton (ed.) *Learning in likely places: varieties of apprenticeship in Japan*, Cambridge: Cambridge University Press, pp. 226–38; R. Smethurst (2000) 'Takahashi Korekiyo's economic policies in the Great Depression and their Meiji roots', in *Politics and the Economy in Pre-War Japan*, London: Suntory Centre, London School of Economics, pp. 1–24; and R. Smethurst (2002) 'Takahashi Korekiyo's fiscal policy and the rise of militarism in Japan during the Great Depression', in Bert Edstrom (ed.) *Turning points in Japanese history*, Richmond, Surrey: Japan Library, pp. 163–79.
3. Cyrus Adler (1929) *Jacob H. Schiff: his life and letters*, London: William Heinemann, 2 vols. In preparing his two-volume biography of Schiff, Adler asked Finance Minister Takahashi to provide a chapter on his dealings with Schiff during the Russo–Japanese War. Takahashi in turn passed the task on to Eigo Fukai, who had been his assistant in 1904/5, but by the early 1920s was a director of the Bank of Japan. Judging by the handwriting of the changes made in the pre-publication manuscript, I surmise that Takahashi added personal touches to Fukai's manuscript before sending it to Adler in New York. See also, Naomi Cohen (1999) *Jacob H. Schiff: a study in American Jewish leadership*, Hanover, New Hampshire, and London: Brandeis University Press; Gary Dean Best (1972) 'Financing a foreign war: Jacob H. Schiff and Japan, 1904–05', *American Jewish Historical Quarterly*, 61, pp. 313–24; A. J. Sherman (1983) 'German–Jewish bankers in world politics: the financing of the Russo–Japanese War', *Year Book*, XXVIII, Leo Baeck Institute, pp. 59–73; *Takahashi Korekiyo jiden* (Autobiography of Takahashi Korekiyo) (1976) Tokyo: Chūkō bunko, vol. 11, pp. 178–300; Techō (Diary) (22 February–17 December 1904), *Takahashi Korekiyo monjo*, 135, Tokyo: National Diet Library.
4. *Takahashi Korekiyo jiden* (1976) vol. 11, pp. 190–1.
5. Ibid., p. 192.
6. Ibid., pp. 193, 199; ING Baring Archives, Baring Journals (2001) 87: 4, 14, 19,

25, 26, 28, 30; Toshio Suzuki (1994) *Japanese government loans on the London capital market, 1870–1913*, London: Athlone Press, pp. 31, 88, 92.

7. Olive Checkland and Norio Tamaki (1997) 'Alexander Allan Shand, 1844–1930: a banker the Japanese could trust', in Ian Nish, *Biographical portraits*, vol. 11, Richmond, Surrey: Japan Library, pp. 65–78; Norio Tamaki (1995) *Japanese banking: a history 1859–1958*, Cambridge: Cambridge University Press, pp. 34–7, 95; Techō (7 April 1904); Umekichi Yoneyama (1927) *Alexander A. Shand: a friend of Nippon: interesting chapters from a banker's reminiscences*, Tokyo: Japan Times, pp. 2–10. Parr's Bank later merged with the London County and Westminster Bank, which in turn merged with National Provincial and District Banks to become NatWest -- thus Parr's papers are found in the NatWest archive.
8. *Takahashi Korekiyo jiden* (1976) vol. 11, pp. 201–2; Techō (7–18 April 1904).
9. *Takahashi Korekiyo jiden* (1976) vol. 11, p. 202.
10. Suzuki 1994; Imamura Takeo (1948) *Hyōden Takahashi Korekiyo* (A critical biography of Korekiyo Takahashi), Tokyo: Jiji Tsūshinsha, p. 67.
11. Techō (22 April and 16 December 1904). Takahashi refers to Ernest Cassel as 'Earnest Cassel' and 'Earnest Castle' or 'Casttle' at different places in his diary.
12. Techō (3 May 1904).
13. Cohen 1999, pp. 1–144.
14. Techō (3–10 May 1904). More than a year later, on 31 July 1905, Takahashi went to Buckingham Palace for his own audience with the king. Edward VII asked Takahashi how his efforts to sell war bonds had worked out. When Takahashi answered, 'The outcome was excellent and I am greatly pleased', the king replied, 'I am highly gratified'. He then went on to ask Takahashi and Japan's minister in London, Tadasu Hayashi, about the prospects for peace (*Takahashi Korekiyo jiden* 1976, vol. 11, pp. 259–61).
15. *Takahashi Korekiyo jiden* 1976, vol. 11, pp. 203–4.
16. Ibid., p. 203.
17. See, for example, Haru Matsukata Reischauer (1986) *Samurai and silk: a Japanese and American heritage*, Cambridge, Massachusetts, and London: The Belknap Press of Harvard University Press; and Ben-Ami Shillony (1991) *The Jews and the Japanese: the successful outsiders*, Rutland, Vermont and Tokyo: Charles E. Tuttle Company, pp. 147–9.
18. Cohen 1999, p. 124.
19. Ibid., p. 134.
20. I write 'apparently' because in his memoirs, written three decades later, Takahashi wrote that he first met Cassel in London in April 1904. (*Takahashi Korekiyo jiden* 1976, vol. 11, p. 194.) There is no evidence of such a meeting in Takahashi's London diary entries.
21. Anthony Allfrey (1991) *Edward VII and his Jewish court*, London: Weidenfeld & Nicolson, pp. 137–51, 215; Cohen 1999, pp. 11–12; Pat Thane (1986) 'Financiers and the British state: the case of Sir Ernest Cassel', *Business History*, XXVIII–1, January, pp. 80–99.
22. Allfrey 1991, p. 215.
23. Baring journals (2001) 87: 39, pp. 33, 34, 35, 39, 45.
24. Allfrey 1991, *Edward VII and his Jewish court*, p. 215; *Takahashi Korekiyo jiden* 1976, vol. 11, pp. 222–4.
25. Matsuo Papers, Bank of Japan Archive. I have not seen Cassel's original letter. The excerpt above is my retranslation of Takahashi's translation of

Cassel's original letter, quoted in a letter from Takahashi to the elder statesman Kaoru Inoue, written on 11 July 1905.

26. Baring Journals (2001) 87:39; Techō (12 May 1904).
27. Takeo (1948), p. 71. Again I am retranslating a letter originally written in English.
28. Schiff wrote an account of his trip to Japan, *Our Journey to Japan*, which was privately published as a surprise to Schiff in 1907. It is available at the American Jewish Archive in Cincinnati.

Chapter 2. Britain and the Japanese Economy during the First World War by *Janet Hunter*

1. M. Barnhart (1987) *Japan prepares for total war: the search for economic security 1919–1941*, Ithaca, New York: Cornell University Press; A. Best (1995) *Britain, Japan and Pearl Harbour: avoiding war in East Asia*, London: Routledge; J. Sharkey (2000) 'Economic diplomacy in Anglo–Japanese relations, 1931–41', in Ian Nish and Yōichi Kibata (eds) *History of Anglo–Japanese relations, 1600–2000*, vol. 2, *The political-diplomatic dimension, 1931–2000*, London: Ithaca Press for the Middle East Centre at St Antony's College, Oxford; H. Shimizu (1986) *Anglo–Japanese trade rivalry in the Middle East in the inter-war period*, London: Ithaca Press for the Middle East Centre at St Antony's College, Oxford.
2. On the impact of the First World War on the international economy, see C. Wrigley (2000) 'The war and the international economy', in C. Wrigley (ed.) *The First World War and the international economy*, Cheltenham: Edward Elgar.
3. Except where indicated, this account relies for Britain on K. Brown (1998) *Britain and Japan: a comparative economic and social history since 1900*, Manchester: Manchester University Press, Chapter 2; J. Lawrence (1994) 'The First World War and its aftermath', in P. Johnson (ed.) *20th century Britain: economic, social and cultural change*, London: Longman; and S. Pollard (1992) *The development of the British economy, 1914–1990*, 4th edition, London: Edward Arnold, Chapter 1. For Japan, see Kenneth Brown (2000) 'The impact of the First World War on Japan', in C. Wrigley (ed.) *The First World War and the international economy*, Cheltenham: Edward Elgar.; T. Nakamura (1971) *Economic growth in prewar Japan*, New Haven: Connecticut, Yale University Press, Chapter 1, passim; Y. Nakamura and K. Odaka (1989) 'Gaisetsu 1914–1937', in T. Nakamura and K. Odaka (eds) *Nijū kōzō*, vol. 6 of *Nihon keizai shi*, Tokyo: Iwanami Shoten; H. Takeda (1983) 'Kokusai kankyō', in 1920 Nendaishi Kenkyūkai (ed.) *Nijūnendai no Nihon shihonshugi*, Tokyo: University of Tokyo Press.
4. Between 1913 and 1920 Germany's share of world trade decreased from 13.1 per cent to 4.7 per cent, while that of the USA increased from 11.2 per cent to 21.1 per cent (Takeda 1983, p.6). The Japanese also recognized that the removal of German competition could be of lasting benefit to both Britain and Japan, as well as being morally desirable. See K. Yamasaki (1916–17) 'Resources of Japan in their relation to British commerce after the war', *Transactions and Proceedings of the Japan Society of London*, XV.
5. Nihon Tōkei Kyōkai (1988) *Nihon chōki tōkei sōran*, vol. 3, p.69.
6. Nakamura and Odaka 1989, p. 20. The figures in the source cited in note 4 suggest a slightly lower proportion, but still nearly 50 per cent.
7. *Economist*, 30 September 1916, pp. 565–6.

8. For this dispute, see *Economist*, 23 December 1916, p. 1178; 21 April 1917, p. 699; 12 May 1917, pp. 815–16.
9. F. W. Hurst (1934) *The consequences of the war to Great Britain*, London and New Haven: Oxford University Press and Yale University Press, p. 265.
10. Nihon Tōkei Kyōkai 1988, vol. 3, pp. 69, 73.
11. Ibid., p. 73.
12. The information in this section is based on data given in the Statistical Office, Customs and Excise Department 1922, vol. IV, pp. 353–61. It should be noted that these figures are not discounted for inflation and so exaggerate increases in the volume of trade. I plan to undertake more in-depth analysis of commodity trading patterns for a future article.
13. In 1913 Japan had six shipyards and had constructed a total tonnage of 51,525. By the autumn of 1918 there were 57 shipyards, which had produced 626,695 tons. See Yoshio Andō (1975) *Kindai Nihon keizai shi yōran*, Tokyo: University of Tokyo Press.
14. Oriental Economist (ed.) (1935) *Foreign trade of Japan*, Tokyo: Toyo Keizai Shinposha.
15. Takeda 1983, p. 6.
16. This situation is described in Junnosuke Inouye (1931) *Problems of the Japanese exchange, 1914–1926*, London: Macmillan, pp. 4–6.
17. Oriental Economist 1935, p. 449.
18. Quoted in the *Economist*, 26 September 1914, p. 524. Hemp and straw braids accounted for nearly 9 per cent of Japan's exports to Britain in 1914 to a yen value of over 4.5 million and Britain received nearly 0.5 million yen worth of shell buttons that year. See *The Times Japanese Supplement*, 15 July 1916, p. 18.
19. Osaka Chamber of Commerce report cited in *Board of Trade Journal*, 14 January 1915, p. 92.
20. See, for example, *Economist* of, 25 March 1916, pp. 578–80; 19 May 1917, pp. 852–3; and 29 September 1917, p. 460.
21. This was predicted very near the start of the war when it was noted that the industry was even in 1914 growing insufficiently rapidly to meet demand, and Japan was being forced to increase imports of paper. See *Board of Trade Journal*, 14 October 1915, p. 130 and 22 February 1917, p. 578; and *Economist*, 2 June 1917, p. 1030.
22. *Economist*, 27 April 1916, p. 247; 29 September 1917; 13 October 1917; 12 January 1918.
23. *Board of Trade Journal*, 14 October 1915, p. 130 and 22 February 1917, p. 578; and *Economist*, 2 June 1917, p. 1030.
24. *Economist*, 3 May 1917, p. 268.
25. *Economist*, 7 March 1918, pp. 278–9.
26. *The Times*, 3 December 1915, p. 11; model pistols and rifles were said to be proving particularly popular.
27. *Economist*, 1 March 1919, p. 368.
28. Ibid., see particularly the issues of 30 December 1916, pp. 1224–5; 12 May 1917, pp. 815–16; and 17 November 1917, p. 808.
29. *The Times*, 6 September 1917, p. 11.
30. Cited in the *Economist*, 9 June 1917, p. 1074.
31. *Board of Trade Journal*, 7 March 1918, p. 279. There was agreement over trademark protection in Japan itself, but not in third countries such as China.

32. Cited in *Board of Trade Journal*, 17 June 1920, p. 793. Crowe had been undertaking a tour of businesses in Britain to assess their approach to Japan. His report is in 'Feeling of commercial community in Britain towards Japan' (Public Record Office, FO/371/5359, F971/119/23), 26 May 1920.
33. Sharkey 2000, p. 261.
34. Quoted in Sadao Oba (1997) 'Japanese businessmen in the UK', in Ian Nish (ed.) *Britain and Japan: biographical portraits*, vol. 2, Richmond: Japan Library, p. 263.
35. *The Times*, 21 August 1918, p. 5; 22 August 1918, p. 5.
36. *Economist*, 9 August 1919, p. 234.
37. *Economist*, 16 August 1919, p. 271.
38. *Economist*, 7 February 1920, p. 263.
39. Quoted in the *Economist*, 11 August 1917, p. 211.
40. For reports in the British press of such initiatives, see, for example, *Board of Trade Journal*, 15 February 1917, p. 495, and 19 July 1917, p. 157; *Economist*, 9 September 1916, pp. 446–7; 24 March 1917, pp. 554–5; 17 November 1917, p. 808; 24 August 1918, p. 245; *The Times*, 6 September 1917, p. 11.
41. 'Eikoku oyobi sono zokuryōchi yori yunyū o hitsuyō to suru butsuhin ni kansuru chōshu sōfu no ken' ('Dispatch of intelligence received in regard to material and goods whose import from England and its dependent territories is thought necessary'), communication from Kamino of Finance Ministry to Shidehara at Ministry of Foreign Affairs, 20 November 1918, reproduced in Gaimushō (Ministry of Foreign Affairs) (1968) *Nihon Gaiko Bunsho*, vol. 1, Tokyo: Gaimusho, pp. 110–44.
42. See, for example, summary of negotiations with Britain regarding the Japan–India commercial treaty contained in Gaimushō 1968, pp. 146–7. For later disputes involving India see Osamu Ishii (2000) 'Rivalries over cotton goods markets, 1930-36', in Ian Nish and Yōichi Kibata (eds) *The history of Anglo–Japanese relations, 1600–2000*, vol. 2, *The political–diplomatic dimension, 1931–2000*, London: Macmillan Press.; and C. Wurm (1993) *Business, politics and international relations: steel, cotton and international cartels in British politics, 1924–1939*, Cambridge: Cambridge University Press.
43. Ishii 2000, p. 950.
44. *Economist*, 30 December 1916, pp. 1224–5.
45. *Economist*, 24 March 1917, pp. 554–5.
46. *Economist*, 11 August 1917, p. 211.
47. *Economist*, 22 June 1918, pp. 1047–8.
48. Horne, H. (1920) *Report of the commercial, industrial and financial situation of Japan, 1914–1919*, British Parliamentary Papers, Cmd. 912, London: Department of Overseas Trade, p. 5.
49. Crowe's report is summarized in *Board of Trade Journal*, 17 June 1920, pp. 793–4. The quotation is from p. 793.
50. *Economist*, 4 December 1915, p. 936.
51. *Board of Trade Journal*, 15 July 1915, p. 175.
52. Report cited in *Board of Trade Journal*, 16 September 1915, p. 820.
53. *Board of Trade Journal*, 28 September 1916, p. 949.
54. *Board of Trade Journal*, 18 April 1918, p. 471.
55. Horne 1920, p. 39.
56. J. Blair (1917-1918) 'The Japanese mercantile marine', *Transactions and proceedings of the Japanese Society of Britain*, XVI, p. 55.
57. There is a vast literature on 'British decline' and its causes, both at the

macro level and in respect to particular industries, especially cotton. In this chapter I do not seek to comment on these debates, but for information on some factors in Britain that have underlined Japan's ability to sustain its gains see, for example, the essays in M. B. Rose (ed.) (1991) *International competition and strategic response in the textile industry since 1870*, London: Frank Cass.

58. Quoted in *Board of Trade Journal*, 4 January 1917, p. 34.
59. See, for example, *Board of Trade Journal*, 22 January 1920, p. 109; 20 February 1920, p. 310.
60. Quoted in *Board of Trade Journal*, 17 June 1920, p. 794.
61. Horne 1920, p. 43.
62. Ibid., p. 15; Horne's report is summarized in *Board of Trade Journal* of 17 June 1920, pp. 793–4.
63. Yamasaki 1916–17, p. 78.
64. *Board of Trade Journal*, 25 January 1917, p. 269. Similar comments were made about Taiwan (Formosa). See *Board of Trade Journal*, 6 December 1917, p. 510.
65. See J. Hunter (2003) 'The Anglo-Japanese alliance and the development of the Japanese economy', in *Studies in the Anglo-Japanese alliance (1902–1923)*, STICERD International Discussion Paper, IS/03/443, London School of Economics.
66. F. W. Hurst (1934) *The consequences of the war to Great Britain*, Book III, Chapter 1, London and New Haven: Oxford University Press and Yale University Press.

Chapter 3. Great Britain and Japanese Views of the International Order in the Interwar Period by *Fumitaka Kurosawa*

1. For instance, deputy foreign secretary B. A. Butler made the following remarks as late as September 1939: 'Japan and the Soviet Union are enemies. In light of our position in India and Asia, it would be in our interest to return to an alliance with Japan. ... I do not believe that it is in our interest to alienate Japan out of solicitude towards the US and view Japan's each and every action with suspicion. I find unsatisfactory our policy towards Japan since the abrogation of the Anglo-Japanese Alliance. I believed, as I still do, that it is possible to obtain Americans' support in our fight against the dictators in the West while improving our relations with Japan' (Peter Lowe (1982) 'Great Britain and the coming of war in Asia', in Chihiro Hosoya (ed.) *Nichiei kankeishi 1917–1949* (History of Japan–UK relations 1917–1949), Tokyo: University of Tokyo Press, p. 162.
2. This chapter is informed by a number of historical studies. I was particularly inspired by the following works: Shigeru Akita and Naoto Kagotani (eds) (2001) *1930 nendai no Ajia kokusai chitsujo* (The Asian international order in the 1930s), Tokyo: Keisuisha; Sadao Asaba (1982) 'Washington kaigi to Nippon no taiō' (The Washington Conference and Japan's response) in Chihiro Hosoya (ed.) *Nichiei kankeishi* (Japan–UK relations), Tokyo: University of Tokyo Press; J. B. Crowley (1978) 'Nichiei kyōchō e no mosaku' (The search for Japanese–British cooperation), in Chihiro Hosoya and Saitō Makoto (eds) *Washinton taisei to Nichibei kankei*, Tokyo: University of Tokyo Press; Yūichi Hasegawa (ed.) (2001) *Taishōki Nippon no Amerika ninshiki* (Taishō-era Japan and perceptions of America), Tokyo: Keiō Gijuku Daigaku Shuppankai (Keiō Gijuku University Press);

Chihiro Hosoya (1978) 'Washington taisei no tokushitsu to hen'yō' (The Washington system's characteristics and transformation), in Chihiro Hosoya and Saitō Makoto (eds) *Washington taisei to Nichibei kankei*, Tokyo: University of Tokyo Press; Chihiro Hosoya (1982) 'Nippon no Eibeikan to senkanki no higashi Ajia' (Japan's perceptions of England and America, and Eastern Asia in the interwar period), in Chihiro Hosoya (ed.) *Nichiei kankeishi* (Japan–UK relations), Tokyo: University of Tokyo Press; Chihiro Hosoya (1988) *Ryōtaisenkan no Nippon gaikō* (Japanese diplomacy between the two great wars), Tokyo: Iwanami Shoten; Chihiro Hosoya and Ian Nish (eds) (2000/1), *Nichiei kōryūshi 1600–2000* (The history of Anglo-Japanese relations 1600–2000), 5 vols, Tokyo: University of Tokyo Press; Toshikazu Inoue (1994) *Kiki no naka no kyōchō gaikō* (Cooperative diplomacy amid crisis), Tokyo: Yamakawa Shuppansha; Akira Iriye (1984) 'Sōron: senkanki no rekishiteki igi' (Overview: the historical significance of the interwar period), in Akira Iriye and Tadashi Aruga (eds) *Senkanki no Nippon gaikō* (Japanese diplomacy in the interwar period), Tokyo: University of Tokyo Press; Kagotani, Naoto (2001) 'Senkanki Nippon to Ajia tsūshōmō' (Japan between the wars and Asian trade networks), in Tetsuo Furuya and Shin'ichi Yamamuro (eds), *Kindai Nippon ni okeru higashi Ajia mondai* (The East Asian problem in modern Japan), Tokyo: Yoshikawa Kōbunkan; Yōko Katō (1993) *Mosaku suru 1930 nendai* (The growing 1930s), Tokyo: Yamakawa Shuppansha; Hidekazu Kawai (1978) 'Hokubatsu e no Igirisu no taiō' (Britain's response to [China's] Northern Expedition [against the Beijing government in the mid-1920s]), in Chihiro Hosoya and Saitō Makoto (eds) *Washington taisei to Nichibei kankei*, Tokyo: University of Tokyo Press; Yōichi Kibata (1998) '1930 nendai no Nichiei kankei' (Japan–UK relations in the 1930s), *Gaikō Shiryōkanpō*, no. 12; Lowe 1982; Ian Nish (1982) 'Igirisu senkanki (1917–1937) kokusai taiseikan ni okeru Nippon' (Japan and the British views on the international system during the interwar period 1917–1937), in Chihiro Hosoya (ed.) *Nichiei kankeishi* (Japan–UK relations), Tokyo: University of Tokyo Press; Tetsuya Sakai (1993) 'Eibei kyōchō to Nitchū teikei' (UK–US cooperation and Japan–China collaboration), in Kindai Nippon Kenkyūkai (Society for the Study of Modern Japan) (ed.) *Kyōchō seisaku no genkai: Nichibei kankei shi 1905–1960* (The limits of a cooperative policy: the history of Japan–US relations 1905–1960), Tokyo: Yamakawa Shuppansha; Katsumi Usui (1982) 'Nippon no taiei imēji to taiheiyō sensō' (Japanese Images of Britain and the Pacific War), in Chihiro Hosoya (ed.) *Nichiei kankeishi* (Japan–UK relations), Tokyo: University of Tokyo Press; Katsumi Usui (1982) 'Satō gaikō to Nitchū kankei' (The Satō diplomacy and Japan–China relations), in Chihiro Hosoya (ed.) *Nichiei kankeishi* (Japan–UK relations), Tokyo: University of Tokyo Press.

3. Statement by Nobuaki Makino before the Emergency Foreign Policy Research Commission, 8 December 1918. See Tatsuo Kobayashi (ed.) (1966) *Diaries of Miyoji Itō, Suiusō nikki* (Diary kept by Makino), Tokyo: Hara Shobō, p. 335.
4. Iriye 1984, p.18.
5. Iriye 1984, p. 13.
6. Kobayashi 1966, pp. 334–5. Makino made this remark before the Emergency Foreign Policy Research Commission before leaving for the Paris Peace Conference.
7. Tsuyoshi Inukai, president of the Rikken Kokumintō Party and a member of

the Emergency Foreign Policy Research Commission, understood Makino's aforementioned remark as criticism of the 'expansionist' policy Japan had practised. See Kobayashi 1966, pp. 336–7, 340.

8. Makino's statement before the Emergency Foreign Policy Research Commission, 2 December 1918. Kobayashi 1966, pp. 326–7.
9. Shidehara Peace Foundation (ed.), 1955, Shidehara Kijūrō, Tokyo: Shidehara Heiwa Zaidan, pp. 259, 263.
10. Asaba 1982, p. 55. See also Hosoya 1978.
11. Shidehara Peace Foundation (ed.) (1955) *Shidehara Kijuro*, Tokyo: Shidehara Heiwa Zaidan, p. 259.
12. Tobe, Ryōichi (2001) 'Ugaki Kazushige no Amerika ninshiki' (Kazushige Ugaki's views of America), in Yūichi Hasegawa (ed.), *Taishōki nippon no Amerika ninshiki*, Tokyo: Keiō Gijuku Daigaku Shuppankai.
13. Hara, Takashi (Kei) (1921) 'Kōkyū heiwa no senketsu kōan: Washinton kaigi ni saishite Nippon kokumin no sekaikan o nobu' (A top-priority plan for permanent peace: expressing the Japanese people's worldview on the occasion of the Washington Conference), *Gaikō Jihō*, no. 34, 15 September, pp. 32–44; Asaba 1982, p. 40.
14. For this point, see Hosoya 1982.
15. Shōji, Jun'ichirō, 'Konoe Fumimaro no taibeikan' (Fumimaro Konoe's Views of the United States), in Yūichi Hasegawa (ed.), *Taishōki Nippon no Amerika ninshiki* (Taishō-era Japan and perceptions of America), Tokyo: Keiō Gijuku Daigaku Shuppankai (Keiō Gijuku University Press).
16. Iriye 1984, p. 10.
17. Asaba 1982, p. 51.
18. Toyohiko Yosihida (Major-General) (1919) 'Kōgyō dōin to busshi to no kankei' ('The relationship between industrial mobilization and commodities'), *Kaikōsha kiji*, no. 541, supplement, September, p. 1. *Kaikōsha kiji* is the internal organ of Kaikōsha, the research and fraternal organization of army generals and officers. As a primary source, it does not directly bear on the policy making process but it is useful in reconstructing the general milieu in which army generals articulated their ideas and concerns among themselves.
19. For the impact of the First World War on the Japanese army, especially its views on total war preparedness and the free trade versus autarky dilemma, see Fumitaka Kurosawa (2000) *Taisenkanki no Nippon rikugun* (The Japanese army between the wars), Tokyo: Misuzu Shobō. I have also written about these questions in Fumitaka Kurosawa (1993) 'A prelude to disaster', in *Beginnings of the Soviet–German and the US–Japanese war and 50 years after*, Tokyo: Sophia University, pp. 19–36; and Fumitaka Kurosawa (1999) 'Das System von 1940 und das Problem der politischen Führung in Japan' (The system of 1940 and the problem of political leadership in Japan), *Zeitschrift für Geshichtswissenshaft*, Berlin, pp. 130–52.
20. Rinji Gunji Chōsa Iin (Emergency Military Affairs Research Commission) (1920) *Kokka sōdōin ni kansuru iken* (Opinions on National Total Mobilization), pp. 55–6. This report was written by Major Tetsuzan Nagata, a member of the Special Committee. He was assassinated by his opponents within the army in 1935.
21. Hisakazu Tanaka (First Lieutenant) (1920) 'Taiheiyō ni okeru teikoku no shōrai' (The future of the [Japanese] Empire in the Pacific Ocean), *Kaikōsha kiji*, no.546, supplement, February, pp. 2, 42–3.
22. Ibid., p. 2.

23. Colonel Kōhei Kashii (1925) 'Nichidoku kokujō no hikaku' (A comparison of the national situations in Japan and Germany), *Kaikōsha kiji*, no. 605, supplement, February, p.9.
24. Department of the Chief of the Imperial General Staff [Kuniaki Koiso] (ed.) (1917) *Teikoku kokubō shigen* (Resources for the empire's national defence), pp. 9, 12, 19, 93–4, 209, 219, 269, 271.
25. Rinji Gunji Chōsa Iin (Emergency Military Affairs Research Commission) (1918) *Kōsen shokoku no rikugun ni tsuite* (Report on the armies of the countries taking part in the war), p. 57.
26. Rinji Gunji Chōsa Iin (1919) 'Doitsu kuppuku no gen'in' (The reasons for Germany's surrender), *Kaikōsha kiji*, no. 537, supplement, May, p. 16.
27. Kawai 1978, p. 157.
28. For this point, see Hosoya 1978 p. 19; and Hosoya 1982, p. 10.
29. For this point, see Hosoya 1978, pp. 24–32; and Hosoya 1982, pp. 10–13.
30. For this point, see Kurosawa 2000, Chapter 7.
31. In this regard, I agree with Anthony Best's following proposition: 'The idea of achieving Japanese dominance over East Asia did not ... mean that the Gaimushō wished to evict Britain completely, as there was a belief that a British financial and commercial presence in the region could be useful as long as Britain did not attempt to sow division between Japan and China. The problem was obviously how to get Britain to accept this diminished role for itself and recognize Japan's regional pre-eminence.' See Anthony Best (2000a) 'Taiketsu e no michi' (The road toward confrontation), in *Nichiei Kōryūshi* (The history of Anglo–Japanese relations, 1600–2000), vol. 2, p. 34. For an English translation, see Best (2000b) 'The road to Anglo–Japanese confrontation, 1931–41', in I. Nish and Y. Kibata (eds.), *The history of Anglo–Japanese relations, 1600–2000*, vol. 2, *The political-diplomatic dimension, 1931–2000*, London: Macmillan.
32. Inoue 1994, p. 286.

Chapter 4. Britain and the World Engineering Congress: Tokyo 1929 by *Christopher Madeley*

Acknowledgements: I would like to thank Chaucer College Canterbury for its support in the preparation of this chapter. In addition, I would like to thank the institutions, institutes and other professional bodies that helped me in the search for records of their members' participation in and reactions to the World Engineering Congress, notably the Institution of Civil Engineers. The staff of the Kelvin Smith Library, Case Western Reserve University kindly supplied information from the Fred H. Colvin Collection in their Department of Special Collections. Bedfordshire and Luton Archives and Records Service were similarly helpful with regard to the Allen Company archives. The major source of information concerning the World Engineering Congress is the published Proceedings of the Congress. British preparations for, participation in and reactions to the Congress are documented in File BT60/17/1 World Engineering Congress Japan 1929: representation of Great Britain at, held at the Public Record Office, London. The transactions, proceedings, journals and other records of participating British institutions, institutes and other professional bodies contain further information.

1. Ayako Hotta-Lister (1999) *The Japan–British Exhibition of 1910: gateway to the island empire of the Far East*, Richmond, Surrey: Japan Library Curzon Press.

2. Hotta-Lister 1999.
3. World Engineering Congress (1931) *World Engineering Congress Tokyo 1929: Proceedings*, vol. 1, Tokyo: World Engineering Congress.
4. *Journal of the Institute of Fuel*, volume 2, 1929, London: Institute of Fuel.
5. Andrew Cobbing (1998) *The Japanese discovery of Victorian Britain: early travel encounters in the far west*, Richmond, Surrey: Japan Library Curzon Press.
6. BT60/17/1. Board of Trade papers, Public Record Office.
7. Richard W. Allen (1930a) 'World tour: September 1929–January 1930', *The Queen's Engineering Works Magazine*, Bedford: W. H. Allen Sons & Company Limited.
8. World Engineering Congress 1931.
9. World Engineering Congress 1931.
10. Sir John Tilley (1942) *London to Tokyo*, London: Hutchinson & Company.
11. Embree John F. (1946) *A Japanese village: Suye Mura*, London: Kegan Paul, Trench, Trubner.
12. Embree 1946.
13. BT60/17/1.
14. BT60/17/1.
15. *The Times*, 22 December 1928.
16. Ibid.
17. BT60/17/1.
18. H. J. Jones (1980) *Live machines: hired foreigners and Meiji Japan*, Tenterden, Kent: Paul Norbury Publications.
19. Janet Hunter and Shinya Sugiyama (2002b) 'Economic relations in historical perspective', in Chihiro Hosoya and Ian Nish (eds) *The history of Anglo–Japanese relations 1600–2000*, vol. IV, *Economic and business relations*, Houndmills: Palgrave.
20. Ian Ruxton (1998) 'Britain 17 August–16 December 1872: the Mission's aims, objectives and results', in Ian Nish (ed.) *The Iwakura Mission in America and Europe: a new assessment*, Richmond, Surrey: Japan Library Curzon Press.
21. Hunter and Sugiyama 2002b.
22. Oriental Economist 1935.
23. Kozo Yamamura (1986) 'Japan's deus ex machina: Western technology in the 1920s', *Journal of Japanese Studies*, vol. 12, no. 1.
24. Wilkins, Mira (1974) *The maturing of multinational enterprise: American business abroad from 1914 to 1970*, Cambridge, Massachusetts: Harvard University Press.
25. *Engineering* (1929) London: Charles Robert Johnson, 10 May.
26. BT60/17/1.
27. BT60/17/1.
28. BT60/17/1.
29. World Engineering Congress 1931, vol. I
30. World Engineering Congress 1931, vol. IX.
31. World Engineering Congress 1931, vol. VII.
32. World Engineering Congress 1931, vol. XVIII.
33. World Engineering Congress 1931, vol. I.
34. Ibid.
35. *Japan Times and Mail*, 6 November 1929.
36. World Engineering Congress 1931, vol. I.
37. *The Times*, 8 November 1929.
38. World Engineering Congress 1931, vol. I.
39. Ibid.

40. Ibid.
41. Richard W. Allen (1930b) 'World Engineering Congress, Tokyo: October–November 1929', *The Queen's Engineering Works Magazine*, Bedford: W. H. Allen Sons & Company Limited.
42. BT60/17/1.
43. Ibid.
44. Ibid.
45. *Transactions of the Institute of Marine Engineers*, vol. 42, London: Institute of Marine Engineers, now Institute of Marine Engineering, Science and Technology, 1930.
46. Ibid.
47. Ibid.
48. Ibid.
49. Ibid.
50. BT60/17/1.
51. Ibid.
52. Ibid.
53. See Allen 1930b.
54. Michael R. Lane (1995) *The story of Queen's Engineering Works Bedford: a history of W. H. Allen Sons and Company Limited*, London: Unicorn Press.
55. 'Visit of Japanese engineers to the Queen's Engineering Works', in *The Queen's Engineering Works Magazine*, Bedford: W. H. Allen Sons & Company Limited, 1918.
56. *Engineering* (1929) vol. 128, London: Charles Robert Johnson.
57. Ibid.
58. Ibid.
59. *Engineering* (1930) vol. 129, London: Charles Robert Johnson.
60. *Engineering* (1929) vol. 128, London: Charles Robert Johnson.
61. *Engineering* (1930) vol. 129, London: Charles Robert Johnson.
62. *American Machinist* (1930) vols 72 and 73, New York: McGraw-Hill Publishing Company.
63. *Industrial Japan: a collection of papers by specialists on various branches of industry in Japan* (1929) Tokyo: World Engineering Congress.
64. *Industries of Japan* (1929) Osaka and Tokyo: Industrial Japan Publishing Company.
65. Oriental Economist (1935) *Foreign Trade of Japan*, Tokyo: Toyo Keizai Shinposha.
66. Ibid.
67. Tilley, *London to Tokyo*.
68. Fred. H. Colvin (1947) *60 years with men and machines: an autobiography*, New York: McGraw-Hill Book Company Inc.
69. Ibid.

Chapter 5. Japan's Commercial Penetration into British India and the Cotton Trade Negotiations in the 1930s by *Naoto Kagotani*

1. Alex J. Robertson (1991) 'Lancashire and the rise of Japan', in Mary B. Rose (ed.) *International competition and strategic response in the textile industries since 1890*, London: Frank Cass; also Kaoru Sugihara (1989) 'Japan's industrial recovery 1931–1936', in Ian Brown (ed.) *The economies of Africa and Asia during the interwar depression*, London: Routledge.

2. Kaoru Sugihara (1998) 'Intra-Asian trade and East Asia's industrialization, 1919-1939', in Gareth Austin (ed.) *Industrial growth in the Third World, c.1870–c.1990: depressions, intra-regional trade, and ethnic networks*, LSE Working Papers in Economic History, 44/98, London: London School of Economics and Political Science.
3. Naoto Kagotani (2000) *Ajia kokusai tsūshō chitsujo to kindai Nihon* (The Asian international trading order and modern Japan), Nagoya: Nagoya University Press, Chapter 6.
4. Osamu Ishii (2000) 'Rivalries over cotton goods markets, 1930–36', in Ian Nish and Yōichi Kibata (eds) *The history of Anglo-Japanese relations, 1600–2000*, vol. 2, *The political-diplomatic dimension, 1931–2000*, London: Macmillan Press.
5. Osamu Ishii (1977) *Cotton-textile diplomacy: Japan, Great Britain and the United States, 1930–1936*, Ann Arbor, Michigan: University of Michigan Press.
6. Hiroshi Nishikawa (1987) *Nihon teikokushugi to mengyō* (Japanese imperialism and the cotton industry), Kyoto: Mineruva Shobō.
7. Ishii 1977; also Shin'ya Sugiyama (1995) 'The expansion of Japan's cotton textile exports into South-East Asia', in Shin'ya Sugiyama and Ian Brown (eds) *International rivalry in South-East Asia in the interwar period*, New Haven: Yale University Press.
8. Japan Cotton Spinners' Association (ed.) *The statistics of cotton trade, 1919–1936*. These statistical records are kept in the library of the Japan Cotton Spinners' Association (Osaka).
9. P. J. Cain and A. G. Hopkins (2001) *British imperialism, 1688–2000*, (2nd edn), London: Longman, Chapters 20, 23 and 25.
10. Basudev Chatterji (1992) *Trade, tariff and empire: Lancashire and British policy in India 1919–1939*, Oxford: Oxford University Press, Chapter 7; see also *Nichi-in Kyōkai kaihō* (Journal of the Indo-Japanese Association), no. 57, 1935, p. 186.
11. Kagotani 2000, Chapter 5.
12. Dietmar Rothermund (1992) *India in the Great Depression 1929–1939*, New Delhi: Manohar, Chapter 2.
13. Ragnar Nurkse (1944) *International currency experience: lessons of the inter-war period*, Geneva: League of Nations, Chapter 3.
14. Jūrō Hashimoto (1984) *Daikyōkōka no Nihon shihonshugi* (Japanese capitalism during the Great Depression), Tokyo: University of Tokyo Press, Chapter 3.
15. Kagotani 2000, Chapters 6 and 7.
16. Chatterji 1992, p. 333.
17. B. R. Tomlinson (1979) *The political economy of the raj 1914–1947: the economics of decolonization in India*, London: Macmillan Press, Chapter 3. For the case of the Netherlands East Indies, see Ann Booth (1990) 'The evolution of fiscal policy and the role of government in the colonial economy', in Ann Booth, W. J. O'Malley and Ann Weidemann (eds), *Indonesian economic history in the Dutch colonial era*, New Haven: Yale University Southeast Asia Studies. See also Ian Brown (1997) *Economic change in South-East Asia, c.1830–1980*, Oxford: Oxford University Press, Chapter 13.
18. Chatterji 1992, pp. 377–81.
19. Memorandum by G. B. Sansom, 8 June 1933, FO371/17160.
20. N. Chamberlain to Samuel Hoare, 1 December 1933, CAB27/556, p. 20.
21. Viceroy to HM SoS for India Office, 3 December 1933, CAB27/556, p. 42.

22. The first meeting of the Cabinet Committee, 28 November 1933, CAB27/556, p.6.
23. Viceroy to HM SoS for India Office, 24 November 1933, CAB27/556, p. 65.
24. N. Chamberlain to Samuel Hoare, 1 December 1933, CAB27/556, p. 14.
25. Thomas M. Ainscough (senior trade commissioner in India) to A. Edgcumbe (Department of Overseas Trade), 27 October 1933, FO371/17164,f7065, p. 166.
26. Ibid. p.18.
27. John Sharkey (2000) 'Economic diplomacy in Anglo–Japanese relations, 1931–41', in Ian Nish and Yōichi Kibata (eds) *The history of Anglo–Japanese relations, 1600–2000*, vol. 2, *The political-diplomatic dimension, 1931–2000*, London: Macmillan Press, pp. 84–5.
28. Keizō Kurata (1934) *Nichi-in kaishō ni kansuru denpō ōfuku hikae* (File of telegrams exchanged in Indo–Japanese cotton trade negotiations), Osaka: Japan Cotton Spinners' Association, April; also Yasuo Tawa (1935) *Nichiran kaishō no keika* (The process of Dutch–Japanese cotton trade negotiations), Osaka: Japan Cotton Spinners' Association, March. These documents are kept in the library of The Japan Cotton Spinners' Association (Osaka).
29. Keizō Kurata, telegram to Osaka headquarters dated 30 December 1933, in Kurata 1934. See also Kagotani 2000, Chapters 4, 6 and 7.
30. A. Best (2000b) 'The road to Anglo–Japanese confrontation, 1931–41', in I. Nish and Y. Kibata (eds), *The history of Anglo–Japanese relations, 1600–2000*, vol. 2, *The political-diplomatic dimension, 1931–2000*, London: Macmillan.

Chapter 6. Paul Einzig and the Japanese Empire in 1943
by *Philip Towle*

I am indebted to the Churchill College archives for permission to use the Einzig and Bracken papers in their possession.

1. Anonymous review of Einzig's autobiography, *In the centre of things*, in *The Times Literary Supplement*, 30 September 1960; a copy is found in the Einzig Papers, Churchill College Archives, Cambridge, ENZG 6/3/2.
2. Paul Einzig (1960) *In the centre of things*, London: Hutchinson, Chapters 19 and 25. See also the letter to the editor of *Financial News*, 5 February 1944 in ENZG 1/14.
3. *American Economic Review*, December 1963; copy in the Einzig papers, loc. cit.
4. Paul Einzig (1943) *The Japanese new order in Asia*, Basingstoke, Macmillan.
5. Einzig 1960, Chapter 5; Charles Edward Lysaght (1979) *Brendan Bracken*, London: Allen Lane, pp. 127 ff. and the Bracken papers in Churchill College Archive, Cambridge BBKN 2/3, particularly Einzig's interview of 3 January 1973. See also Andrew Boyle (1974) *Poor dear Brendan: the quest for Brendan Bracken*, London: Hutchinson.
6. Einzig only heard after the war that his family was safe; see telegram of 9 January 1945 from his father in ENZG 7/1. See also Richard Crocket (1990) *My Dear Max: the letters of Brendan Bracken to Lord Beaverbrook*, London: Historians Press, p. 5. For Einzig's relations with Dalton see Ben Pimlott (1986) *The political diary of Hugh Dalton: 1945–1960*, London: Jonathan Cape, p. 327.
7. Lysaght 1979, loc cit.

8. See the interviews in the Bracken papers in Churchill College, BBKN 2/2, particularly with Eric Whelpton on 30 August 1973.
9. Letter from Brendan Bracken to Einzig, 29 January 1942, ENZG 1/14.
10. Letter from Keynes to Einzig, 27 May 1943 in ENZG 1/14.
11. See the unpublished manuscript of 'Parliament in War' in ENZG 2/3.
12. Einzig 1960, Chapter 22, titled 'My Finest Hour.'
13. Einzig 1960, Chapter 9, titled 'Parliament'. For public attitudes, see *Public Opinion Quarterly*, Princeton, 1942, p. 156 and 1943, p. 330.
14. Einzig 1943, p. 90.
15. A. V. Alexander (1937) 'Changing forces in the Pacific', *International Affairs*, January–February; see also Sadao Saburi (1929) 'Japan's position in the Far East', *Royal United Service Institution Journal*, August.
16. Yūsuke Tsurumi (1937) 'Japan today and tomorrow', *International Affairs* (London), May–June.
17. Captain M. D. Kennedy (1924) *The military side of Japanese life*, London: Constable; Captain M. D. Kennedy (1930) *The changing fabric of Japan*, London: Constable.
18. Paul Einzig (1942) *Can we win the peace?* London: Macmillan, p. vi.
19. Einzig 1943, p. 17.
20. Ibid., pp. 5–17.
21. Ibid., p. 73.
22. Ibid., p. 144.
23. Ibid., p. 67.
24. Ibid., p. 68. Synthetic oil production was disappointing to the Japanese authorities; see Alvin D. Coox (1988) 'The effectiveness of the Japanese military establishment in the Second World War', in Allan R. Millett and Murray Williamson (eds), *Military effectiveness*, vol. III, Boston, Allen & Unwin, p. 20.
25. Einzig 1943, p. 70.
26. Ibid., p. 71.
27. Ibid., p. 72.
28. Ibid., p. 74.
29. Ibid., p. 57.
30. Ibid., p. 60.
31. Ibid., p. 59.
32. Ibid., p. 61.
33. Ibid.
34. Ibid., p. 80.
35. Ibid., p. 81.
36. Ibid.
37. Ibid., p. 86.
38. Winton, John (1983) *Convoy: the defence of seaborne trade 1880–1990*, London: Michael Joseph, p. 310.
39. Einzig 1943, pp. 92 and 140.
40. Hector C. Bywater (1927) *Navies and nations: a review of naval developments since the Great War*, London: Constable, especially pp. 154 and 206–7. See also William H. Honan (1990) *Bywater: the man who invented the Pacific War*, London: Macdonald.
41. Einzig 1943, p. 140.
42. On oil supplies see ibid., p. 69.
43. Einzig 1943, p. 142. For a recent appraisal of the effect of shipping losses on

the Japanese economy, see Akira Hara (1998) 'Japan: guns before rice', in Mark Harrison, *The economics of World War II*, Cambridge: Cambridge University Press, p. 245: 'Insufficient shipping capacity [was] the most important factor restricting the wartime economy of mainland Japan.'

44. The United States Strategic Bombing Survey (USSBS) (1976) vol. VII, New York: Garland Publishing, p. 11. On the authors of the survey, see J. K. Galbraith (1983) *A life in our times*, London: Corgi, pp. 244–6, and Paul H. Nitze (1989) *From Hiroshima to glasnost: at the centre of decision*, London: Weidenfeld & Nicolson, Chapter 2.
45. USSBS, volume IX, pp. 2 and 6. For Brassey's, see L. H. Hordern (1986) 'The submarine war on merchant shipping', in Bryan Ranft (ed.) *Ironclad to Trident*, London: Brassey's Defence Publishers. On Japanese naval successes in the Mediterranean in the First World War, see Paul G. Halpern (1987) *The naval war in the Mediterranean*, London: Allen & Unwin, p. 388.
46. Jerome B. Cohen (2000) *Japan's economy in war and reconstruction*, edited by Janet Hunter, London: Routledge, p. xi; Commander D. W. Waters (1988) 'Japan: defeat through blockade, 1941–1945', *The Naval Review*, July. See also Captain D. Conley (2000) 'US submarine warfare in the Pacific, 1942–1945', *The Naval Review*, January.
47. On Anglo-American differences over strategy see Christopher Thorne (1978) *Allies of a kind: the United States, Britain and the war against Japan, 1941–1945*, London: Hamish Hamilton, pp. 207 ff. For a sympathetic account of British weakness, see Robert E. Sherwood (1948) *The White House papers of Harry L. Hopkins*, London: Eyre & Spottiswoode, pp. 806 ff. For a critical appraisal of British 'defensiveness' in the Pacific, see Henry H. Adams (1985) *Witness to power: the life of Fleet Admiral William D. Leahy*, Annapolis, Maryland: Naval Institute Press, pp. 201–2.
48. Churchill to Roosevelt, 16 December 1941, in Warren F. Kimball (1984) *Churchill and Roosevelt: the complete correspondence*, vol. I, Princeton, New Jersey: Princeton University Press, pp. 294 ff. See also Winston S. Churchill (1950) *The Second World War*, vol. III, *The grand alliance*, London: Reprint Society, pp. 505 ff.; Martin Gilbert (1986) *Winston S. Churchill: road to victory*, vol. VII, London: Heinemann, Chapter 1.
49. For an excellent summary of the whole Asian war, see Louis Allen (1990) 'The campaigns in Asia and the Pacific', *Journal of Strategic Studies*, March. See also Peter Calvocoressi, Guy Wint and John Pritchard (1989) *Total war*, vol. II, London: Penguin. On MacArthur, see William Manchester (1979) *American Caesar: Douglas MacArthur 1880–1964*, London: Arrow.
50. Hadley Cantril and Mildred Strunk (1951) *Public opinion 1935–1946*, Princeton, New Jersey: Princeton University Press, pp. 1063 ff.
51. 'Report of the Maritime Air Defence Committee to the Chiefs of Staff', in John B Hattendorf et al. (1993) *British naval documents 1204–1960*, Aldershot: Scholar Press/Navy Record Society, pp. 873 ff.
52. On Japanese naval preparations for war, see Stephen E. Pelz (1974) *Race to Pearl Harbor*, Cambridge, Massachusetts: Harvard University Press, Chapter 2; Jerome Cohen 2000, pp. 250 ff. For German comments on the Japanese obsession with great battles, see Cohen 2000, p. 261. See also Parillo, Mark P. (1993) *The Japanese merchant marine in World War II*, Annapolis: Naval Institute Press, pp. 9–10. For Mahan's views see Mahan, Captain Alfred Thayer (1911) *Naval strategy*, London: Samson, Low & Marston.

53. On Blackett, see his obituary in *The Times*, 15 July 1974; P. M. S. Blackett (1962) *Studies of war*, London: Oliver & Boyd; Peter Hore (2003) *Patrick Blackett: sailor, scientist, socialist*, London: Frank Cass, particularly Chapters 9 and 11.
54. Cohen 2000, p. 265; Parillo 1993, pp. 24 3ff.; Winton 1983, p. 315.
55. Chay Blair (1978) *Combat patrol*, New York: Bantam, p. 380. For the postwar focus on major surface battles, see Jeffrey S. Barlow (1989) 'US and Japanese naval strategies', in Colin S. Gray and Roger W. Barnett (eds) *Seapower and strategy*, London: Tri-Service Press, pp. 249 ff.
56. Cohen 2000, p. 48. For quarrels between the Japanese armed forces, see Parillo 1993, p. 18ff.
57. Cohen 2000, p. 48.
58. Blair 1978, pp. 170–82. See also Winton 1983, p. 314.
59. Ibid.
60. Winton 1983, p. 313; Parillo 1993, on 'paths not taken', see p. 222.
61. Winton, 1983, p. 380.
62. Kimball 1984, vol. III, p. 13.
63. Blair 1978, p. 381; Winton 1983, p. 319. Winton suggests 108,000 Japanese seamen were killed or missing. See also Parillo 1993, p. 207.
64. Blair 1978, pp. 155, 208, 223.
65. One of the first books to argue to this effect was P. M S. Blackett (1948) *Military and political consequences of atomic energy*, London: Turnstile Press.
66. Barton J. Bernstein (1995) 'Compelling Japan's surrender without the A-bomb, Soviet entry or invasion: reconsidering the US Bombing Survey's early surrender conclusions', *Journal of Strategic Studies*, June. Cohen 2000, p. 107 quotes the chief secretary of the Japanese cabinet reporting in the spring of 1945 on the desperate shortage of food and raw materials. See also Coox 1988, p. 20, quoting Premier Higashikuni as saying 'the basic cause of the defeat was the loss of transport shipping.'
67. Cohen 2000, p. 35.
68. Parillo 1993, pp. 208–18. See also the comments on the effects of the war on Asian living standards in Hara 1998, pp. 245 and 256.
69. For Iraqi complaints about the effects of UN sanctions on mortality rates, see UN documents S/25657 (letter dated 20 April 1993 from the permanent representative of Iraq) and S/25775 (letter dated 11 May 1993 from the permanent representative of Iraq).
70 John Morris (1943) *Traveller from Tokyo*, Harmondsworth: Penguin.
71. Hugh Byas (1942) *The Japanese enemy: his power and his vulnerability*, London: Hodder & Stoughton, p. 86.
72. Harcourt-Smith, Simon (1942) *Japanese frenzy*, London: Hamish Hamilton, pp. 205 and 213.
73. Einzig Papers, ENZG 2/1. Between July 1943 and June 1944 *The Japanese New Order in Asia* sold just 127 copies and was reviewed in the *News Chronicle* (London), 5 May 1943.
74. Churchill 1950, pp. 311, 385, 651; Cordell Hull (1948) *The memoirs of Cordell Hull*, vol. II, London: Hodder & Stoughton, pp. 1046–50; Lord Hastings Lionel Ismay (1960) *The memoirs of Lord Ismay*, London: Heinemann, pp. 280, 286, 295, 299; Henry L. Stimson and McGeorge Bundy (1948) *On active service in peace and war*, New York: Harper, pp. 508–18.

Chapter 7. Britain and the Recovery of Japan post-1945 by *Peter Lowe*

1. See John Dower (1999) *Embracing defeat: Japan in the aftermath of World War II*, London: Allen Lane; and Christopher Thorne (1978) *Allies of a kind: the United States, Britain and the war against Japan, 1941–1945*, London: Hamish Hamilton.
2. See Roger Buckley (1982) *Occupation diplomacy: Britain, the United States and Japan, 1945–52*, Cambridge: Cambridge University Press; and R. B. Finn (1992) *Winners in peace: MacArthur, Yoshida and postwar Japan*, Berkeley: University of California.
3. Buckley, Roger (1992) 'A particularly vital issue? Harry S. Truman and Japan, 1945–52', in T. G. Fraser and Peter Lowe (eds) *Conflict and amity: essays in honour of Ian Nish*, London: Macmillan, pp.143–62.
4. See Peter Lowe (1994) 'Sir Alvary Gascoigne in Japan, 1946–1951', in Ian Nish (ed.) *Britain and Japan: biographical portraits*, Folkestone: Japan Library, pp.279–94, 340–2.
5. Peter Lowe (1997) *Containing the cold war in East Asia: British policies towards Japan, China and Korea, 1948–53*, Manchester: Manchester University Press, pp.12, 15–22.
6. James D. Clayton (1985) *The years of MacArthur*, vol. III, *Triumph and disaster, 1945–1964*, Boston: Houghton Mifflin, pp.193–217.
7. Lowe 1997, pp.15–17.
8. See Sir Alec Cairncross (1987) *Years of recovery: British economic policy, 1945–51*, London: Methuen, p. 20.
9. D. A. Farnie and Abe Takeshi (2000) 'Japan, Lancashire and the Asian market for cotton manufactures, 1890–1990', in D. A Farnie, A. Takeshi, N. Tetsuro and J. F. Wilson, *Region and strategy in Britain and Japan: business in Lancashire and Kansai, 1890–1990*, London: Routledge, p. 151.
10. For a wide-ranging discussion of the evolution of thinking in Lancashire, including the challenge to free trade, see Peter Clarke (1972) *Lancashire and the new liberalism*, Cambridge: Cambridge University Press.
11. D. A. Farnie and Tetsurō Nakaoka (2000) 'Region and nation', in D. A Farnie, A. Takeshi, N. Tetsuro and J. F. Wilson, *Region and strategy in Britain and Japan: business in Lancashire and Kansai, 1890–1990*, London: Routledge, p. 25
12. Ibid., p. 42. See also John Sharkey (2000) 'Economic diplomacy in Anglo-Japanese relations, 1931–41', in Ian Nish and Yōichi Kibata (eds) *The history of Anglo-Japanese relations, 1600–2000*, vol. II, *The political-diplomatic dimension, 1931–2000*, London: Macmillan, pp. 78–111.
13. Farnie and Takeshi 2000, p. 134.
14. Ibid., p. 137.
15. Lowe 1997, pp. 18, 72.
16. Farnie and Takeshi 2000, pp. 142, 146–7.
17. Ibid., p. 116.
18. Foreign Office to Tokyo, 18 March 1948, FO 371/69885/4043, Public Record Office, Kew.
19. See Marguerite Dupree (ed.) (1987) *Lancashire and Whitehall: the diary of Sir Raymond Streat*, 2 vols, Manchester: Manchester University Press, vol. 2, pp. 423–615.
20. Farnie and Nakaoka 2000, p. 34.
21. Minute by C. P. Scott, 8 July 1951, FO 371/92616/5.

22. San Francisco to Foreign Office, 12 September 1951, FO 371/92616/5.
23. Lowe 1997, pp. 61–2.
24. Farnie and Nakaoka 2000, p. 36.
25. Lowe 1997, p. 61.
26. Farnie and Nakaoka 2000, p. 112.
27. Tōru Takamatsu and Ken Warren (2000) 'A comparison of Cammel Laird and Hitachi Zōsen as shipbuilders', in D. A Farnie, A. Takeshi, N. Tetsuro and J. F. Wilson, *Region and strategy in Britain and Japan: business in Lancashire and Kansai, 1890–1990*, London: Routledge, p. 212.
28. Ibid.
29. Memorandum by Morrison, CP(51)234, 30 July 1951, Cab 129/47.
30. Ibid.
31. Cabinet minutes, 57(51)5, 1 August 1951, Cab 128/20.
32. Takamatsu and Warren 2000, pp. 214–15, 222.
33. Ibid, p. 212.
34. Lowe 1997, p. 61.
35. Cabinet minutes, 22(51)3, 22 March 1951, Cab 128/19.
36. See John Dower (1979) *Empire and aftermath: Yoshida Shigeru and the Japanese experience, 1878–1954*, Harvard: Harvard University Press, pp. 292–368.
37. For a valuable discussion of the treatment of POWs, see Flower, Sybilla Jane (2000) 'British prisoners of war of the Japanese, 1941–45', in Ian Nish and Yōichi Kibata (eds) *The history of Anglo–Japanese relations, 1600–2000*, vol. II, *The political–diplomatic dimension, 1931–2000*, London: Macmillan, pp. 149–73.
38. Treasury memorandum by A. J. Phelps, 6 June 1951, FO 371/92557/564A.
39. Record of meeting held in the House of Commons, 8 June 1951, FO 371/92552/516.
40. Cabinet minutes, 43(51)3, 14 June 1951, Cab 128/19.
41. Ibid.
42. Letter from Dening to Scott, 21 January 1952, FO 371/99441/1.
43. Sir Hugh Cortazzi (1992) 'Britain and Japan: a personal view of postwar economic relations', in T. G. Fraser and Peter Lowe (eds) *Conflict and amity: essays in honour of Ian Nish*, London: Macmillan, pp. 163–81.
44. Ibid., p. 166.
45. Ibid., p. 172.
46. Ibid., pp. 176–7.
47. Christopher Braddick (2000) 'Distant friends: Britain and Japan since 1958 – the age of globalization', in Ian Nish and Yōichi Kibata (eds) *History of Anglo–Japanese relations, 1600–2000*, vol. 2, *The political-diplomatic dimension, 1931–2000*, London: Macmillan, p. 300.

Chapter 8. Shipping and Shipbuilding by *John Weste*

1. See, for example, J. Tomaru (2000) *The postwar rapprochement of Malaya and Japan, 1945–1961: the roles of Britain and Japan in South-East Asia*, New York: St Martin's; J. Weste (2002) 'Facing the unavoidable: Great Britain, the sterling area and Japan', in J. Hunter and S. Sugiyama (eds) *Economic and business relations*, vol. 4, *The history of Anglo–Japanese relations, 1600–2000*, Basingstoke: Palgrave, pp. 283–313; and N. White (1998) 'Britain and the return of Japanese economic interests to South East Asia after the Second World War', *South East Asia Research*, vol. 6, no. 3, pp. 281–307.

2. L. Johnman and H. Murphy (2002) *British shipbuilding and the state since 1918*, Exeter: University of Exeter Press, p. 103.
3. Janet Hunter and Shinya Sugiyama (2002a) 'Introduction', in J. Hunter and S. Sugiyama (eds) *Economic and business relations*, vol. 4, *The history of Anglo–Japanese relations, 1600–2000*, Basingstoke: Palgrave, pp. 57–9.
4. Cited in G. Daniels (1982) 'Britain's view of post-war Japan, 1945–9', in I. Nish (ed.) *Anglo–Japanese alienation, 1919–1952*, Cambridge: Cambridge University Press, pp. 260–1.
5. Ibid., pp. 262–3.
6. M. Dupree (ed.) *Lancashire and Whitehall: the diary of Sir Raymond Streat*, vol. 2, Manchester: Manchester University Press, pp. 460–1.
7. Malcolm MacDonald Papers, University of Durham 22/10/24 'Anthony Eden to Malcolm MacDonald', 23 May 1952.
8. Minutes of Meeting of the Council of the Chamber of Shipping, (hereafter, CCS), 31st May 1951, p. 5.
9. Chamber of Shipping of the United Kingdom, Annual Reports, 1955–6, p. 80.
10. During the 1945–52 occupation, Japan was not a sovereign nation and thus was unable to be officially accredited with embassies, hence the designnation 'liaison mission'.
11. FCO 371/63736, UKLM to Foreign Office D. F. McDermot, 13 January 1947, p. 1.
12. On Japan and Southeast Asia, see W. Borden (1984) *The Pacific alliance: United States foreign economic policy and Japanese trade recovery, 1947–1955*, Madison: University of Wisconsin Press. The movement away from, for example zaibatsu dissolution, to promoting economic growth is often regarded as being one example of the 'reverse course'. While generally recognized as a gradual yet irregular shift in policy from the reform Japanese institutions to stabilization, the term attracts much debate in studies of occupied Japan in terms of what actually constitutes the reverse course and, indeed, the date from which it can be said to have commenced. All of the above concerns, it should be observed, were widely and publicly discussed at the time. See, for example, 'Japanese comeback', *The Economist*, 17 September 1949, pp. 595–6. The designation SCAP refers to both General Douglas MacArthur, the Supreme Allied Commander in Japan, and to the bureaucratic organization he commanded.
13. Ibid.
14. FO 371/76233 MT to FCO, 13 January 1949, p. 1.
15. Ibid., UK Liaison Mission to MT, 'Japanese shipping and shipbuilding', 2 March 1949, p. 1.
16. FO 371/76233 MT to FCO, 13 January 1949, p. 1.
17. MT 73/174 'Confidential: Report No. 3', 2 March 1949, p. 1.
18. Ibid.
19. Ibid., p. 3.
20. FO 371/63736 D. L. M. MacFarlane to General Money, 16 September 1947, pp. 1–2.
21. Ibid., p. 2.
22. FO 371/76233, J. V. Clyne, chairman, Canadian Maritime Commission to Sir Gilmour Jenkins, permanent secretary MT, 28 January 1949, p. 1.
23. MT 73/174 MT to FCO, 24 March 1950, pp. 3–4. As it transpired, their estimates were wildly conservative with Japan producing 2,300,000 tons in

1957 alone as its percentage share in the world export market between 1956 and 1960 all but trebled to 32 per cent as Britain's fell by an inverse proportion to 7 per cent. See Johnman and Murphy 2002, p. 103; and K. Warren (1998) *Steel, ships and men: Cammell Laird, 1824–1993*, Liverpool: Liverpool University Press, p. 276.

24. 'Tickets for Tokyo', *Economist*, 14 June 1947, p. 932.
25. FO 371/63736 Report from SS *Cape Howe*, 30 November 1946, pp. 1–2.
26. FO 371/63736 Draft [MT] memorandum, 24 January 1947, p.1.
27. Ibid.
28. Ibid., p. 4.
29. Ibid., UKLM to FCO, 'Japanese trade', 22 May 1947; and Tokyo to FCO, 'Discrimination against British shipping', 1 July 1949, p. 1.
30. FO 371/76233 UKLM to MT, 'Japanese shipping and shipbuilding', 2 March 1949, p. 6. GARIOA funds were used to provide supplies to ensure that occupied nations did not starve and could meet basic living conditions; Japan received $2140 million in total. The relief was not a gift, but it was not until 1962 that a US–Japanese agreement on repayment was concluded.
31. FO 371/63736, MT, London to FCO (untitled), 17 July 1947, p. 1.
32. See, for example, T. Remme (1995) *Britain and regional cooperation in South-East Asia, 1945–49*, London: Routledge; and White 1998.
33. FO 371/84004, UKLM to MacDonald (untitled), 22 February 1950, p. 2; see also: FO 371.84005, 'Japanese trade arrangements: shipping', 11 June 1950, pp. 1–2.
34. Ibid., p. 1.
35. FO 371/84005, Secretary of State of the Colonies to North Borneo, Sarawak, Federation of Malaya, Singapore, Fiji and Brunei, 'Japanese merchant shipping', 6 May 1950, pp. 1–2; and Ibid., 'Japanese merchant shipping' (Singaporean response to the above), 26 May 1950, pp. 1–2.
36. MT 59/3046, Sir John Masson, John Swire & Sons to Morris, 'Australia/Japan', 8 March 1954, pp.1–2.
37. Ibid., 'Note of meeting', undated (probably 27 August 1953), p. 1.
38. FO 371/110436 'Problems affecting UK relations with Japan – memorandum: commercial policy of the United Kingdom towards Japan', 1954, p. 1.
39. MT 59/3046 'Note of a meeting held in the Secretary's room on 23rd October 1951', p. 1.
40. Chamber of Shipping of the United Kingdom: annual reports, 1954–5, p. 64.
41. FO 371/76234, Shipbuilding advisory committee minutes, 25 August 1949, p. 3.
42. MT 73/174 MT, UK shipping representative for the Far East, to MT, 'Confidential report, No. 3', p. 11.
43. FO 371/76233, Untitled document, MT to FCO, 27 January 1949, p. 1. The Convention of the IMCO was established in 1948. The core objectives of the organization included: (a) to provide machinery for cooperation among governments in the field of governmental regulation and practices relating to technical matters of all kinds affecting shipping engaged in international trade, and to encourage the general adoption of the highest practicable standards in matters concerning maritime safety and efficiency of navigation; (b) to encourage the removal of discriminatory action and unnecessary restrictions by governments affecting shipping engaged in international trade so as to promote the availability of shipping services to

the commerce of the world without discrimination; the assistance and encouragement a government gives for the development of its national shipping and for the purposes of security do not in themselves constitute discrimination, provided such assistance and encouragement are not based on measures designed to restrict the freedom of shipping of all flags.

44. FO 371/84005, 'Japanese merchant shipping', 6 May 1950, pp. 1–2.
45. FO 371/76233, untitled, 5 April 1949, p. 1.
46. MT 73/174 MT to FCO, untitled, 24 March 1950, p. 2.
47. The Far Eastern Commission (FEC) was an eleven-, later thirteen-, member advisory board to SCAP. It met in Washington, far removed from actual events in Japan.

Chapter 10. Military and Economic Power: Complementing Each Other's National Strength by *Reinhard Drifte*

1. On this subject see my book, Reinhard Drifte (2000) *Japan's quest for a permanent Security Council seat: a matter of pride or justice?* Basingstoke: Macmillan and St Antony's College (in Japanese, *Kokuren Ampori to Nihon. Joninrijikoku iri mondai no kiseki*, Tokyo: Iwanami Shoten, 2000).
2. European Commission (1994) *Towards a new Asia strategy*, COM(94) 314 final, Brussels: Commission of the European Communities, p. 1.
3 Ibid., p. 7.
4. European Commission (1995 updated 2001) *Europe and Japan: the next steps*, COM(95) 73 final, 08.03, Brussels: Commission of the European Communities, 2001 edition, p. 3.

Chapter 11. Bilateral Stability, Global Instability: The Political Economy of Contemporary Anglo-Japanese Economic Relations by *Simon Lee*

1. C. Johnson (1982) *MITI and the Japanese miracle: the growth of industrial policy, 1925–1975*, Stanford: Stanford University Press, p.17.
2. K. Sheridan (1994) *Governing the Japanese economy*, Cambridge: Polity Press, p. 31.
3. G. C. Allen (1981) *A short economic history of modern Japan*, 4th edn, London: Macmillan, p. 43.
4. P. Francks (1992) *Japanese economic development: theory and practice*, London: Routledge, pp. 182–3.
5. See C. Freeman (1987) *Technology and economic performance: lessons from Japan*, London: Pinter.
6. See K. Smith (1984) *The British economic crisis: its past and future*, Harmondsworth: Penguin.
7. Invest–UK (2003) *Invest–UK: operations review 2003*, London: Department of Trade and Industry, p. 1.
8. J. Williamson (1993) 'Democracy and the "Washington Consensus"', *World Development*, vol. 21, no. 8, pp. 1329–36.
9. FCO (2002) 'The UK and Japan: "natural business partners"', Foreign and Commonwealth press release, 30 October, London: Foreign and Commonwealth Office, p. 1.
10. FCO (1999) 'Action Agenda 21: the UK and Japan in the 21st century', Foreign and Commonwealth Office News Release, 6 September, London: Foreign and Commonwealth Office, p. 3.

11. European Commission (2001) *Shaping our common future: an action plan for EU–Japan cooperation*, Brussels, European Commission, p.9.
12. European Commission (2003) *EU priority proposals for regulatory reform in Japan*, Brussels: European Commission, p.3.
13. European Commission (2002) Chair's statement: ASEM 4th Economic Ministers Meeting (EMM 4), Copenhagen, 18/19 September, Brussels: European Commission, p. 3.
14. Invest–UK 2003, p.7.
15. ONS (2003) *United Kingdom balance of payments: the Pink Book 2003*, London: The Stationery Office, p. 16.
16. S. Lee (1998) 'Managed or mismanaged trade? US–Japan trade relations during the Clinton Presidency', in I. Cook, M. Doel, R. Li and Y. Wang (eds) *Dynamic Asia: business trade and economic development in Pacific Asia*, Aldershot: Ashgate, pp. 209–33.
17. Williamson 1993, pp. 1329–36.
18. IMF (2003a) *World economic outlook: growth and institutions*, Washington, DC: International Monetary Fund, p. 13.
19. IMF (2003b) *United Kingdom: 2002 Article IV consultation*, Washington, DC: International Monetary Fund Country Report No. 03/48, p. 12.
20. K. Krugman (1998) 'Saving Asia: it's time to get radical', *Fortune*, 7 September, pp. 27–32.
21. R. Higgott (1998) 'The Asian economic crisis: a study in the politics of resentment', *New Political Economy*, vol. 3, no. 3, p. 333.
22. R. Wade and F. Veneroso (1998) 'The Asian crisis: the high debt model versus the Wall Street–Treasury–IMF complex', *New Left Review*, vol. 228, March–April, pp. 3–34.
23. G8 (2003) *Co-operative G8 action on trade*, Ottawa: G8 Information Centre, p. 1.
24. World Bank (2003) *Global economic prospects 2004: realizing the development prospects of the Doha agenda*, Washington, DC: World Bank, p. 205.
25. IMD (2003) *World Competitiveness Scoreboard 2003: executive summary*, Lausanne: Institute for Management Development.
26. ONS (2003) *International Comparisons of productivity*, London: Office of National Statistics, p. 1.
27. OECD (2003) *Economic survey of Japan, 2002: policy brief*, Paris: Organization for Economic Co-operation and Development, p. 2.
28. CEA (2003) *Economic indicators: December 2003. Prepared for the Joint Economic Committee by the Council of Economic Advisers*, Washington, DC: United States Government Printing Office, p. 16.
29. UNCTAD (2003) *World Development Report 2003. Country fact sheet: Japan*, New York: United Nations Conference on Trade and Development, p. 1.
30. UNCTAD (2003) *World Investment Report 2003. Country fact sheet: United Kingdom*, New York: United Nations Conference on Trade and Development, p. 1.
31. B. Audretsch and R. Thurik (2001) *Linking entrepreneurship to growth*, Paris: Organization for Economic Cooperation and Development, pp. 5–29.
32. World Bank (2002) *Building institutions for markets: world development report 2002*, Washington, DC: World Bank.
33. Williamson 1993, pp. 1329–36.
34. OECD (2001) *The new economy: beyond the hype. Final report on the OECD growth report*, Paris: Organization for Cooperation and Development, p. 87.

35. GEM (2002) *Global Entrepreneurship Monitor: 2002 executive report*, London: Global Entrepreneurship Monitor, p. 15.
36. D. Archibugi and J. Michie (1997) 'Technological globalization and national systems of innovation: an introduction', in D. Archibugi and J. Michie (eds) *Technology, globalisation and economic performance*, Cambridge: Cambridge University Press, pp. 1–23.
37. Porter, M. and C. Ketels (2003) *UK competitiveness: moving to the next stage. DTI economics paper No. 3*, London: Department of Trade and Industry and Economic and Social Research Council, p. 42.
38. M. Porter, H. Takeuchi and M. Sakakibara (2000) *Can Japan compete?* London: Macmillan, pp. 33–44.
39. Porter and Ketels 2003, pp. 7, 11–3.
40. S. Lee (1997) 'Part B: explaining Britain's relative economic performance', in A. Cox, S. Lee and J. Sanderson, *The political economy of modern Britain*, Cheltenham: Edward Elgar, pp. 65–253.
41. Porter and Ketels 2003, p.30.
42. Ibid.
43. Porter et al. 2000, p. 139.
44. Ibid., pp. 140–1, 159.
45. Porter and Ketels 2003, pp. 43–4.
46. F. Allen and D. Gale (2000) 'Bubbles and crises', *The Economic Journal*, vol. 110, pp. 236–7.
47. OECD 2003, p. 3.
48. HMT (2003) *Budget 2003: building a Britain of economic strength and social justice*, London: Her Majesty's Treasury, pp. 21, 33.
49. HMT/DFID (2003) *International Finance Facility*, London: Department for International Development and Her Majesty's Treasury.
50. HMT (2002) *Tackling poverty: a global new deal: a modern Marshall Plan for the developing world*, London: Her Majesty's Treasury, p. 2.
51. HMT/DFID 2003, sections 3.4–3.9, 5.
52. World Bank (1993) *The East Asian miracle: economic growth and public policy*, Oxford: Oxford University Press, p. 312.
53. S. Lee (2003) 'Asia-Pacific economic regionalism: global constraints and opportunities', in C. Dent (ed.) *Asia-Pacific economic and security cooperation: new regional agendas*, London: Palgrave Macmillan, pp. 19–33.
54. Lee, S. (2002) 'Global monitor: the International Monetary Fund', *New Political Economy*, vol. 7, no. 2, p. 285.
55. IMF (2002) *World economic outlook: recessions and recoveries*, Washington, DC: International Monetary Fund, p. 5.
56. IMF (2003c) *Republic of Korea: financial system stability assessment*, Washington, DC: International Monetary Fund Country Report No. 03/81, p. 9.
57. World Bank (2000) *East Asia: recovery and beyond*, Washington, DC: World Bank, p. 110.
58. World Bank (1997) *The state in a changing world: World Development Report 1997*, Washington, DC: The World Bank, p. 3.

Chapter 12. Japan and the UK at the G8 Summit, 1975 to 2006 by *Hugo Dobson*

1. John J. Kirton (1989) 'Introduction: the significance of the seven-power summit', in Peter I. Hajnal (ed.) *The seven-power summit: documents from the*

summit of industrialized countries, 1975–1989, Millwood, New York: Kraus International Publications, p. xxi.

2. G. John Ikenberry (1993) 'Salvaging the G7', *Foreign Affairs*, vol. 72, no. 2, p. 132.
3. Michael R. Hodges (1999) 'The G8 and the new political economy', in Michael R. Hodge, John J. Kirton and Joseph P. Daniels (eds) *The G8's role in the new millennium*, Aldershot: Ashgate, p. 69.
4. This chapter is based on previous research supported by the Japan Foundation Endowment Committee (grant number 173), and Hōsei University, Japan and published in Hugo Dobson (2004) *Japan and the G7/8, 1975–2002*, London: Routledge Curzon, and Hugo Dobson (2006) *The Group of 7/8*, London: Routledge.
5. Dobson 2004.
6. John J. Kirton (1998) 'The emerging pacific partnership: Japan, Canada, and the United States at the G7 summit', in Michael Fry, John J. Kirton and Mitsuru Kurosawa (eds) *The North Pacific Triangle: the United States, Japan and Canada at century's end*, Toronto: University of Toronto Press, pp. 301–2.
7. See the cartoon in *Mainichi Shinbun*, 17 May 1998. As host of the 1998 Birmingham summit, Tony Blair looks on bemused while Hashimoto Ryūtarō attempts to include Asian issues such as Indian nuclear testing and unrest in Indonesia in the summit communiqué, as well as provide the funds to support any initiatives.
8. See the cartoon in *Asahi Shinbun*, 12 June 1984. Margaret Thatcher cleans up after the 1984 London summit as Nakasone Yasuhiro bids farewell. His return the following year (like Ronald Reagan) was dependent upon his re-election as president of the Liberal Democratic Party.
9. Nobuhiko Shima (2000) *Shunō gaiko: senshinkoku samitto no rimenshi* (Prime ministerial diplomacy: a behind-the-scenes history of the summit of the most industrialised nations) Tokyo: Bungeishunjū, p. 69.
10. *Japan Times*, 5 June 1983.
11. Nicholas Bayne (2002) 'Impressions of the Genoa summit, 20–22 July 2001', in Michele Fratianni, Paolo Savona and John J. Kirton (eds) *Governing global finance: new challenges, G7 and IMF contributions*, Aldershot: Ashgate, p. 200.
12. Risto E. J. Penttilä (2003) *The role of the G8 in international peace and security*, Oxford: Oxford University Press, p. 54.
13. *Asahi Shinbun*, 23 June 1980.
14. *Japan Times*, 5 May 1986.
15. *Mainichi Shinbun*, 7 May 1986.
16. *Japan Times*, 22 June 1997.
17. *Asahi Shinbun*, 27 June 2002.
18. *Japan Times*, 5 June 1984.
19. *Asahi Shinbun*, 9 July 1990 evening edition.
20. *Japan Times*, 15 July 1991; The Japan Times, 18 July 1991.
21. *Japan Times*, 5 July 1992.
22. *Yomiuri Shinbun*, 21 July 2000.
23. See Chatan Town's Homepage: http://www.chatan.jp/chatan/summit_flame.html
24. *Japan Times*, 24 April 1977.
25. *Japan Times*, 1 May 1977.
26. *Asahi Shinbun*, 9 May 1977 evening edition.
27. *Japan Times*, 23 July 1981.

28. *Asahi Shinbun*, 10 June 1987.
29. *Yomiuri Shinbun*, 15 July 1989; Shima 2000, pp. 66–7.
30. *Yomiuri Shinbun*, 5 June 1982 evening edition.
31. *Yomiuri Shinbun*, 6 June 1982.
32. *Mainichi Shinbun*, 5 June 1982.
33. *Asahi Shinbun*, 22 July 2001.
34. *Mainichi Shinbun*, 16 November 1975.
35. *Japan Times*, 6 June 1991.
36. *Japan Times*, 8 June 1991.
37. *Japan Times*, 13 January 1993.
38. *Asahi Shinbun*, 3 June 2003.
39. *Japan Times*, 25 July 2000.
40. Robert D. Putnam and Nicholas Bayne (1984) *Hanging together: the seven-power summits*, Cambridge, Massachusetts: Harvard University Press, p. 141.
41. Nicholas Bayne (2000) *Hanging in there: the G7 and G8 summit in maturity and renewal*, Aldershot: Ashgate, pp. 61–2, 113–16.
42. Nicholas Bayne (2005) *Staying together: the G8 summit confronts the 21st century*, Aldershot: Ashgate, p. 149.
43. *Japan Times*, 8 April 1993.
44. Peter I. Hajnal (2002) 'Partners or adversaries? The G7/8 encounters civil society', in John J. Kirton and Junichi Takase (eds) *New directions in global political governance: the G8 and international order in the twenty-first century*, Aldershot: Ashgate, pp. 209–22.
45. G8 (1998) Response by the presidency on behalf of the G8 to the Jubilee 2000 petition, 16 May 1998. Available on-line at: http://www.g8.utoronto. ca/summit/1998birmingham/2000.htm, visited on 19 August 2004.
46. Hajnal 2002, p. 217.
47. *Japan Times*, 22 July 2000.
48. Kitazawa, Yōko (2000) 'Jubilee 2000 Japan: the first but revolutionary step', *Ampo: Japan-Asia Quarterly Review*, vol. 29, no. 3, p. 5.
49. *Japan Times*, 22 July 2000.
50. *Japan Times*, 25 July 2000.

Chapter 13. The Pressure of the Past on Anglo–Japanese Relations by *Nobuko Margaret Kosuge*

1. This chapter reflects research that was supported in part by a grant from the Japan Society for the Promotion of Sciences.
2. On the Far Eastern prisoners of war issue, see specifically Philip Towle, N. Margaret Kosuge and Yōichi Kibata (eds) (2000) *Japanese prisoners of war*, London: Hambledon Press; also Yōichi Kibata, Nobuko Kosuge and Philip Towle (eds) (2003) *Sensō no kioku to horyo mondai* (War memories and the Far Eastern prisoners of war), Tokyo: University of Tokyo Press.
3. Louis Allen and Yūji Aida (1990) 'Āron shūyōjo o megutte' (Thinking about the Alon camp), in Ikeda Masayuki (ed.) *Igirisujin no Nihonjinkan*, (British perceptions of the Japanese), Tokyo: Kawai Shuppan, pp. 360–78.
4. Sadaaki Numata (1998) 'Imēji to genjitsu: Nichi-Ei kankei seijuku no 30 nen' (Image and reality: thirty years of maturation in Anglo–Japanese relations), *Gaikō Fōramu* (Forum on Foreign Affairs), May.
5. Kibata Yōichi (2000) *Teikoku no tasogare: reisenka no Igirisu to Ajia*, (Twilight of empire: Britain and Asia in the cold war era), Tokyo: University of Tokyo

Press, Chapters 3 and 4, pp. 81-118; Peter Lowe (2000) 'Uneasy readjustment, 1945-1958', translated by Tetsu Kobayashi as 'Konnan na saichōsei', in *Nichi-Ei kōryūshi*, vol. 2, pp. 195–231.

6. Akanezawa Tetsuo (1992) *Nihon no GATT kanyū mondai*, Tokyo: University of Tokyo Press, Chapters 2 and 3, pp. 43–110.
7. John Weste (2000) *Anglo-Japanese economic and trading relations: jet engines and the energy sector, 1950–1960*, Durham East Asian Papers, vol. 10; John Weste (2001) 'Southeast Asia, jet engine and energy', translated by Miki Sayako as 'Tōnan Ajia, jetto enjin, enerugī: 1950-nendai no Nichi-Ei kankei,' in *Nichi-Ei kōryū-shi*, vol. 4, Tokyo: University of Tokyo Press, pp. 275-302.
8. John Weste and Nobuko M. Kosuge (2003) 'The crisis of Durham: the ditching of Japanese studies,' *UP Journal*, University of Tokyo Press, December.
9. Asakai Kōichirō (1988) *Hanamizuki no niwa nite: aru gaikokan no kaisō* (In the dogwood garden: a diplomat's memoir), Asakai Kōichirō Kaikoroku Henshū Iinkai, pp. 100–2.
10. Ibid., pp. 102–3.
11. Hiroyuki Ikeda and D Douglas Lummis (1985) *Nihonjin-ron no shinsō* (The deeper meanings of 'theories about the Japanese') Tokyo: Haru Shobō, pp. 41–101, 176–91.
12. Nobuhiko Ushiba and Yasushi Hara (1979) *Nihon keizai gaikō no keifu* (Genealogy of Japanese economic diplomacy) Tokyo: Asahi Evening News, p. 183.
13. *Daily Express*, 6 October 1971.
14. Ibid.; *Guardian*, 8 October 1971.
15. *Daily Express*, 4 October 1971
16. *Guardian*, 8 October 1971.
17. Ibid.
18. *Asahi Evening News*, 1 November 1971.
19. *Economist* (London) 17 April 1973.
20. Ushiba and Hara 1979, pp. 190–5.
21. It was only after the 1970s that notes, memoirs and diaries by former British POWs, perhaps most notably J. F. Cook and Ernest Gordon, were translated and published in Japan. Gordon's *Miracle on the River Kwai* (London: Collins, 1963), which relates how the British inmates in a Japanese camp tried to regain and maintain their humanity using the support that their mutual friendships could offer, was superbly translated by literary scholar Kazuaki Saitō and first published in 1976. Other fairly recent translations of memoirs by former British war prisoners include Jack Edwards (1991) *Banzai you Bastards!* Japanese edition 1992; Robert Hardie (1984) *The Burma–Siam Railway*, London: Quadrant Books, Japanese edition 1993; and Eric Lomax (1995) *The Railway Man*, London: Jonathan Cape, Japanese edition 2000.
22. *Daily Express*, 7 October 1971
23. In Japan as well, many investigations were made into foreign reactions to the death of Emperor Hirohito. See Yui Daizaburō and Nobuko Kosuge (1993) *Rengōkoku horyo gyakutai to sengo sekinin* (The mistreatment of allied POWs and Japan's postwar responsibility), Tokyo: Iwanami Shoten.
24. Morris-Suzuki, Tessa (2000) 'The myth of the harmless monarchy,' translated by Nobuko Kosuge as 'Mugai na kunshusei to shite no tennōsei wa ikinokoreru ka' (Can the emperor system as a harmless type of monarchy survive?), *Sekai*, January.

25. Speech by Ian Bruce, House of Commons, *Hansard*, 24 November 1988.
26. Statement by Robert Rhodes James in *Hansard*, 6 June 1991. Later it was reported in the *Observer* (18 January 1998) that the British government had rejected a study of the possibility of further compensation. It was revealed that Lord Reading had agreed on 26 May 1955 that the government should not take advantage of Article 26 of the same treaty, which provided for further claims if Japan should conclude agreements with other countries more advantageous than the original signatory countries. His footnote said: 'We are at present unpopular enough with the Japanese without trying to exert further pressure which would be likely to cause the maximum resentment for the minimum advantage.' Since November 2000, the British government has made payment of a special gratuity for ex-POWs of the Japanese and their widows 'in gratitude for all they suffered in captivity on behalf of their country'. Perhaps this can be seen as a meaningful achievement of domestic reconciliation between the 'forgotten' ones and their government (Royal British Legion, 'Background briefing for parliamentarians on the claim for a special gratuity for former Far East prisoners of war (FEPOWs)').
27. Yoshino, Shūichirō (1998) 'Kinō no teki wa kyō no tomo' (Yesterday's enemy is today's friend), in *Bessatsu rekishi tokuhon, eikyū hozonban* (History Reader Supplement, 'permanent preservation edition') Yomiuri Shimbunsha.
28. Statement by Alaistair Goodlad in *Hansard*, 23 February 1955, col. 281.
29. Toshiko Marks (1996) *Senshōkoku Igirisu e, Nihon no iibun* (What Japan has to say to Britain the victor), Tokyo: Sōshisha, p. 10. See also Nobuko Kosuge (1997) 'Eigun horyo-tachi no owaranai sensō' (The endless war of the FEPOWs), *Sekai*, November, pp. 161–71; and Nobuko Kosuge (1998) 'Endless war of the British ex-POWs II', *Sekai*, June 1998, pp. 219–26.
30. Speech by Alaistair Goodlad, House of Commons, *Hansard*, 10 May 1995.
31. Written answer by Hanley to question by Alfred Morris, 13 January 1997.
32. *Daily Mail*, 26 May 1998. See also Tony Blair (1998) 'Why we must welcome the Emperor of Japan to Britain today', *Sun*, 26 May.
33. *Mainichi Shimbun*, 23 May 1998.
34. For instance, see Michiko Nakahara (1998) 'Horyo to rōmushi no aida' (Between being a war prisoner and death from forced labour), *Sekai*, June, pp. 227–30.
35. Stephen Gomersall (2001) 'Eikoku no kaikaku no keiken wa Nihon no yaku ni tatsu deshō', (England's reform experiences can likely help Japan), *Gaikō Fōramu* (Forum on Foreign Affairs), October, pp. 28–34.
36. *Financial Times*, 27 May 1998.

NOTES ON CONTRIBUTORS

SIR JOHN BOYD is Master of Churchill College, Cambridge and Chairman of the British Museum. He is a former British ambassador in Tokyo.

HUGO DOBSON is senior lecturer in Japan's international relations in the School of East Asian Studies at the University of Sheffield, UK. His research interests are in global governance, the G8, the aesthetic turn in international relations and Japan's international relations. He has published numerous articles and books including *Japan and United Nations peacekeeping: new pressures, new responses* (RoutledgeCurzon, 2003); *Japan and the G7/8, 1975–2002* (RoutledgeCurzon, 2004); and (with Glenn D. Hook, Julie Gilson and Christopher W. Hughes) *Japan's international relations: politics, economics and security* (Routledge, 2005, second edition); and *The Group of 7/8* (Routledge, 2006).

REINHARD DRIFTE is emeritus professor of Japanese politics at the University of Newcastle, visiting research fellow at the London School of Economics and regularly visiting professor at Japanese and French universities. His main research interests are Japan's foreign and security policy, security issues in Northeast Asia, and EU–Northeast Asian relations. He has published numerous articles and books and many of them have been translated into East Asian languages as well, including *Japan's security relations with China since 1989: from balancing to bandwagoning?* (Routledge, 2003); *Japan's quest for a permanent Security Council seat: a matter of pride or justice?* (Macmillan, 1999); and *Japan's foreign policy in the 1990s: from economic superpower to what power?* (Macmillan, 1996, reprinted 1998).

JANET HUNTER is Saji professor of economic history in the economic history department of the London School of Economics. She has published widely on the economic and social development of modern Japan. She has recently been co-editor, with S. Sugiyama, of a volume on British–Japanese economic and business relations for the Anglo–Japanese History Project (*Economic and Business Relations*, vol. 4 of *The History of Anglo–Japanese Relations, 1600–2000*, Palgrave, 2002), and author of a monograph on prewar Japan (*Women and the labour market in Japan's industrialising economy: the textile industry before the Pacific War*, RoutledgeCurzon, 2003).

NAOTO KAGOTANI is professor of the economic history of modern Japan in the Institute for Research in Humanities at the University of Kyoto. His research interests are in modern Japan and the international trading order in Asia. His numerous publications include *Ajia kokusai tūshotitsujo to kindai nihon* (The international trading order in Asia and modern Japan), University of Nagoya Press, Japan, 2000; 'The international order in Asia in the 1930s', in S. Akita (ed.) *Gentlemanly capitalism, imperialism, and global history*, Palgrave, 2002; and 'The Chinese merchant community in Kobe and the development of the Japanese cotton industry, 1890–1941', in K. Sugihara (ed.) *Japan, China and the growth of the Asian international economy, 1850–1949*, Harvard University Press, 2005.

NOBUKO MARGARET KOSUGE is professor in international relations in the faculty of law at Yamanashi Gakuin University, Japan. Her research interests are in humanitarianism in war and postwar peacemaking, Japan's postwar reconciliation and the controversies over the unrecognized protective emblems in the Middle East and Asia from a post-colonial perspective. Her recent publications include *Post-war Reconciliation* (Chūōkōron-shinsha, Tokyo, 2005); 'Non-religious Red Cross emblem and Japan', *International Review of the Red Cross*, no. 849, Geneva, March 2003; (with Yōichi Kibata and Philip Towle) *War memories and the Far Eastern prisoners of war* (University of Tokyo Press, 2003) and (again with Towle and Kibata) *Japanese prisoners of war* (London, Hambledon 2000).

FUMITAKA KUROSAWA is professor in the department of cultural studies at Tokyo Woman's Christian University. His field is modern Japanese history and modern Japanese studies. His major publications include *The Imperial Japanese Army during the interwar years* (Misuzu Shobo, 2000); *Diaries of Hamaguchi Osachi* (Misuzu Shobo, 1991); *Memoirs of Nara Takezi*, 4 vols (Kashiwa Shobo, 2000) and *Modern Japan and international environment*, co-edited with Seiji Saito and Yoshiki Sakurai (Fuyoshobo Publisher, 2001).

SIMON LEE is lecturer in politics in the department of politics and international studies at Hull University where he is co-director of the Centre for Democratic Governance. His principal research interests are in the field of political economy. His recent publications include *Blair's third way* (Palgrave, 2005); 'Asia-Pacific economic regionalism: global constraints and opportunities', in C. Dent (ed.), *Asia-Pacific economic and security cooperation* (Palgrave, 2003); and 'The political economy of the third way: the relationship between globalisation and national economic policy', in J. Michie (ed.), *The handbook of globalisation* (Cheltenham: Edward Elgar, 2003).

PETER LOWE is reader in history at the University of Manchester. He has written widely on East Asian history. His most recent publications include *British policies towards Japan, China and Korea, 1945–1953* (Manchester University Press, 1997) and *The origins of the Korean War* (Palgrave, 2000). He is currently working on a monograph on British policy towards Southeast Asia between 1945 and 1965.

CHRISTOPHER MADELEY is a lecturer and administrator at Chaucer College Canterbury. He lived for 11 years in Japan where he began to study Japan's industrialization and Britain's part in it. His publications include contributions to *Britain and Japan: biographical portraits*, vol. III and to the *History of Anglo-Japanese relations 1600–2000*, vol. 1V.

RICHARD J. SMETHURST is research professor and professor of history in the University Centre for International Studies at the University of Pittsburgh. His interests are in modern Japanese economic and social history. His major publications include *A social basis for prewar Japanese militarism* (California, 1974). *Agricultural development and tenancy disputes in Japan, 1870–1940* (Princeton, 1986), 'Japan's first experiment with democracy, 1868–1940', in George Reid Andrews and Herrick Chapman, *The social construction of democracy, 1870–1940* (NYU, 1995), 'The self-taught bureaucrat: Takahashi Korekiyo and economic policy during the Great Depression', in John Singleton, *Learning in likely places* (Cambridge, 1998), and 'Takahashi Korekiyo's fiscal policy and the rise of militarism in Japan during the Great Depression', *Kindai Nihon Kenkyu* (2001). He is currently writing a biography of Takahashi Korekiyo.

HIDEYA TAIDA is executive vice-president and executive director of the Japan Foundation Centre for Global Partnership. He is a member of the board of trustees of the Japan Economic Foundation and a professor in the global business programme at Akita International University. Until June 2001 he was senior vice-president and a board member of Marubeni Corporation, a leading Japanese general trading house that he represented for many years in London. He is author of a number of publications including *Eikoku business guide* and *Europe's view of Japan*.

PHILIP TOWLE is reader in international relations at the Centre of International Studies in Cambridge. His most recent books include *Enforced disarmament from the Napoleonic campaigns to the Gulf War* (Clarendon, Oxford, 1997) and *Democracy and peacemaking: negotiations and debates 1815–1973* (Routledge, 2000). He was co-editor with Nobuko Margaret Kosuge and Yōichi Kibata of *Japanese prisoners of war* (Hambledon, 2000); and *War memories and the Far Eastern prisoners of war* (University of Tokyo Press, 2003).

JOHN WESTE was lecturer in Japanese studies at the department of East Asian studies, University of Leeds. His publications include 'Facing the unavoidable - Great Britain, the sterling area and Japan: economic and trading relations 1950–60', in J. Hunter and S. Sugiyama (eds), vol. 4 of *The history of Anglo–Japanese relations* (Palgrave, 2002); 'Tonanajia, Jetto Enjin to Enerugi', in *Nichiei kôryûshi 1600–2000*, vol. 4 (University of Tokyo Press, 2001); 'Bakumatsu Japan', an introduction to the *Iwakura Mission, Durham East Asia Series*, 2001; 'Staging a comeback: *Kyûgunjin* and rearmament planning in occupied Japan', *Japan Forum*, vol. 11, no. 2, 1999; and 'Salvation from without: mutual security assistance and the military-industry lobby in postwar Japan', *Japan Forum*, vol. 4, no. 2, 1992.

REFERENCES

Adams, Henry H. (1985) *Witness to power: the life of Fleet Admiral William D. Leahy*, Annapolis, Maryland: Naval Institute Press.

Adler, Cyrus (1929) *Jacob H. Schiff: his life and letters*, London: William Heinemann, 2 volumes.

Akanezawa Tetsuo (1992) *Nihon no GATT kanyū mondai*, Tokyo: University of Tokyo Press.

Akita, Shigeru and Naoto Kagotani (eds) (2001) *1930 nendai no Ajia kokusai chitsujo* (The Asian international order in the 1930s), Tokyo: Keisuisha.

Alexander, A. V. (1937) 'Changing forces in the Pacific', *International Affairs*, January–February

Allen, F. and D. Gale (2000) 'Bubbles and crises', *The Economic Journal*, vol. 110, pp. 236–55.

Allen, G. C. (1981) *A short economic history of modern Japan*, 4th edn, London: Macmillan.

Allen, Louis (1990) 'The campaigns in Asia and the Pacific', *Journal of Strategic Studies*, March.

Allen, Louis and Yūji Aida (1990) 'Āron shūyōjo o megutte' (Thinking about the Alon camp), in Ikeda Masayuki (ed.) *Igirisujin no Nihonjinkan*, (British perceptions of the Japanese), Tokyo: Kawai Shuppan.

Allen, Richard W. (1930a) 'World tour: September 1929–January 1930', *The Queen's Engineering Works Magazine*, Bedford: W. H. Allen Sons & Company Limited.

(1930b) 'World Engineering Congress, Tokyo: October–November 1929', *The Queen's Engineering Works Magazine*, Bedford: W. H. Allen Sons & Company Limited.

Allfrey, Anthony (1991) *Edward VII and his Jewish court*, London: Weidenfeld & Nicolson.

American Machinist (1930) vols 72 and 73, New York: McGraw-Hill Publishing Company.

Andō, Y. (1975) *Kindai Nihon keizai shi yōran* (Handbook of modern Japanese economic history), Tokyo: University of Tokyo Press.

Archibugi, D. and J. Michie (1997) 'Technological globalization and national systems of innovation: an introduction', in D. Archibugi and J. Michie (eds) *Technology, globalisation and economic performance,* Cambridge: Cambridge University Press.

Asaba, Sadao (1982) 'Washington kaigi to Nippon no taiō' (The Washington Conference and Japan's response), in Chihiro Hosoya (ed.) *Nichiei kankeishi* (Japan–UK relations), Tokyo: University of Tokyo Press.

Audretsch, B. and R. Thurik (2001) *Linking entrepreneurship to growth,* Paris: Organization for Economic Cooperation and Development.

Barlow, Jeffrey S. (1989) 'US and Japanese naval strategies', in Colin S. Gray and Roger W. Barnett (eds) *Seapower and strategy,* London: Tri-Service Press.

Barnhart, M. (1987) *Japan prepares for total war: the search for economic security 1919–1941,* Ithica: Cornell University Press.

Bayne, Nicholas (2000) *Hanging in there: the G7 and G8 summit in maturity and renewal,* Aldershot: Ashgate.

(2002) 'Impressions of the Genoa summit, 20–22 July 2001', in Michele Fratianni, Paolo Savona and John J. Kirton (eds), *Governing global finance: new challenges, G7 and IMF contributions,* Aldershot: Ashgate.

(2005) *Staying together: the G8 summit confronts the 21st century,* Aldershot: Ashgate.

Bernstein, Barton J. (1995) 'Compelling Japan's surrender without the A-bomb, Soviet entry or invasion: reconsidering the US Bombing Survey's early surrender conclusions', *Journal of Strategic Studies,* June.

Best, A. (1995) *Britain, Japan and Pearl Harbour: avoiding war in East Asia,* London: Routledge.

(2000a) 'Taiketsu e no michi' (The road toward confrontation), in *Nichiei Kōryūshi* (The history of Anglo–Japanese relations, 1600–2000), vol. 2

(2000b) 'The road to Anglo–Japanese confrontation, 1931–41', in I. Nish and Y. Kibata (eds), *The History of Anglo–Japanese relations, 1600–2000,* vol. 2, *The Political-Diplomatic Dimension, 1931–2000,* London: Macmillan.

Best, Gary Dean (1972) 'Financing a foreign war: Jacob H. Schiff and Japan, 1904–05', *American Jewish Historical Quarterly,* 61, pp. 313–24.

Blackett, P. M S. (1948) *Military and political consequences of atomic energy,* London: Turnstile Press

(1962) *Studies of war,* London: Oliver & Boyd

Blair, Chay (1978) *Combat patrol,* New York: Bantam.

Blair, J. (1917–1918) 'The Japanese mercantile marine', *Transactions and proceedings of the Japan Society of London,* XVI.

Blair, Tony (1998) 'Why we must welcome the Emperor of Japan to Britain today', *Sun,* 26 May.

Booth, Ann (1990) 'The evolution of fiscal policy and the role of government in the colonial economy', in Ann Booth, W. J. O'Malley and Ann Weidemann (eds), *Indonesian economic history in the Dutch colonial era,* New Haven: Yale University Southeast Asia Studies.

Borden, W. (1984) *The Pacific alliance: United States foreign economic policy and Japanese trade recovery, 1947–1955*, Madison: University of Wisconsin Press.

Boyle, Andrew (1974) *Poor dear Brendan: the quest for Brendan Bracken*, London: Hutchinson.

Braddick, Christopher (2000) 'Distant friends: Britain and Japan since 1958 – the age of globalization', in Ian Nish and Yōichi Kibata (eds) *History of Anglo-Japanese relations, 1600–2000*, vol. 2, *The political-diplomatic dimension, 1931–2000*, London: Macmillan.

Brown, Ian (1997) *Economic change in South-East Asia, c.1830–1980*, Oxford: Oxford University Press.

Brown, K. (1998) *Britain and Japan: a comparative economic and social history since 1900*, Manchester: Manchester University Press.

(2000) 'The impact of the First World War on Japan', in C. Wrigley (ed.) *The First World War and the international economy*, Cheltenham: Edward Elgar.

Buckley, Roger (1982) *Occupation diplomacy: Britain, the United States and Japan, 1945–52*, Cambridge: Cambridge University Press.

(1992) 'A particularly vital issue? Harry S. Truman and Japan, 1945–52', in T. G. Fraser and Peter Lowe (eds) *Conflict and amity: essays in honour of Ian Nish*, London: Macmillan.

Byas, Hugh (1942) *The Japanese enemy: his power and his vulnerability*, London: Hodder & Stoughton

Bywater, Hector C. (1927) *Navies and nations: a review of naval developments since the Great War*, London: Constable.

Cain, P. J. and A. G. Hopkins (2001) *British imperialism, 1688–2000* (2nd edn), London: Longman.

Cairncross, Sir Alec (1987) *Years of recovery: British economic policy, 1945–51*, London: Methuen.

Calvocoressi, Peter, Guy Wint and John Pritchard (1989) *Total war*, vol. II, London: Penguin.

Cantril, Hadley and Mildred Strunk (1951) *Public opinion 1935–1946*, Princeton, New Jersey: Princeton University Press.

CEA (2003) *Economic indicators: December 2003. Prepared for the Joint Economic Committee by the Council of Economic Advisers*, Washington, DC: United States Government Printing Office.

Chatterji, Basudev (1992) *Trade, tariff and empire: Lancashire and British policy in India 1919–1939*, Oxford: Oxford University Press.

Checkland, Olive and Norio Tamaki (1997) 'Alexander Allan Shand, 1844–1930: a banker the Japanese could trust', in Ian Nish, *Biographical portraits*, vol. 11, Richmond Surrey: Japan Library.

Churchill, Winston S. (1950) *The Second World War*, vol. III, *The grand alliance*, London: Reprint Society.

Clarke, Peter (1972) *Lancashire and the new liberalism*, Cambridge: Cambridge University Press.

Clayton, James D. (1985) *The years of MacArthur*, vol. III, *Triumph and disaster, 1945–1964*, Boston: Houghton Mifflin.

Cobbing, Andrew (1998) *The Japanese discovery of Victorian Britain: early travel encounters in the far west*, Richmond, Surrey: Japan Library Curzon Press.

Cohen, Jerome B. (2000) *Japan's economy in war and reconstruction*, edited by Janet Hunter, London: Routledge.

Cohen, Naomi (1999) *Jacob H. Schiff: a study in American Jewish leadership*, Hanover and London: Brandeis University Press.

Colvin, Fred. H. (1947) *60 years with men and machines: an autobiography*, New York: McGraw-Hill Book Company Inc.

Conley, Captain D. (2000) 'US submarine warfare in the Pacific, 1942–1945', *The Naval Review*, January.

Coox, Alvin D. (1988) 'The effectiveness of the Japanese military establishment in the Second World War', in Allan R. Millett and Murray Williamson (eds) *Military effectiveness*, vol. III, Boston, Allen & Unwin.

Cortazzi, Sir Hugh (1992) 'Britain and Japan: a personal view of postwar economic relations', in T. G. Fraser and Peter Lowe (eds) *Conflict and amity: essays in honour of Ian Nish*, London: Macmillan.

Crocket, Richard (1990) *My Dear Max: the letters of Brendan Bracken to Lord Beaverbrook*, London: Historians Press.

Crowley, J. B. (1978) 'Nichiei kyōchō e no mosaku' (The search for Japanese–British cooperation), in Hosoya Chihiro and Saitō Makoto (eds) *Washinton taisei to Nichibei kankei*, Tokyo: University of Tokyo Press.

Daniels, G. (1982) 'Britain's view of post-war Japan, 1945–9', in I. Nish (ed.) *Anglo–Japanese alienation, 1919–1952*, Cambridge: Cambridge University Press.

Department of the Chief of the Imperial General Staff [Kuniaki Koiso] (ed.) (1917) *Teikoku kokubō shigen* (Resources for the empire's national defence), pp. 9, 12, 19, 93–4, 209, 219, 269, 271.

Dobson, Hugo (2004) *Japan and the G7/8, 1975–2002*, London: Routledge Curzon.
(2006) *The Group of 7/8*, London: Routledge.

Dower, John (1979) *Empire and aftermath: Yoshida Shigeru and the Japanese experience, 1878–1954*, Harvard, Massachusetts: Harvard University Press.
(1999) *Embracing defeat: Japan in the aftermath of World War II*, London: Allen Lane.

Drifte, Reinhard (2000) *Japan's quest for a permanent Security Council seat: a matter of pride or justice?* London: Macmillan and St Antony's College (in Japanese) *Kokuren Ampori to Nihon. Joninrijikoku iri mondai no kiseki*, Tokyo: Iwanami Shoten.

Dupree, Marguerite (ed.) (1987) *Lancashire and Whitehall: the diary of Sir Raymond Streat*, 2 vols, Manchester: Manchester University Press.

Edwards, Jack (1991) *Banzai, you Bastards!* London: Souvenir Press, Japanese edition 1992. N.B. Two years after its publication in English *Banzai you Bastards!* appeared in Japanese as *Kutabare Jap Yaroh!* [Drop Dead, Jap!] (1993)

Einzig, Paul (1942) *Can we win the peace?* London: Macmillan

(1943) *The Japanese new order in Asia*, Basingstoke: Macmillan.

(1960) *In the centre of things*, London: Hutchinson.

Embree John, F. (1946) *A Japanese village: Suye Mura*, London: Kegan Paul, Trench, Trubner.

Engineering (1929) vol. 128, London: Charles Robert Johnson, 10 May.

Engineering (1930) vol. 129, London: Charles Robert Johnson.

European Commission (1994) *Towards a new Asia strategy*, COM(94) 314 final, Brussels: Commission of the European Communities.

(1995 updated 2001) *Europe and Japan: the next steps*, COM(95) 73 final, 08.03, Brussels: Commission of the European Communities.

(2001) *Shaping our common future: an action plan for EU–Japan cooperation*, Brussels, European Commission, p.9.

(2002) *Chair's statement: ASEM 4th Economic Ministers Meeting (EMM 4), Copenhagen, 18/19 September*, Brussels: European Commission.

(2003) *EU priority proposals for regulatory reform in Japan*, Brussels: European Commission.

Farnie, D. A. and Tetsurō Nakaoka (2000) 'Region and nation', in D. A Farnie, A. Takeshi, N. Tetsuro and J. F. Wilson, *Region and strategy in Britain and Japan: business in Lancashire and Kansai, 1890–1990*, London: Routledge.

Farnie, D. A. and Abe Takeshi (2000) 'Japan, Lancashire and the Asian market for cotton manufactures, 1890–1990', in D. A Farnie, A. Takeshi, N. Tetsuro and J. F. Wilson, *Region and strategy in Britain and Japan: business in Lancashire and Kansai, 1890–1990*, London: Routledge.

FCO (1999) 'Action Agenda 21: the UK and Japan in the 21st century', Foreign and Commonwealth Office News Release, 6 September, London: Foreign and Commonwealth Office.

(2002) 'The UK and Japan: "natural business partners"', Foreign and Commonwealth press release, 30 October, London: Foreign and Commonwealth Office, p. 1.

Finn, R. B. (1992) *Winners in peace: MacArthur, Yoshida and postwar Japan*, Berkeley: University of California.

Flower, Sybilla Jane (2000) 'British prisoners of war of the Japanese, 1941–45', in Ian Nish and Yōichi Kibata (eds) *The history of Anglo-Japanese relations, 1600–2000*, vol. II, *The political-diplomatic dimension, 1931–2000*, London: Macmillan, pp. 149–73.

Francks, P. (1992) *Japanese economic development: theory and practice*, London: Routledge.

Freeman, C. (1987) *Technology and economic performance: lessons from Japan*, London: Pinter.

G8 (2003) *Co-operative G8 action on trade*, Ottawa: G8 Information Centre.

Gaimushō (Ministry of Foreign Affairs) (1968) *Nihon Gaiko Bunsho*, vol. 1, Tokyo: Gaimusho.

Galbraith, J. K. (1983) *A life in our times*, London: Corgi.

GEM (2002) *Global Entrepreneurship Monitor: 2002 executive report*, London: Global Entrepreneurship Monitor

Gilbert, Martin (1986) *Winston S. Churchill: road to victory*, vol. VII, London: Heinemann.

Gomersall, Stephen (2001) 'Eikoku no kaikaku no keiken wa Nihon no yaku ni tatsu deshō', (England's reform experiences can likely help Japan), *Gaikō Fōramu* (Forum on Foreign Affairs), October, pp. 28–34.

Gordon, Ernest (1963) *Miracle on the River Kwai*, London: Collins.

Gotō Shin'ichi (1977) *Takahashi Korekiyo: Nihon no Keinzu* (Takahashi Korekiyo: Japan's Keynes), Tokyo: Nihon keizai Shinbunsha.

Hajnal, Peter I. (2002) 'Partners or adversaries? The G7/8 encounters civil society', in John J. Kirton and Junichi Takase (eds) *New directions in global political governance: the G8 and international order in the twenty-first century*, Aldershot: Ashgate.

Halpern, Paul G. (1987) *The naval war in the Mediterranean*, London: Allen & Unwin.

Hara, Akira (1998) 'Japan: guns before rice', in Mark Harrison, *The economics of World War II*, Cambridge: Cambridge University Press.

Hara, Takashi (Kei) (1921) 'Kōkyū heiwa no senketsu kōan: Washinton kaigi ni saishite Nippon kokumin no sekaikan o nobu' (A top-priority plan for permanent peace: expressing the Japanese people's worldview on the occasion of the Washington Conference), *Gaikō Jihō*, no. 34, 15 September.

Harcourt-Smith, Simon (1942) *Japanese frenzy*, London: Hamish Hamilton.

Hardie, Robert (1983) *The Burma–Siam Railway: the secret diary of Robert Hardie, 1942–45*, London: Quadrant Books, Japanese edition 1993.

Hasegawa, Yūichi (ed.) (2001) *Taishōki Nippon no Amerika ninshiki* (Taishō-era Japan and perceptions of America), Tokyo: Keiō Gijuku Daigaku Shuppankai (Keiō Gijuku University Press).

Hashimoto, Jūrō (1984) *Daikyōkōka no Nihon shihonshugi* (Japanese capitalism during the Great Depression), Tokyo: University of Tokyo Press.

Hattendorf, John B. et al. (1993) *British naval documents 1204–1960*, Aldershot: Scholar Press/Navy Record Society.

Higgott, R. (1998) 'The Asian economic crisis: a study in the politics of resentment', *New Political Economy*, vol. 3, no. 3.

HMT (2002) *Tackling poverty: a global new deal: a modern Marshall Plan for the developing world*, London: Her Majesty's Treasury.

(2003) *Budget 2003: building a Britain of economic strength and social justice*, London: Her Majesty's Treasury.

HMT/DFID (2003) *International Finance Facility*, London: Department for International Development and Her Majesty's Treasury.

Hodges, Michael R. (1999) 'The G8 and the new political economy', in Michael R. Hodge, John J. Kirton and Joseph P. Daniels (eds) *The G8's role in the new millennium*, Aldershot: Ashgate.

Honan, William H. (1990) *Bywater: the man who invented the Pacific War*, London: Macdonald.

Hordern, L. H. (1986) 'The submarine war on merchant shipping', in Bryan Ranft (ed.) *Ironclad to Trident*, London: Brassey's Defence Publishers.

Hore, Peter (2003) *Patrick Blackett: sailor, scientist, socialist*, London: Frank Cass

Horne, H. (1920) *Report of the commercial, industrial and financial situation of Japan, 1914–1919*, British Parliamentary Papers, Cmd. 912, London: Department of Overseas Trade.

Hosoya, Chihiro (1978) 'Washington taisei no tokushitsu to hen'yō' (The Washington system's characteristics and transformation), in Hosoya Chihiro and Saitō Makoto (eds) *Washington taisei to Nichibei kankei*, Tokyo: University of Tokyo Press.

(1982) 'Nippon no Eibeikan to senkanki no higashi Ajia' (Japan's perceptions of England and America, and Eastern Asia in the interwar period), in Chihiro Hosoya (ed.), *Nichiei kankeishi* (Japan-UK Relations), Tokyo: University of Tokyo Press.

(1988) *Ryōtaisenkan no Nippon gaikō* (Japanese diplomacy between the two great wars), Tokyo: Iwanami Shoten.

Hosoya, Chihiro and Ian Nish (eds) (2000/1), *Nichiei kōryūshi 1600–2000* (The history of Anglo-Japanese relations 1600–2000), 5 vols, Tokyo: University of Tokyo Press.

Hotta-Lister, Ayako (1999) *The Japan–British Exhibition of 1910: gateway to the island empire of the Far East*, Richmond, Surrey: Japan Library Curzon Press.

Hull, Cordell (1948) *The memoirs of Cordell Hull*, vol. II, London: Hodder & Stoughton.

Hunter, J. (2003) 'The Anglo-Japanese alliance and the development of the Japanese economy', in *Studies in the Anglo-Japanese alliance (1902–1923)*, STICERD International Discussion Paper, IS/03/443, LSE.

Hunter, Janet and Shinya Sugiyama (2002a) 'Introduction', in J. Hunter and S. Sugiyama (eds) *Economic and business relations*, vol. 4, *The history of Anglo–Japanese relations, 1600–2000*, Basingstoke: Palgrave.

(2002b) 'Economic relations in historical perspective', in Chihiro Hosoya and Ian Nish (eds) *The history of Anglo–Japanese relations 1600–2000*, vol. IV, *Economic and business relations*, Houndmills: Palgrave.

Hurst, F. W. (1934) *The consequences of the war to Great Britain*, London and New Haven: Oxford University Press and Yale University Press.

Ikeda, Hiroyuki and D Douglas Lummis (1985) *Nihonjin-ron no shinsō* (The deeper meanings of 'theories about the Japanese') Tokyo: Haru Shobō.

Ikenberry, G. John (1993) 'Salvaging the G7', *Foreign Affairs*, vol. 72, no. 2.

IMD (2003) *World Competitiveness Scoreboard 2003: executive summary*, Lausanne: Institute for Management Development.

IMF (2002) *World economic outlook: recessions and recoveries*, Washington, DC: International Monetary Fund.

(2003a) *World economic outlook: growth and institutions*, Washington, DC: International Monetary Fund.
(2003b) *United Kingdom: 2002 Article IV consultation*, Washington, DC: International Monetary Fund Country Report No. 03/48.
(2003c) *Republic of Korea: financial system stability assessment*, Washington, DC: International Monetary Fund Country Report No. 03/81.

Industrial Japan: a collection of papers by specialists on various branches of industry in Japan (1929) Tokyo: World Engineering Congress.

Industries of Japan (1929) Osaka and Tokyo: Industrial Japan Publishing Company.

Inoue, Toshikazu (1994) *Kiki no naka no kyōchō gaikō* (Cooperative diplomacy amid crisis), Tokyo: Yamakawa Shuppansha.

Inouye, Junnosuke (1931) *Problems of the Japanese exchange, 1914–1926*, London: Macmillan.

Invest-UK (2003) *Invest-UK: operations review 2003*, London: Department of Trade and Industry.

Iriye, Akira (1984) 'Sōron: senkanki no rekishiteki igi' (Overview: the historical significance of the interwar period), in Akira Iriye and Tadashi Aruga (eds) *Senkanki no Nippon gaikō* (Japanese diplomacy in the interwar period), Tokyo: University of Tokyo Press.

Ishii, Osamu (1977) *Cotton-textile diplomacy: Japan, Great Britain and the United States, 1930–1936*, Ann Arbor, Michigan: University of Michigan Press.
(2000) 'Rivalries over cotton goods markets, 1930–36', in Ian Nish and Yōichi Kibata (eds) *The history of Anglo-Japanese relations, 1600–2000*, vol. 2, *The political-diplomatic dimension, 1931–2000*, London: Macmillan Press.

Ismay, Lord Hastings Lionel (1960) *The memoirs of Lord Ismay*, London: Heinemann.

Japan Cotton Spinners' Association (ed.) *The statistics of cotton trade, 1919–1936*. Housed in the Japan Cotton Spinners' Association library in Osaka.

Johnman, L. and H. Murphy (2002) *British shipbuilding and the state since 1918*, Exeter: University of Exeter Press.

Johnson, C. (1982) *MITI and the Japanese miracle: the growth of industrial policy, 1925–1975*, Stanford: Stanford University Press.

Jones, H. J. (1980) *Live machines: hired foreigners and Meiji Japan*, Tenterden, Kent: Paul Norbury Publications.

Kagotani, Naoto (2000) *Ajia kokusai tsūshō chitsujo to kindai Nihon* (The Asian international trading order and modern Japan), Nagoya: Nagoya University Press.
(2001) 'Senkanki Nippon to Ajia tsūshōmō' (Japan between the wars and Asian trade networks), in Tetsuo Furuya and Shin'ichi Yamamuro (eds), *Kindai Nippon ni okeru higashi Ajia mondai* (The East Asian problem in modern Japan), Tokyo: Yoshikawa Kōbunkan.

Kashii, Kōhei (Colonel) (1925) 'Nichidoku kokujō no hikaku' (A comparison of the national situations in Japan and Germany), *Kaikōsha kiji*, no. 605, supplement, February.

Katō, Yōko (1993) *Mosaku suru 1930 nendai* (The growing 1930s), Tokyo: Yamakawa Shuppansha.

Kawai, Hidekazu (1978) 'Hokubatsu e no Igirisu no taiō' (Britain's response to [China's] northern expedition [against the Beijing government in the mid-1920s]), in Hosoya Chihiro and Saitō Makoto (eds) *Washington taisei to Nichibei kankei*, Tokyo: University of Tokyo Press.

Kennedy, Captain M. D. (1924) *The military side of Japanese life*, London: Constable.

(1930) *The changing fabric of Japan*, London: Constable.

Kibata Yōichi (1998) '1930 nendai no Nichiei kankei' (Japan–UK relations in the 1930s), *Gaikō Shiryōkanpō*, no. 12.

(2000) *Teikoku no tasogare: reisenka no Igirisu to Ajia*, (Twilight of empire: Britain and Asia in the cold war era), Tokyo: University of Tokyo Press.

Kibata Yōichi, Nobuko Kosuge and Philip Towle (eds) (2003) *Sensō no kioku to horyo mondai* (War memories and the Far Eastern prisoners of war), Tokyo: University of Tokyo Press.

Kimball, Warren F. (1984) *Churchill and Roosevelt: the complete correspondence*, 3 vols, Princeton, New Jersey: Princeton University Press.

Kirton, John J. (1989) 'Introduction: the significance of the seven-power summit', in Peter I. Hajnal (ed.) *The seven-power summit: documents from the summit of industrialized countries, 1975–1989*, Millwood, New York: Kraus International Publications.

(1998) 'The emerging pacific partnership: Japan, Canada, and the United States at the G7 summit', in Michael Fry, John J. Kirton and Mitsuru Kurosawa (eds) *The North Pacific Triangle: the United States, Japan and Canada at century's end*, Toronto: University of Toronto Press.

Kitazawa Yōko (2000) 'Jubilee 2000 Japan: the first but revolutionary step', *Ampo: Japan-Asia Quarterly Review*, vol. 29, no. 3.

Kobayashi, Tatsuo (ed.) (1966) *Diaries of Miyoji Itō, Suiusō nikki* (Diary kept by Makino), Tokyo: Hara Shobō.

Kōichirō, Asakai (1988) *Hanamizuki no niwa nite: aru gaikokan no kaisō* (In the dogwood garden: a diplomat's memoirs), Asakai Kōichirō Kaikoroku Henshū Iinkai.

Kosuge, Nobuko (1997) 'Eigun horyo-tachi no owaranai sensō' (The endless war of the FEPOWs), *Sekai*, November, pp. 161–71

(1998) 'Endless war of the British ex-POWs II', *Sekai*, June, pp. 219–26.

Krugman, K. (1998) 'Saving Asia: it's time to get radical', *Fortune*, 7 September, pp. 27-32.

Kurata, Keizō (1934) *Nichi-in kaishō ni kansuru denpō ōfuku hikae* (File of telegrams exchanged in Indo-Japanese cotton trade negotiations), Osaka: Japan Cotton Spinners' Association, April.

Kurosawa, Fumitaka (1993) 'A prelude to disaster,' in *Beginnings of the Soviet–German and the US–Japanese war and 50 years after*, Tokyo: Sophia University.

(1999) 'Das System von 1940 und das Problem der politischen Führung in Japan' (The system of 1940 and the problem of political leadership in Japan), *Zeitschrift für Geshichtswissenshaft*, Berlin.

(2000) *Taisenkanki no Nippon rikugun* (The Japanese army between the wars), Tokyo: Misuzu Shobō.

Lane, Michael R. (1995) *The story of Queen's Engineering Works Bedford: a history of W. H. Allen Sons and Company Limited*, London: Unicorn Press.

Lawrence, J. (1994) 'The First World War and its aftermath' in P. Johnson (ed.) *20th century Britain: economic, social and cultural change*, London: Longman.

Lee, S. (1997) 'Part B: explaining Britain's relative economic performance', in A. Cox, S. Lee and J. Sanderson, *The political economy of modern Britain*, Cheltenham: Edward Elgar, pp. 65–253.

(1998) 'Managed or mismanaged trade? US–Japan trade relations during the Clinton Presidency', in I. Cook, M. Doel, R. Li and Y. Wang (eds) *Dynamic Asia: business trade and economic development in Pacific Asia*, Aldershot: Ashgate.

(2002) 'Global monitor: the International Monetary Fund', *New Political Economy*, vol. 7, no. 2.

(2003) 'Asia-Pacific economic regionalism: global constraints and opportunities', in C. Dent (ed.) *Asia-Pacific economic and security cooperation: new regional agendas*, London: Palgrave Macmillan, pp. 19–33.

Lomax, Eric (1995) *The Railway Man*, London: Jonathan Cape, Japanese edition 2000.

Lowe, Peter (1982), 'Great Britain and the coming of war in Asia', in Chihiro Hosoya (ed.) *Nichiei Kankeishi 1917–1949* (History of Japan–UK relations 1917–1949), Tokyo: University of Tokyo Press.

(1994) 'Sir Alvary Gascoigne in Japan, 1946–1951', in Ian Nish (ed.) *Britain and Japan: biographical portraits*, Folkestone: Japan Library.

(1997) *Containing the cold war in East Asia: British policies towards Japan, China and Korea, 1948–53*, Manchester: Manchester University Press.

(2000) 'Uneasy readjustment, 1945–1958', translated by Kobayashi Tetsu as 'Konnan na saichōsei', in *Nichi-Ei kōryūshi*, vol. 2, pp. 195–231.

Lysaght, Charles Edward (1979) *Brendan Bracken*, London: Allen Lane

Mahan, Captain Alfred Thayer (1911) *Naval strategy*, London: Samson, Low & Marston.

Manchester, William (1979) *American Caesar: Douglas MacArthur 1880–1964*, London: Arrow.

Marks, Toshiko (1996) *Senshōkoku Igirisu e, Nihon no iibun* (What Japan has to say to Britain, the victor), Tokyo: Sōshisha.

Morris, John (1943) *Traveller from Tokyo*, Harmondsworth: Penguin

Morris-Suzuki, Tessa (2000) 'The myth of the harmless monarchy', translated by Nobuko Kosuge as 'Mugai na kunshusei to shite no tennōsei wa ikinokoreru ka' (Can the emperor system as a harmless type of monarchy survive?), *Sekai*, January.

Nakahara, Michiko (1998) 'Horyo to rōmushi no aida' (Between being a war prisoner and death from forced labour), *Sekai*, June, pp. 227–30.

Nakamura, T. (1971) *Economic growth in prewar Japan*, New Haven, Connecticut: Yale University Press.

Nakamura, Y. and K. Odaka (1989) 'Gaisetau 1914–1937' (overview 1914–1937), in T. Nakamura and K. Odaka (eds) *Niju Kozo* (The dual structure), vol. 6 of *Nihon keizai shi* (Japanese economic history), Tokyo: Iwanami Shoten.

Nichi-in Kyōkai kaihō (Journal of Indo-Japanese Association) (1935) no. 57.

Nihon Tōkei Kyōkai (Japan Statistical Society) (1988) *Nihon chōki tōkei sōran* (Long-term statistical handbook of Japan), vol. 3.

Nish, Ian (1982) 'Igirisu senkanki (1917–1937) kokusai taiseikan ni okeru Nippon' (Japan and the British views on the international system during the interwar period 1917–1937), in Chihiro Hosoya (ed.) *Nichiei kankeishi* (Japan–UK relations), Tokyo: University of Tokyo Press.

Nishikawa, Hiroshi (1987) *Nihon teikokushugi to mengyō* (Japanese imperialism and the cotton industry), Kyoto: Mineruva Shobō.

Nitze, Paul H. (1989) *From Hiroshima to glasnost: at the centre of decision*, London: Weidenfeld & Nicolson.

Numata, Sadaaki (1998) 'Imēji to genjitsu: Nichi-Ei kankei seijuku no 30 nen' (Image and reality: thirty years of maturation in Anglo-Japanese relations), *Gaikō Fōramu* (Forum on Foreign Affairs), May.

Nurkse, Ragnar (1944) *International currency experience: lessons of the inter-war period*, Geneva: League of Nations.

Oba, Sadao (1997) 'Japanese businessmen in the UK', in Ian Nish (ed.) *Britain and Japan: biographical portraits*, vol. 2, Richmond: Japan Library.

OECD (2001) *The new economy: beyond the hype. Final report on the OECD growth report*, Paris: Organization for Cooperation and Development

(2003) *Economic survey of Japan, 2002: policy brief*, Paris: Organization for Economic Co-operation and Development.

ONS (2003) *International Comparisons of productivity*, London: Office of National Statistics.

(2003) *United Kingdom balance of payments: the Pink Book 2003*, London: The Stationery Office

Oriental Economist (ed.) (1935) *Foreign trade of Japan*, Tokyo: Toyo Keizai Shinposha.

Parillo, Mark P. (1993) *The Japanese merchant marine in World War II*, Annapolis: Naval Institute Press.

Pelz, Stephen E. (1974) *Race to Pearl Harbor*, Cambridge, Massachusetts: Harvard University Press.

Penttilä, Risto E. J. (2003) *The role of the G8 in international peace and security*, Oxford: Oxford University Press.

Pimlott, Ben (1986) *The political diary of Hugh Dalton: 1945–1960*, London: Jonathan Cape.

Pollard, S. (1992) *The development of the British economy, 1914–1990*, 4th edition, London: Edward Arnold.

Porter, M. and C. Ketels (2003) *UK competitiveness: moving to the next stage, DTI economics paper No. 3*, London: Department of Trade and Industry and Economic and Social Research Council

Porter, M., H. Takeuchi and M. Sakakibara (2000) *Can Japan compete?* London: Macmillan.

Putnam, Robert D. and Nicholas Bayne (1984) *Hanging together: the seven-power summits*, Cambridge, Massachusetts: Harvard University Press.

Reiscauer, Haru Matsukata (1986) *Samurai and silk: a Japanese and American heritage*, Cambridge, Massachusetts and London: The Belknap Press of Harvard University Press.

Remme, T. (1995) *Britain and regional cooperation in South-East Asia, 1945–49*, London: Routledge

Rinji Gunji Chōsa Iin (Emergency Military Affairs Research Commission) (1918) *Kōsen shokoku no rikugun ni tsuite* (Report on the armies of the countries taking part in the war).

(1919) 'Doitsu kuppuku no gen'in' (The reasons for Germany's surrender), *Kaikōsha kiji*, no. 537, supplement, May, p. 16.

(Emergency Military Affairs Research Commission) (1920) *Kokka sōdōin ni kansuru iken* (Opinions on national total mobilization.

Robertson, Alex J. (1991) 'Lancashire and the rise of Japan', in Mary B. Rose (ed.) *International competition and strategic response in the textile industries since 1890*, London: Frank Cass.

Rose, M. B. (ed) (1991) *International competition and strategic response in the textile industry since 1870*, London: Frank Cass.

Rothermund, Dietmar (1992) *India in the Great Depression 1929–1939*, New Delhi: Manohar.

Ruxton, Ian (1998) 'Britain 17 August–16 December 1872: the Mission's aims, objectives and results', in Ian Nish (ed.), *The Iwakura Mission in America and Europe: a new assessment*, Richmond, Surrey: Japan Library Curzon Press.

Saburi, Sadao (1929) 'Japan's position in the Far East', *Royal United Service Institution Journal*, August.

Sakai, Tetsuya (1993) 'Eibei kyōchō to Nitchū teikei' (UK–US cooperation and Japan–China collaboration), in Kindai Nippon Kenkyūkai (Society for the Study of Modern Japan) (ed.) *Kyōchō seisaku no genkai: Nichibei kankei shi 1905–1960* (The limits of a cooperative policy: the history of Japan–US relations 1905–1960), Tokyo: Yamakawa Shuppansha.

Sharkey, John (2000) 'Economic diplomacy in Anglo-Japanese relations, 1931–41', in Ian Nish and Yoichi Kibata (eds) *The history of Anglo-Japanese relations, 1600-2000*, vol. 2, *The political-diplomatic dimension, 1931-2000*, London: Ithaca Press for the Middle East Centre at St Antony's College, Oxford.

Sheridan, K. (1994) *Governing the Japanese economy*, Cambridge: Polity Press.

Sherman, A. J. (1983) 'German–Jewish bankers in world politics: the financing of the Russo-Japanese War', *Year Book*, XXVIII, Leo Baeck Institute.

Sherwood, Robert E. (1948) *The White House papers of Harry L. Hopkins*, London: Eyre & Spottiswoode.

Shidehara Peace Foundation (ed.) (1955) *Shidehara Kijuro*, Tokyo: Shidehara Heiwa Zaidan.

Shillony, Ben-Ami (1991) *The Jews and the Japanese: the successful outsiders*, Rutland, Vermont and Tokyo: Charles E. Tuttle Company.

Shima Nobuhiko (2000) *Shunō gaiko: senshinkoku samitto no rimenshi* (Prime ministerial diplomacy: a behind-the-scenes history of the summit of the most industrialised nations), Tokyo: Bungeishunjū

Shimizu, H. (1986) *Anglo–Japanese trade rivalry in the Middle East in the inter-war period*, London: Ithaca Press for the Middle East Centre at St Antony's College, Oxford.

Shōji, Jun'ichirō (2001) 'Konoe Fumimaro no taibeikan' (Fumimaro Konoe's views of the United States), in Yūichi Hasegawa (ed.), *Taishōki Nippon no Amerika ninshiki* (Taishō-era Japan and perceptions of America), Tokyo: Keiō Gijuku Daigaku Shuppankai (Keiō Gijuku University Press).

Smethurst, R. (1998) 'The self-taught bureaucrat: Takahashi Korekiyo and economic policy during the Great Depression', in J. Singleton, *Learning in likely places: varieties of apprenticeship in Japan*, Cambridge: Cambridge University Press.

(2000) 'Takahashi Korekiyo's economic policies in the Great Depression and their Meiji roots', *Politics and the Economy in Pre-War Japan*, London: Suntory Centre, London School of Economics.

(2002) 'Takahashi Korekiyo's fiscal policy and the rise of militarism in Japan during the Great Depression', in Bert Edstrom (ed.) *Turning points in Japanese history*, Japan Library.

Smith, K. (1984) *The British economic crisis: its past and future*, Harmondsworth: Penguin.

Stimson, Henry L. and McGeorge Bundy (1948) *On active service in peace and war*, New York: Harper.

Sugihara, Kaoru (1989) 'Japan's industrial recovery 1931–1936', in Ian Brown (ed.) *The economies of Africa and Asia during the interwar depression*, London: Routledge

(1998) 'Intra-Asian trade and East Asia's industrialization, 1919–1939', in Gareth Austin (ed.) *Industrial growth in the Third World, c.1870–c.1990: depressions, intra-regional trade, and ethnic networks*, LSE Working Papers in Economic History, 44/98, London: London School of Economics and Political Science.

Sugiyama, Shin'ya (1995) 'The expansion of Japan's cotton textile exports into South-East Asia', in Shin'ya Sugiyama and Ian Brown (eds) *International rivalry in South-East Asia in the interwar period*, New Haven: Yale University Press.

Suzuki, Toshio (1994) *Japanese government loans on the London capital market, 1870–1913*, London: Athlone Press.

Takahashi Korekiyo jiden (Autobiography of Takahashi Korekiyo) (1976) Tokyo: Chukõ bunko, vol. 11.

Takamatsu, Tōru and Ken Warren (2000) 'A comparison of Cammel Laird and Hitachi Zõsen as shipbuilders', in D. A Farnie, A. Takeshi, N. Tetsuro and J. F. Wilson, *Region and strategy in Britain and Japan: business in Lancashire and Kansai, 1890–1990*, London: Routledge.

Takeda, H. (1983) 'Kokosai kankyo' (The international environment), in 1920 Nendai Shi Kenkyukai (ed.) *Nijūnendai no Nihon shihonshugi* (Japanese capitalism in the 1920s), Tokyo: University of Tokyo Press.

Takeo, Imamura (1948) *Hyõden Takahashi Korekiyo* (A critical biography of Takahashi Korekiyo) Tokyo: Jiji Tsūshinsha.

Tamaki, Norio (1995) *Japanese banking: a history 1859–1958*, Cambridge: Cambridge University Press.

Tanaka, Hisakazu (First Lieutenant) (1920) 'Taiheiyō ni okeru teikoku no shōrai' (The future of the [Japanese] Empire in the Pacific Ocean), *Kaikōsha kiji*, no.546, supplement, February.

Tawa, Yasuo (1935) *Nichiran kaishō no keika* (The process of Dutch–Japanese cotton trade negotiations), Osaka: Japan Cotton Spinners' Association, March.

Techō (22 February–17 December 1904), *Takahashi Korekiyo monjo*, 135, Tokyo: National Diet Library.

Thane, Pat (1986) 'Financiers and the British state: the case of Sir Ernest Cassel', *Business History*, XXVIII-1 (January).

Thorne, Christopher (1978) *Allies of a kind: the United States, Britain and the war against Japan, 1941–1945*, London: Hamish Hamilton.

Tilley Sir John (1942) *London to Tokyo*, London: Hutchinson & Company.

Tobe, Ryōichi (2001) 'Ugaki Kazushige no Amerika ninshiki' (Kazushige Ugaki's views of America), in Yūichi Hasegawa (ed.), *Taishōki nippon no Amerika ninshiki*, Tokyo: Keiō Gijuku Daigaku Shuppankai.

Tomaru, J. (2000) *The postwar rapprochement of Malaya and Japan, 1945–1961: the roles of Britain and Japan in South-East Asia*, New York: St Martin's.

Tomlinson, B. R. (1979) *The political economy of the raj 1914–1947: the economics of decolonization in India*, London: Macmillan Press.

Towle, Philip, N. Margaret Kosuge and Yōichi Kibata (eds) (2000) *Japanese prisoners of war*, London: Hambledon Press.

Tsurumi, Yūsuke (1937) 'Japan today and tomorrow', *International Affairs* (London), May–June.

UNCTAD (2003) *World Development Report 2003. Country fact sheet: Japan*, New York: United Nations Conference on Trade and Development.

Ushiba, Nobuhiko and Yasushi Hara (1979) *Nihon keizai gaikō no keifu* (Genealogy of Japanese economic diplomacy) Tokyo: Asahi Evening News.

Usui, Katsumi (1982) 'Nippon no taiei imēji to taiheiyō sensō' (Japanese Images of Britain and the Pacific War), in Chihiro Hosoya (ed.) *Nichiei kankeishi* (Japan–UK relations), Tokyo: University of Tokyo Press.

(1982) 'Satō gaikō to Nitchū kankei' (The Satō diplomacy and Japan–China relations), in Chihiro Hosoya (ed.) *Nichiei kankeishi* (Japan–UK relations), Tokyo: University of Tokyo Press.

Wade, R. and F. Veneroso (1998) 'The Asian crisis: the high debt model versus the Wall Street–Treasury–IMF complex', *New Left Review*, vol. 228, March–April, pp. 3-34.

Warren K, (1998) *Steel, ships and men: Cammell Laird 1824–1993*, Liverpool, Liverpool University Press.

Waters, Commander D. W. (1988) 'Japan: defeat through blockade, 1941-1945', *The Naval Review*, July.

Weste, John (2000) *Anglo-Japanese economic and trading relations: jet engines and the energy sector, 1950–1960*, Durham East Asian Papers, vol. 10.

(2001) 'Southeast Asia, jet engine and energy', translated by Miki Sayako as 'Tōnan Ajia, jetto enjin, enerugī: 1950-nendai no Nichi-Ei kankei,' in *Nichi-Ei kōryū-shi*, vol. 4, Tokyo: University of Tokyo Press.

(2002) 'Facing the unavoidable: Great Britain, the sterling area and Japan', in J. Hunter and S. Sugiyama (eds) *Economic and business relations*, vol. 4, *The history of Anglo-Japanese relations, 1600–2000*, Basingstoke: Palgrave, pp. 283–313.

Weste, John and Nobuko M. Kosuge (2003) 'The crisis of Durham: the ditching of Japanese studies,' *UP Journal*, University of Tokyo Press, December.

White, N. (1998) 'Britain and the return of Japanese economic interests to South East Asia after the Second World War', *South East Asia Research*, vol. 6, no. 3, pp. 281–307.

Wilkins, Mira (1974) *The maturing of multination enterprise: American business abroad from 1914–1970*, Cambridge, Mass: Harvard University Press.

Williamson, J. (1993) 'Democracy and the "Washington Consensus"', *World Development*, vol. 21, no. 8, pp. 1329–36.

Winton, John (1983) *Convoy: the defence of seaborne trade 1880–1990*, London: Michael Joseph.

World Bank (1993) *The East Asian miracle: economic growth and public policy*, Oxford: Oxford University Press.

(1997) *The state in a changing world: World Development Report 1997*, Washington, DC: The World Bank.

(2000) *East Asia: recovery and beyond*, Washington, DC: World Bank.

(2002) *Building institutions for markets: world development report 2002*, Washington, DC: World Bank.

(2003) *Global economic prospects 2004: realizing the development prospects of the Doha agenda*, Washington, DC: World Bank.

World Engineering Congress (1931) *World Engineering Congress Tokyo 1929: Proceedings*, vol. 1, Tokyo: World Engineering Congress.

Wrigley, C. (2000) 'The war and the international economy', in C. Wrigley (ed.) *The First World War and the international economy*, Cheltenham: Edward Elgar.

Wurm, C. (1993) *Business, politics and international relations: steel, cotton and international cartels in British politics, 1924–1939*, Cambridge: Cambridge University Press.

Yamamura, Kozo (1986) 'Japan's deus ex machina: Western technology in the 1920s', *Journal of Japanese Studies*, vol. 12, no. 1.

Yamasaki, K. (1916–17) 'Resources of Japan in their relation to British commerce after the war', *Transactions and Proceedings of the Japan Society of London*, vol. XV.

Yoneyama, Umekichi (1927) *Alexander A. Shand: a friend of Nippon: interesting chapters from a banker's reminiscences*, Tokyo: Japan Times.

Yosihida, Toyohiko (Major-General) (1919) 'Kōgyō dōin to busshi to no kankei' ('The relationship between industrial mobilization and commodities'), *Kaikōsha kiji*, no. 541, supplement, September.

Yoshino, Shūichirō (1998) 'Kinō no teki wa kyō no tomo' (Yesterday's enemy is today's friend), in *Bessatsu rekishi tokuhon, eikyū hozonban* (History Reader Supplement, 'permanent preservation edition'), Yomiuri Shimbunsha.

Yui Daizaburō and Nobuko Kosuge (1993) *Rengōkoku horyo gyakutai to sengo sekinin* (The mistreatment of allied POWs and Japan's postwar responsibility), Tokyo: Iwanami Shoten.

INDEX